G000152856

The BATTLE of the CONSCIENCE

A Psychiatric Study of the Inner Working of the Conscience

✦

BY

EDMUND BERGLER, M.D.

WASHINGTON INSTITUTE OF MEDICINE

WASHINGTON, D. C.

COPYRIGHT 1948

BY EDMUND BERGLER

ALL RIGHTS RESERVED

*Printed in United States of America by Monumental Printing Co.,
Baltimore, Md.*

"... And like a devilish Engine back recoils
Upon himself; horror and doubt distract
His troubl'd thoughts, and from the bottom stir
The Hell within him. ...

... Now conscience wakes despair
That slumbered, wakes the bitter memorie
Of what he was, what is, and what must be
Worse; of worse deeds worse suffering must ensue."

MILTON, *Paradise Lost,* Book V.

The author wishes to express his thanks to the editors of

Quarterly Review of Psychiatry and Neurology

The Psychiatric Quarterly

The Psychoanalytic Review

The Psychoanalytic Quarterly

Medical Record

Journal of Criminal Psychopathology

for permission to reprint papers previously published in these journals.

PREFACE

An old medical practitioner stated once that a hundred remedies for a specific disease, based on the same number of theories, were proof positive that ignorance and therapeutic helplessness were the real state of affairs. Applying that rule to the problem of the conscience (though with modification, since the conscience is the opposite of a disease, working rather as "preventive medicine"), we must come to the conclusion that little is known about the working of the inner conscience. We find a series of theories whose common denominator is only—contradiction. One group asserts that conscience is an inborn tendency; another describes people allegedly without conscience; another speaks of "temporary extinction" in specific circumstances of that inner institution; and still another substitutes external fear of punishment for inner conscience.

The cynic, "the man who knows the price of everything and the value of nothing," to quote Oscar Wilde, who should have known, tells us that inner conscience is just a fable that everybody agrees on. He uses for his argument criminals with or without acknowledged social position, whose "hardboiled" actions can hardly be described as being influenced or restricted by conscience. And still, interestingly enough, the majority of outstanding criminals of the political or simple murder variety, end in the electric chair, on gallows, or before firing squads. In other words, the cynic does not look far enough; he focuses his attention on the *initial* action, not taking into account the fact that these actions are possible only with the *unconscious* condition that *final* detection and punishment must be reckoned with. Every criminal bargains *unconsciously* for the electric chair. Of course, he is not aware that he does so, with the result that the cynic (nobody is more easily fooled than the cynic!) comes to false conclusions, believing the criminal's rationalization.

Psychiatric-psychoanalytic investigations confirm the consoling intuitive belief of humanity that *everyone has an inner conscience and is constantly under the influence of that inner department of the personality*. A feeling of guilt follows every person like his shadow, whether or not he knows it. This statement may sound absurd if one looks only at the initial actions and is taken in by the braggadocio of the wrong-doers, expressed in their actions, appearance, words, and posture. If one looks at such an individual with the analytic microscope, however, an entirely different picture appears. Every member of the detective force knows that the most clever criminal will make his "little mistake" somewhere, leading to detection. No "perfect crime" is possible because of the counteraction of the *unconscious* part of the conscience, demanding detection and punishment that the criminal tries so hard to avoid consciously. The old saying, "You can get away with murder," is not borne out by statistics of detected and undetected criminals.

The cynic concentrates too much on his chief but spurious argument—criminality—and overlooks, in so doing, two facts. First, that his own cynicism has unconscious reasons, too. Second, that the real psychologic problem of determining the existence of conscience is not whether people react *immediately* to the influence of conscience, undoubtedly the ideal situation, but whether they have to use devious unconscious means to appease this conscience. This is a fertile field for investigation to which the cynic is blind. No less blind is he in differentiating between the *conscious* and the *unconscious* parts of the conscience.

Action proves the man—only insofar as he is not too neurotic. As far as the majority of neurotics are concerned—and neurotics comprise a sizable part of the population—one cannot understand their inner structure from their actions alone; one must know the unconscious background and what self-punishment they are unconsciously intending.

The purpose of this book is to investigate the genesis and working ramifications of the normal conscience and also the technique of neurotic appeasement of the *unconscious* part of the conscience.

E. BERGLER.

New York, April, 1946.

TABLE OF CONTENTS

PAGE

Preface vii

CHAPTER I

Origin of the Pre-Stages of Conscience............................ 1

CHAPTER II

The Janus Face of Our Conscience................................... 7

CHAPTER III

Normal and Neurotic Feeling of Guilt............................. 14

CHAPTER IV

A Great Poet's Opinion of the Development of the Conscience.... 39

CHAPTER V

A Few Typical Examples of Neurotic Guilt, Including Suicide.... 58

CHAPTER VI

The "Injustice Collector"... 89

CHAPTER VII

Tender Love—the Classical Normal Antidote for Feeling of Guilt 110

CHAPTER VIII

Other Normal Antidotes: Work, Sublimation, Rationalization,
    "Pathos" 118

CHAPTER IX

Paradigms of Neurotic Antidotes for Feeling of Guilt: the Triad
    —Cynicism, Hypocrisy, Self-derision.......................... 150

CHAPTER X

Identification and Sense of Inner Guilt............................ 190

Contents

Chapter XI

Success Without Blessing of Conscience Spells—Depression of a
Specific Type 211

Chapter XII

"Poetic Justice" and the Unconscious Background 220

Chapter XIII

"Small Change" of Guilty Feelings 225

Chapter XIV

Torturing Dreams and Insomnia Caused by Inner Guilt 230

Chapter XV

The Neurotic Who Unconsciously Bargains for the Electric
Chair: the Criminal 261

Chapter XVI

"Let Your Conscience Be Your Guide"—Especially in the
Atomic Age 293

CHAPTER I

ORIGIN OF THE PRE-STAGES OF CONSCIENCE

The religious and scientific approaches to the genesis of conscience start, of necessity, at different points. The religious approach assumes an act or manifestation of God as the basis of conscience. The scientific approach describes clinically observable facts. There is no contradiction between the two approaches; belief and clinical observation work on completely different psychic levels. When a religious man, of whatever denomination, asserts to the scientist that, without the preordained help of God, education and inner psychic mechanisms could not build up the phenomenon of conscience, no objection can be made—his assertion is simply outside of scientific-clinical observation. It cannot be scientifically denied or proven, it is outside the realm of science.

The psychiatric-psychoanalytic approach starts with clinically observable facts. These facts are: The infant doesn't show any manifestations of conscience without two influences, education and later internalized education, in the form of identifications and defense mechanisms.

The first visible pre-stages of conscience are traceable to the restrictions imposed on the child—continence and, even earlier, restraint from biting and tearing of the mother's breast, or breast equivalents. (If the child is bottle fed, regulation of this restraint is not so vigorously enforced.) The former set of rules, which Ferenzi called "sphinctermorality," is forced upon the child in the first two years and later becomes a specific part of his educational program. We know of the horror of mothers when their children are bed wetters until an advanced age, and of the deep feeling of guilt connected with this habit in the child. The same applies to the unavoidable masturbation of the child.

The child's cruelty toward siblings and animals is another point in question. Education restricts this and implants in the child the idea of guilt if he carries out unjustified and unwarranted aggressions. Pity, gratitude, commiseration, and a sense of justice are acquired by the child, as far as is observable, only on the basis of identifications with the demands of the educators. The *first* reason for abstaining from aggressive acts prohibited by the educator is

1

fear of the loss of love or fear of punishment. *Secondarily* the educators are internalized, and thus the pre-stages of inner conscience are built up.

But the origin of conscience goes deeper than that. A general characteristic of instincts seems to be that they must be discharged. They are comparable to rivers; if a dam prevents the flow of the river in one direction, another is used. The strange thing about instincts is that if their discharge is prevented they even turn against the possessor himself. Discharge of instincts, *per se*, seems to be more important than the direction of discharge. Thus, a certain canalization of aggressive drives toward the person himself is prepared. Now, the infant's aggressive drive is highly restricted by reality factors and education, first because of the motoric helplessness of the infant and later because of external restrictions stemming from education. The next step in restriction comes, instead of from external sources, from internal ones. In other words, the educator is internalized. Instead of the warning voice from the *outside*, the warning voice from the *inside* is heard. This is the observable beginning of an inner conscience.

In the first months of life, the child has a peculiar misconception of reality. He doesn't differentiate between his own body and the outer world. Hence, he misconstrues reality. He perceives nourishment, loving care, attention, not as such, but as the product of his own megalomania and ideas of grandeur.[1] The question might be asked as to how we have that knowledge of the "autarchic fantasy," since the baby can't reveal his fantasies. The knowledge is gleaned from the observation of the behavior of adult neurotics, which permits us to reconstruct the stages of development. We can state that the fight to retain childlike megalomania and exaggerated narcissism has first priority in the human being, and the gradual collapse of that fantasy constitutes one of the most painful human experiences.

A great poet, Romain Rolland, caught a glimpse of that tragedy. In "Jean Christophe" he describes a little boy as follows:

> "He is a magician, too. . . . He commands the clouds. He wants them to go more to the right. But they continue their way to the left. He scolds them and repeats his command

[1] Following hints from Freud, Ferenczi was the first to draw attention to that fact.

more urgently. He observes with high pulses whether at least one little cloud obeys him. But they continue to run to the left. He stamps with his foot, menaces them with his little stick and—changes his command. He now wants them to go more to the left, and this time the clouds obey. He is happy and proud of his power. . . ."

The poet describes, as if he were dealing with a clinical case, a transitory phase. The child acknowledges, at last, that he is not an omnipotent magician, but he wants to save, trrough sanction *post facto*, at least a part of his fiction of omnipotence. It is as if someone, looking at his watch 60 seconds before 6 o'clock, were to command the watch to point to six in one minute, and to observe that the watch "obeys."

Why does the child "internalize" the educator? The child's education is a constant offense to his megalomania, to which he clings desperately. In the long run the strongest child is weaker than even the weakest educator. The child can choose between two alternatives. He can persist in his megalomania ("naughtiness," as it is called by the educator) and risk loss of love and even punishment, or pretend that he is giving up his "naughtiness," not because of external pressure, but because of his "free will." In other words, he can "save face" by pretending that his megalomania is maintained ("I renounce that wish") and at the same time avoid conflict with his educators. Therefore he renounces a specific "naughtiness" in a way in which his childlike megalomania is not too greatly hurt.

In normal conditions the child identifies with the educator also because he wants to be "grown up" and as powerful as the educator. The internalized educator, later the Ego Ideal, is the cornerstone of the inner conscience.

Let's take a clinical example, as follows. Anyone dispassionately observing small children, for instance, knows that the barrier of the sense of shame has not yet been built up in the very little child. So if a child aged between one and a quarter to one and a half years (let us call him Robert) is brought in to see a visitor, he is likely suddenly to lift up his clothes and exhibit his naked body. In this act we see the expression of the exhibitionistic (scoptophilic) instinct. This uncovering of the body is then forbidden on pain of punishment or the displeasure of the educating person. (Threat of the loss of love.) In some way the child hears the well-known cry of "Shame! Nobody does that!" If this demand on the child is made long enough, in time he becomes "good," that is, he will not exhibit his body any more. If we ask the educator, after he has thus been successful, what has happened to the instinct of exhibitionism, he will at first deny that he was dealing with the expression of any instinct at all, and proudly declare that he has driven the "naughtiness" or the "bad habit" out of the child. This naive opinion is wrong, for in the psychic world nothing is lost. Instincts may be modified, led into other channels or directions, sublimated, forced to build up reactions, and above all, they may be repressed. Instincts may do anything but one thing, and that is, disappear. In the case under discussion, the exhibitionistic instinct will be repressed and used to build up a reaction, the sense of shame.

The little Robert of our example has thus built up a reaction and has acquired a sense of shame. Robert, now three years old (to carry on with our example), is again in the living room when another child of one and a half years, Betty, is brought in to see the guests. Betty exhibits herself. And at once Robert calls out, in shocked tones: "Shame! Nobody does that!"

What has happened? Where has Robert's wisdom come from? We say Robert has, in this particular case, identified himself with the people who are bringing him up. But this identification is again an unconscious process, as Robert would be the first to deny that he is an echo of his educators. When Robert has grown to manhood, he will in no way admit that the people with whom he has identified himself are the original models for his own moral convictions. No, he came to these ideas quite by himself. "By chance," however, these original ideas happen to agree with the general standards of collective decency, with which we usually identify ourselves.

This weak child builds up the Ego Ideal for the purpose of adapting to a stronger reality. By identifying with the stronger power, he becomes as "strong" as the educator is in his fantasy.

The inner conscience seems, at first glance, therefore, to be but a photographic copy of the environment and the educators. That impression is erroneous; otherwise a severe education would automatically build up a severe inner conscience in the child, a lenient education a lenient conscience. Clinical experience contradicts precisely this congruity. Therefore other influences must also be at work. They are. First of all, the child does not see reality as it *is*, but through the spectacles of his "projection," as the English school of analysis has proved.

Projection denotes a psychologic process which enables the person, through *unconscious* shifting, to attribute his own feelings to another person. These feelings are always disagreeable, consciously rejected ones. In clinical analysis we can observe these projections constantly. If the analyst shows the patient that he hates his wife, the patient retorts bitterly that the analyst hates his own wife. If the patient's neurotic pessimism is analyzed, the patient "feels" that the analyst is speaking only about himself. And if the patient's self-damaging tendencies (psychic masochism) are scrutinized, the patient discovers that the analyst is a masochist himself. The patient often greets the analyst with the statement: "Why are you angry with me?" when in reality the patient is the angry one, and simply shifts that anger to the physician.

Sometimes these projections are very cleverly concocted. A patient whose psychic masochism was under treatment came to his appointment one day and stated: "I made an important observation which you cannot discard as simply projection. I discovered that you and your colleagues are exquisite masochists, and I can prove it. 'What's the difference between a prisoner and an analyst?' The prisoner changes his jailer every eight hours; the analyst changes his every fifty minutes. . . ."

Another patient, an hysteric girl, once came very apologetically to her appointment, stating that she was ashamed to admit the "crazy" thought she had had about me. Finally she came out with it. It was that my books and papers were written, not by me but by a ghost writer. This mysterious ghost writer was in a Nazi concentration camp. I had left Vienna without bothering about him. "I know it's senseless, I know that I've no grounds for such an assumption; still there it is, and now you will throw me out." I suggested analyzing the thought, and pointed out that a projection might be involved. "Whom did *you* plagiarize?" I suspected that the idea might have had some connection with her dead sister. Then the patient recollected that at the age of twelve she had copied, during a written examination, the paper of her sister, who was a year older but in the same class because she had been out of school with tuberculosis. The unastute teacher believed, upon seeing that the papers were identical, that the patient's sister had done the copying. A year later the tubercular sister died, and the patient went through a protracted period of mourning because of her death wishes toward her. In analysis she projected the conflict upon me, and this projection was the first approach to a recollection.

If, therefore, the child projects a great deal of his own aggression onto his educator, the educator, even though a weak one, becomes "tyrannical and cruel." The educator *as the child sees him*, tinged with the child's own *projected* aggression, not the *real* educator, is introjected.

The second factor proving the *relative* importance only of the reality of "bringing up," at least as far as the inner conscience is concerned, has something to do with the previously discussed general tendency of the discharge of instinct to be more important than the direction of discharge. Every bit of aggression which he cannot discharge, the child turns upon himself, thus increasing the severity of his inner conscience (Freud).

In any case, the child builds up his Ego Ideal finally, an unconscious glorified picture of himself. It contains remnants of his old childlike megalomania, plus the introjected demands of his parents, as he saw them through the spectacles of his own projection. This Ego Ideal, a summary of narcissistically-tinged "Thou shalt," is the first cornerstone of the inner conscience. Its effects on the individual are far-reaching, but not understandable without first introducing the second part of the inner conscience, the Daimonion.

CHAPTER II

THE JANUS FACE OF OUR CONSCIENCE

Socrates assumed that a malignant spirit operated within the human being, and called it Daimonion. The description was mere mythology; the facts, however, correct. The unconscious conscience harbors such a Daimonion.

Analytic terminology of the last twenty years usually applies the term Super Ego to designate the unconscious part of the conscience. The older Freudian conception of the Ego Ideal has become submerged somewhere in the larger concept of the Super Ego, a subsequent Freudian discovery. I believe that a more precise distinction should be made between the two parts constituting the Super Ego,[1] the Ego Ideal and the Daimonion. This is necessary for two reasons: the introduction of Freud's theory of life and death instincts, and clinical observation.

Freud's Eros-Thanatos theory[2] assumes that our whole life consists of a fight between two basic instincts: the "life instinct" (Eros) and the "death instinct" (Thanatos). Eros attempts to discharge upon objects of the outer world the tendency of Thanatos, which is originally turned upon the individual himself. What is manifested as instinct of destruction is genetically the original Thanatos forced into an altered direction by Eros. Guided by Eros, the destructive instinct rages outward instead of inward. Its redirection toward the individual himself is unconsciously regarded by that individual as the greatest possible danger.

Imagine two giants fighting each other. The first wants to kill the second. The second tries to divert the destructive energy of the first towards a third party. Imagine further both giants as operative instincts in the same personality, and you have in a nutshell the Eros-Thanatos theory.

These drives never appear "unmixed." They are combined in quantitative degrees at different times. There is also an "indifferent narcissistic energy," which can be added to one drive or the other,

[1] See the paper "Transference and Love," in collaboration with Freud's oldest pupil, Dr. Ludwig Jekels, Imago, 1934, 1. A partial translation is found in "Thirty Some Years After Ferenczi's 'Stages in the Development of the Sense of Reality,'" Psychoanalyt. Rev., 1945.
[2] Freud, "The Ego and the Id," Ges. Schr., VI.

thus increasing its cathexis. Of course, what we see clinically is not life or death instinct, not even their original mixtures, but only the derivatives of these mixtures. In this sense we can speak of libido and destrudo, assuming that each contains mixtures of both drives, libido more of the derivatives of Eros, destrudo more thanatic elements, but both admixtures of erotic and thanatic elements.

The genesis of the Super Ego,[2] containing the Ego Ideal and the Daimonion, is the following:

Both portions of the same, Ego Ideal ("Thou shalt") and Daimonion ("Thou shalt not") are various as to *instinctual psychology and genesis.* The Ego Ideal has two roots: One of these consists in the attempt of the Ego to put upon objects the aggression of the death-instinct directed against the Ego itself. These objects thus become fear-inspiring, and thus an internal danger is merely exchanged for a projected external danger, an unsuccessful attempt. This achievement of the destructive instincts is parried by Eros by absorbing this object of fear into the Ego, where it becomes the object of the individual's own narcissism. The second root of the Ego Ideal formation is to be sought in a compromising attempt of the Ego to maintain its supposed omnipotence. This fictitious omnipotence is severely shaken by the demands of the outer world (intervals between feedings, training to cleanliness, etc.). Because of his helplessness, the child has the choice of reacting in only two ways: either to give up his infantile megalomania or to take to himself the commands of the parents and then disguise this involuntary act as voluntary, in order to preserve his fictitious omnipotence, and invest the introjected commands with his own narcissism. But if Eros really succeeded in parrying Thanatos by setting up the Ego Ideal by means of identification, then only love would be found there, which, in fact, is not the case. Thanatos parries this stroke by Eros by desexualization, which is known to accompany every identification. Thus, the Ego Ideal is desexualized Eros, and corresponds to the indifferent narcissistic energy postulated by Freud in "The Ego and the Id," which may at times be added to one of the two fundamental instincts and increase the total cathexis of the one or the other instinct. The Ego Ideal thus becomes the real aim of the combat between these two gigantic forces. Like a neutral zone between two parties at war, it becomes the plaything chiefly

[2]According to Jekels and Bergler l.c.

of the Thanatos section of the Super Ego (Daimonion). The formation of the Daimonion is due to the unsuccessful attempt of Eros to divert to objects the aggressions of Thanatos originally directed against the individual's own Ego by means of projection. The projection is unsuccessful to a quantitatively greater or lesser degree: first, because of the helplessness of the individual, as the little child is powerless against its environment, and hardly able to carry out aggressions to any extent; second, because the same objects against which the aggressions of the child are directed—the parents—have already been absorbed into the Ego Ideal, and this results in a decrease of aggression or in aggression against himself. Both cause stasis and redirection of the aggression against the child's own Ego. The Ego, thus endangered, becomes fearful and gives the danger signal. The Ego Ideal, the repository of desexualized Eros, is made use of by the Ego-disturbing tendencies of the Daimonion. The Daimonion causes the Ego to experience feelings of guilt by constantly holding the Ego Ideal up to the Ego as a model, and pointing out the discrepancy between the Ego and the Ego Ideal. The Ego Ideal, which was originally erected to bolster up the child's own threatened narcissism, thus becomes the most dangerous weapon of Thanatos against Eros. This holding up of the Ego Ideal as a model by the Daimonion is far from harmless; every deviation from the self-erected Ego Ideal appears in the Ego in the form of guilt. The remarkable thing about this procedure is that the suffering which the Daimonion causes the Ego always takes the route over the Ego Ideal. It is as though an opponent of the regime in a dictator state stood before a special tribunal; the outcome of the trial is all decided upon beforehand, but the prisoner is condemned "legally," according to certain laws, etc. This comedy of justice is also carried out intrapsychically; a discrepancy between Ego and Ego Ideal must always be demonstrated before guilt and the desire for punishment arise in the Ego. The destructive instinct beats the Eros with its own stick by making use of this desexualized Eros against the Eros itself. It should also be noted that the Ego Ideal is an unhomogeneous formation, a not-at-all completely successful alloy of two substances of unequal value, the original unconquerable narcissism, with the introjection of the parents, to which cannot be attributed anywhere nearly equal resistance.

The mechanism which makes our conscience "tick and click" is therefore typically this: *The Daimonion uses the Ego Ideal for a "silent model," constantly holding it to the frightened Ego with the eternal rebuke: "Have you fulfilled your self-created Ego Ideal demands?" Every discrepancy between Ego and Ego Ideal results in feeling of inner guilt.*

To use a simple example, let us assume a particular person has built up an Ego Ideal demanding that he become the world's most famous chemist. In real life he achieves only the position of clerk in a pharmaceutical house. The discrepancy between "famous scientist" and "clerk" manifests itself on the psychic surface, in consciousness, as dissatisfaction—scientifically speaking, as an unconscious feeling of guilt.

One could object that the adult Ego could reject or modify the high-pitched demands of the self-created, infantile Ego Ideal which has turned from a blessing into a Shylock, demanding his pound of flesh. This reasonable modification is impossible, however, without psychoanalysis, because the whole process is *unconscious*. One could say that the human being pays an exaggerated price for his juvenile narcissism. On the other side of the ledger is the fact that a high-pitched Ego Ideal pushes one to greater achievements. What is popularily described as "ambition" is nothing but the desperate attempt to reach one's Ego Ideal and thus avoid conflict with that department of the personality. Unfortunately, the Ego Ideal is formed at an age when the person has no precise appreciation of real difficulties. Since the real possibilities in life are greatly limited, the Ego Ideal can rarely be fulfilled. The *adult* pays a heavy penalty for his *childlike* megalomania: His Ego Ideal is not impressed with real limitations, and acts as if anyone could be a genius and could achieve everything of which he had dreamt in childhood. The Ego Ideal reflects the popular adage: Give him enough rope and he'll hang himself. . . .

Observing the disposition of psychic energy of normal people, one comes to the conclusion that even they spend a great deal of that energy (libido and especially aggression) in checkmating their conscience. They do it partly by bowing to the demands of conscience, thus becoming a civilized being, and partly in fighting the unreasonable, self-destructive tendencies of their Daimonion.

The old Romans created the image of a God having two faces

looking in *opposite* directions. The conscience, too, has such a Janus face—the benevolent Ego Ideal and the cruel Daimonion. To increase the irony of the situation, even the "benevolent" Ego Ideal is constantly used by the tyrannical Daimonion to torture the Ego. One can definitely state that conscience as a whole is not a benevolent institution. It is necessary but not benevolent. *Man's inhumanity to man is equaled only by man's inhumanity to himself.* For me, there exists no stronger argument for the acceptance of the Eros-Thanatos hypothesis than the working of the inner conscience. Without a self-destructive tendency, the necessary limitations of inner drives in the form of conscience would be quite different. The basic tendency of the Super Ego is its *anti-libidinous* structure. As one patient put it: "This Super Ego is just mean and doesn't allow any pleasure, if possible." One should never be fooled by the happy-go-luckies and their attitude, "Nothing can happen to me." If one doesn't know their inner troubles, even people with conflicts may appear all right on the surface. "There are no winners in the battle of conscience, only half-losers," said the pessimistic patient quoted above.

The generally recognized principle of justice in every civilized country declares that only the wrong-doer may be called upon to expiate the crime. The subjective responsibility for subjective guilt seems a matter of course to our sense of justice. Complicated and long drawn-out methods are used to bring about the conviction of the criminal, from the problematic statements of witnesses to the still more problematic circumstantial evidence. The idea that the person A has committed a crime, and that the person B, who had no part in it whatever, shall be held responsible for it, is unthinkable to our conscious sense of fairness. If anything similar does occur, then, in normal times, the sense of equity of persons having nothing whatever to do with the matter will be aroused against the judicial murder.

Quite different, indeed exactly the opposite, are the methods of the unconscious intropsychic justice. The unconscious seems to consider it of first importance that an instinctive impulse be expressed and eliminated, while the object at which this instinctive drive is directed seems to be rather irrelevant. The principle, "Only the doer is responsible for the deed," is here suspended, and instead of subjective, we find collective responsibility. The motion, pressing forward to consummation, rages against an innocent subject, using the method of chance, without regard for persons. The innocent are called upon to expiate and to suffer in spite of their innocence. Freud, the man of genius who discovered the dynamic Unconscious, illustrated this by the following anecdote: During wartime, in a small village in the warzone, the only shoemaker in the village was condemned to death by court-martial as a spy. Whereupon the burgomaster of the village went to the presiding officer of the court-martial, and said: "We cannot do without the only shoemaker in this place, so please spare his life. However, we have three tailors, so you may hang one of them."

If we make use of the measuring-rod of our conscious sense of equity to measure the unconscious inner lawgiver, we must decide that it is unjust, cruel, bloodthirsty, underhanded, and that above all, it wreaks revenge for alleged crimes on completely innocent persons.

The unconscious reason for that tendency of exchangeability is the phenomenon of "transference." Every neurotic can be compared to a person carrying around constantly *one* phonograph record and constantly on the lookout for a phonograph on which to play his only tune. In this simile the one and only record represents the basic *unconscious* neurotic tendency; the phonograph stands for the other person with whom the neurotic pattern can be repeated. Expressed differently, Freudian psychoanalysis has proven in fifty years of clinical experience that certain unconscious behavior patterns acquired in early childhood become petrified, and under the pressure of the "unconscious repetition compulsion" (Freud) are repeated throughout the remainder of life with eternal monotony—and completely without conscious awareness of that repetition. Thus, the unconscious "repetition machine" reels off the unconscious behavior pattern.

To make the irony of the situation complete, people behave in general in a very arrogant and supercilious manner when conscience is mentioned. The smart and sophisticated set has only irony and scorn for it. These people believe they are "above such nonsense." They are *not; no one* is for that matter. *The inner conscience functions despite conscious awareness or ignorance of it.* Of course, one cannot measure the conscience only by observable signs, such as feeling of guilt, depression, and anxiety. The conscience can be measured thus only in "symptomatic neuroses." In "personality difficulties" or characterologic neuroses none of these symptoms and signs may appear on the surface, and still they are operative.

A person who considers himself outside the "danger zone of conscience," to quote a witty patient, is like a man who says: "True, I lived through the day but I didn't breathe. . . ." Even naiveté should have its limits.

CHAPTER III

NORMAL AND NEUROTIC INNER FEELING OF GUILT

Unconscious feeling of guilt is the result of a discrepancy between Ego and Ego Ideal. The anti-libidinous Daimonion confronts the Ego with the self-created Ego Ideal. Both are contrasted and if something remains on the debit side, guilt is felt.

The whole process just described is, of course, *unconscious*. Its effects are felt in consciousness, however, in the form of feeling of guilt, depression, and inferiority.[1] Often these feelings are displaced, rationalized, and attributed to wrong sources; however, they are a dynamic factor.

The simplest way to avoid conflicts with the Janus-faced Super Ego is to prevent a discrepancy betwen Ego and Ego Ideal from arising. This advice seems as simple as it is difficult in reality, since it presupposes being constantly a "good boy."

The problem of how to be a "bad boy" without experiencing feeling of guilt is, fortunately, insoluble. Still, the unconscious Ego devises a series of techniques which neutralize at least too severe conflicts with the Super Ego, if the deviation between Ego and Ego Ideal is not too great.

Since the unconscious part of the personality consists of the triad, Id, Super Ego and unconscious Ego, an explanation of these terms is necessary. Id denotes the reservoir of repressed unconscious wishes; Super Ego the inner conscience; and unconscious Ego a sort of mediator between Id and Super Ego. Id, Super Ego, and unconscious Ego have often been personified in psychoanalytic literature as the criminal, district attorney, and lawyer, respectively. In *normal* conditions the criminal presents a wish, the district attorney rejects the wish and threatens the criminal so that he dares not put the thought into action. Here the process stops. Nothing happens since the approach to motility is unconsciously inhibited by a strong Ego. In *neurotic* conditions the inner district attorney is corrupt and can be "bribed" (Alexander) by depression, pain, un-

---

[1] "Feeling of inferiority" is an Adlerian misnomer and simplification. It simply means "feeling of guilt," and confuses the outward manifestations and rationalizations with the real problem, which is unconscious.

14

happiness. The go-between is a shyster lawyer (unconscious Ego). To the criminal he says: "You can't fulfill your wish without paying a penalty for it. If you consent to limit your wishes to unconscious fantasy only and to pay with depression and pain, I can fix it with the D. A." He pleads with the district attorney: "My client is a fool but a harmless one. Your main interest is to punish him. He'll take all of the punishment you want, but let him have his unconscious fantasy." On the basis of this neurotic compromise, the neurotic symptom and sign is established. Take, for example, an uncomplicated case of agoraphobia (street fear): The Id wish is exhibitionism. Every time the patient goes out into the street he feels fright, which he rationalizes more or less intelligently (traffic accident, heart attack, etc.). This fright pertains to the exhibitionistic fantasy; the fee to the Super Ego for this fantasy is unhappiness and restriction of normal life.

The problem cannot be explained without first making a precise distinction between "neurosis" and "normality." Neurosis is an anachronistic disease in which unconscious wishes and fantasies, stemming from early childhood, are permitted to manifest themselves in disguise on the condition of suffering. In *normal* conditions an unconscious, typically repressed, Id wish is presented and is refused by the Super Ego; since the outlet to motility is inhibited, the wish returns to the storehouse of the Id and remains either harmlessly deposited there or forms the raw material for sublimation, provokes dreams, or undergoes modifications until it can be expressed in harmless ways. In *neurotic* conditions, the situation is quite different because the Super Ego, the inner conscience, is "corrupt" and can be bribed by pain, depression and unhappiness to permit modifications of the original wish, in disguise under the condition of suffering.

Neurosis is, as Freud proved fifty years ago, an anachronism: it is the perpetuation of unconscious wishes and defense mechanisms stemming from early childhood, which every human being harbors or produces in *transitory* phases in the first five years of life. To use a banal example: Every human being goes through the phase of the oedipus complex. Normally the libidinous and aggressive wishes imbedded in this are given up. However, the hysteric neurotic, who regresses to the oedipal stage, makes out of a transitory phase, a permanent one. Such a neurotic, by sticking to these infantile oedipal wishes, unconsciously identifies every woman with his mother, and as a result has neurotic impotence.

The neurotic symptom, impotence, comprises "substitute gratifications" (Freud) embodied in the unconscious fantasy (of possessing the mother). The pleasure in living out the unconscious fantasy *is paid for by unhappiness.* Here the feeling of guilt enters. The neurotic psyche works on the basis of "bribing" the inner conscience. Neurotic feeling of guilt is one of the cornerstones of neurosis. Only by circumventing, "bribing," appeasing the inner conscience can the neurotic find his *modus vivendi.*

Neurotic symptoms and feeling of guilt are closely interconnected. The predominant part played by unconscious guilt has become known only gradually, even in analysis. Originally, stress was laid more on unconscious wishes. Freud first discovered the libidinous contents of the Id. The inhibiting conscience was first described as the inner "censor" who had to be circumvented in the veiled neurotic symptom. The more psychoanalysis progressed, the greater became the part attributed to the Super Ego, the inner conscience. The role of the unconscious Ego, which creates the defense mechanism, also became more and more pronounced.

I personally believe that every neurotic symptom has a three-layer structure. The original wish never comes to the surface directly. *An Id wish is presented (Layer 1). The Super Ego protests and a defense mechanism is created (Layer 2).* The Super Ego protests, however, even against the defense, and *a second defense mechanism is established (Layer 3).* This second defense mechanism is the neurotic symptom.

This strictly personal assumption differs from the original conceptions of early days of analysis, which were based on the idea that neurotic symptoms constitute a compromise between an unconscious wish and unconscious inhibition; in other words, assumed a two-layer structure. I believe that one of the main difficulties in psychoanalysis is the constant necessity to modify established formulations according to new experience. It is only human that even the analyst wants to cling to certain fixed notions, when ever-new facets of unconscious mechanisms are discovered. As a result, a hiatus is frequently apparent; contradictory views are often not coordinated for a considerable length of time.

A good example is the theory of dreams. The original Freudian formulation for the interpretation of dreams made the dream analogous to the neurotic symptom: According to it, in a dream an unconscious libidinous wish was presented, masked and symbolized to circumvent the "inner censor." Much later the formulation was broadened to include aggressive repressed wishes. And still the part played by the Super Ego was underestimated. When Freud brought forth his theory of life and death instincts, the situation became even more untenable, and still no revision was proposed. Only recently, in 1934, at the Luzerne International Psychoanalytic Convention, in a paper entitled "Instinct Dualism in Dreams,"[2] presented by the author and Dr. L. Jekels, was a necessary revision suggested. We concluded that every dream was "double-tracked," that is, it had to do with repressed libidinous and aggressive Id wishes *and* at the same time with reproaches stemming from the Super Ego. A successful dream copes with both tendencies: It fulfills, in a hallucinatory way, the repressed wishes *and* refutes the reproaches of conscience.[3]

The same approach holds true for neurotic symptoms. Only with great reluctance have I come to the conclusion that a neurotic symptom never "fulfills" the repressed wish, but fulfills only the defense against this wish. I have placed the stress more and more on the dominant part played by the powerful inner conscience.

These ideas had the following development. In the investigation of cases of depersonalization[4] in collaboration with Eidelberg, I found that these neurotics were warding off an exhibitionistic wish. The Super Ego objects, and the inner defense is established by changing from exhibitionism to voyeurism ("peeping"): these sick people observe themselves constantly. But, as usual, the Super Ego rejects the first defense and forces establishment of a second one. Self-voyeurism becomes painful. Self-observation becomes the predomi-

---

[2] Published in Imago, 1934, and Psychoanalyt. Quart. 1940.
[3] For details see Chapter XIV.
[4] "The Mechanism of Depersonalization," Internat. Ztschr. f. Psychoanalyse. 1935. Depersonalization is a strange feeling characterized by P. Schilder, one of the greatest authorities in that field as follows: "To the depersonalized, the world appears foreign, strange, uncanny, dreamlike. . . The tactile attributes of objects seem strangely altered. The patients complain not only about the change of their perceptive functions, their imaginative function seems disturbed as well. The patients feel their own imagination to be colorless. Some of these patients state that they can not imagine things at all. The whole emotional life shows severe disturbances, too. The patients complain that they can feel neither pleasure nor displeasure. Love and hate are 'dead.' "

nant surface symptom of depersonalized people. The next step was the discovery that cases of blushing (erythrophobia) also had a three-layer unconscious mechanism.[5] At that time I suspected that this three-layer structure was a specialty of the scoptophiliac drives (scopophilia comprises exhibitionism and voyeurism). Later experiences, however, seemed to show that this three-layer structure was involved in all human reactions. For instance, in cases of obsessional neurosis I found the same three-layer structure.[6] Instead of going further into theory, let us look at clinical examples.

An obsessional patient had, among many other symptoms, also the compulsion to think about the telephone number of his divorced wife, and often felt obsessional panic lest he forget this number. He had been divorced for twenty years (more precisely, his marriage had been annulled because of his complete impotence), hadn't seen his wife in two decades, didn't know where she lived, or even if she were still alive. The obsessional idea was connected with a telephone number of twenty years' standing; he knew that in the meantime telephone numbers were changed, but never dared look up the number in the telephone directory. The obvious interpretation was that he wished evil to his wife and his Super Ego reproached him because of his death wishes. The inner defense offered his Super Ego was (obsessional neurotics believe in "omnipotence of thoughts"): "Call her up and you will see that she is still alive, that I haven't killed her." In other words, this interpretation assumed, as is usual, in our literature of obsessional cases, a repressed aggressive tendency and an overdimensional feeling of guilt because of that aggression.

At that point a contradiction struck me. How was one to explain that a man so deeply masochistic should fight only against reproaches of aggression, and not of psychic masochism? It dawned on me that this aggression was only pseudo-aggression, that the really decisive Super Ego reproach pertained to exactly the opposite wish—psychic masochism. I assumed, therefore, that a three-layer structure was involved: (1) Wish to be mistreated, counteracted by a Super Ego reproach. (2) First defense mechanism of pseudo-aggression ("I am not masochistic in relation to my wife;

[5]"A New Approach to the Therapy of Erythrophobia," paper read before the XVth Internat. Psychoanalyt. Convention in Paris, 1938, published in Psychoanalyt. Quart., 1944.
[6]"The Forms of Aggression in Obsessional Neurosis," Psychoanalyt. Rev. 1942.

on the contrary, I want to kill her"). (3) Rejection of the defense, too, by the Super Ego, and reproaches to the unconscious Ego, resulting in establishment of a second defense: "I don't want to kill or harm my wife. Call up and you will see that she is unharmed."

The same mechanism could be studied in this patient in another symptom. He hadn't dared to read a newspaper for the last fifteen years. His rationalization was the following: He cared only for the New York Times, and in it the editorials were always arranged on the left side of the sheet, the right side containing death notices. He was magically attracted to the latter, always comparing age and the illness causing death, and worried lest he himself should die of the same illness as the deceased of his own age. This symptom had developed when an acquaintance of his who had swindled him out of money had committed suicide, allegedly after the patient had refused another loan.

The interpretation on the basis of the two-layer structure was obvious. Because of his aggressive wishes, the patient identified all deceased people with his father, later, substitute fathers (the acquaintance, etc.). Because of inner guilt, he believed that the same punishment would overtake him, too. I believe that this interpretation is not sufficient. It was more likely that the *end-result* of his inner conflict in childhood was deep masochistic passivity. His Super Ego reproached him with that passivity, forcing his unconscious Ego to furnish the first defense mechanism: pseudo-aggression in the form of death wishes. That defense, too, was counteracted by guilt feelings, with the result that the patient unconsciously had to produce a new alibi—turning of aggression toward himself.

The advantages which the unconscious Ego derives from the three-layer structure is that, by constantly fighting on a specious front, it can cover and preserve the dynamic wish. Of course, the "return of the repressed material" (Freud) takes place; in reproaching himself, the obsessional neurotic "enjoys" exactly the basically forbidden wish—psychic masochism.

It was "oral" neurosis which convinced me finally that every neurotic symptom has a three-layer structure. I found in analyses of more than twenty-five writers that these neurotics expressed in their writings, not unconscious wishes, but defenses.[7]. To give an

[7]See "On a Clinical Approach to the Psychoanalysis of Writers." The Psychoanalyt. Rev. 31:1, 1944.

example: A patient of mine wanted to write a comedy in which a man accepted the sacrifices of his wife only to learn that his whole life thereafter was made miserable by her resenting her sacrifice. Let us assume that the man had written that aggressive comedy (he never did!) and that one hundred years later a psychoanalytic biographer would make a study of the famous author. He would come to the conclusion that the object of his study was an exceedingly aggressive person to whom nothing, not even sacrifice, was sacred. Actually, however, the patient was an exceedingly passive hypochondriac. What he expressed as his work was not *aggressive Id-wish*, but the defense against his passivity, via pseudo-aggression.

Having come to the conclusion that every neurotic symptom contains a three-layer structure, I had to test that theory on the most superficial neurosis—hysteria. I found that it applied to this neurosis as well, even more, that it offered here the clue to certain therapeutic disappointments. To take an example:

A certain patient produced the symptom of a tremor of the hands. An organic neurologic examination had negative results. He let fall every object that he took hold of, or could hold it only with a noticeable tremor, clearly visible to any observer. The symptom had appeared during his sixth year, and had persisted since that time almost without a change.

Analysis showed that the patient had been especially aggressive from his very earliest childhood. His favorite occupation was tormenting animals, among them chickens and ducks whose necks he twisted around until he literally tore their heads off. And as a child he was equally cruel to his sister. For instance, when he was five years old he suddenly caught hold of the little four-year-old girl while crossing a bridge over a stream, and threw her into the water, then immediately jumped after her and rescued her. When questioned as to why he had done this, he answered that his sister was cowardly about swimming and he wanted in this way to teach her to be brave. ("Rationalization," according to E. Jones.)

Another time, when his sister was just recovering from an appendectomy, he put her on his back and started to climb a tree. The little girl clung to him, unable to make any strenuous movements for fear of tearing open her wound which had not yet healed. Our patient climbed a high tree, deposited the little girl on a branch, then got down himself, and in spite of his sisters' protests and cries, paid no further attention to her. Even when a severe thunderstorm came up soon after, deadening the sound of her screams, and when her parents had looked for her everywhere without success, the boy was not touched and pretended to know nothing about the matter. Only several hours later, after the little girl had almost "died of fright," (to use our patient's own words) and had contracted a bad cold, did he bring her down from the tree. His parents punished him severely, reproaching him for his "bad character." Similar scenes were repeated many times.

At the end of his sixth year the boy began to attend school, and his behavior underwent a radical change. He suddenly became "a good boy," that is, he stopped being directly aggressive, but with equal suddenness then produced the symptom of the trembling of his hands whenever he intended to grasp something. Analysis showed that there, as in every neurotic symptom, unconscious pleasure and unconscious mechanism of punishment were at work. The unconscious wish said: "I want to be aggressive as I was in early childhood and stretch out my hands to choke others, for instance, my sister." The unconscious prohibition of his conscience said: "You must not be aggressive towards your sister." Both tendencies were now satisfied in the symptom, though only symbolically and in the realm of unconscious fantasy. The patient stretched out his hand with aggressive intention, but the aggression was inhibited by the veto of conscience, and the hand trembled. In other words, the aggressive wish of early childhood was repeated but only on the condition of suffering, for the symptom was a real torment to the patient, hampering him in his work and rendering him unfit for society. "At the price of suffering, you may be allowed the aggression you desire," such was the unconscious compromise represented in the tremor of the hands. The objection that the pleasure element was gained in an awkward manner and might have been more comfortably and less dangerously attained in some other way is answered by the fact that conscious thinking had nothing to do with the whole matter.

Nothing changed in the patient's behavior until his aggression, or rather, pseudo-aggression was discarded. His symptom, too, had a passive basis, (wish to be sexually overwhelmed) warded off by pseudo-aggression, warded off in turn by the second defense, the symptom.

Even in simple cases of hysteric potency disturbances, it became clear to me that the oedipal wish was but a defense against the deeper feminine tendencies. Strangely enough, the sequence of events was: The boy regressed to the negative oedipus (feminine identification). This was counteracted by guilt. As a defense, the positive oedipus was mobilized, with resultant symptom of impotence.

How important is the understanding of these facts is shown by the following example: A young man consulted a physician because of his anxiety that he might choke or stab his wife during coitus. He related that a few months previously he had seen in the movies the dramatization of Emile Zola's novel, "The Human Beast," in which the hero shrank from having intercourse with a girl for fear that in his sexual frenzy he might strangle her. This attitude is attributed by Zola, erroneously, to hereditary alcoholism. The patient could not forget this scene, and applied the whole thing to himself, fearing that he also might commit such a crime. He became impotent with his wife, depressed, and felt close to a "nervous breakdown." The physician, who was interested in analysis, sent the patient to me, stating: "The man identifies himself with the murderer." I questioned this immediately, for, had this been his inner conflict, the patient would not have become consciously aware of it. I suspected that the patient rather identified with the endangered girl, warding off this feminine identification with pseudo-aggression. Subsequent analysis proved the correctness of that assumption.

The understanding that only the *defense against the defense* is visible on the psychic surface explains a series of facts never correctly evaluated: instances of intuitive understanding. I would like to exemplify that from the works and lives of two literary geniuses.

Stendhal, the famous French writer, discovered, two generations before Freud, his individual oedipus complex. This was strange, since normally, this complex is repressed. And still, in "La Vie d'Henri Brulard," (written in 1835) we read:

"My mother, Henriette Gagnon, was a charming woman, and *I was in love with her*. I hasten to add that I lost her when I was seven years old. When I loved her, around perhaps 1789, I had the same character as in 1828, at the time I was madly in love with Alberte de Rubempré (a sweetheart of Stendhal's). *The manner in which I go on the hunt for happiness* had scarcely altered except for one thing. In respect to the physical part of love, I was in the same situation as Caesar would have been, had he returned to earth, with regard to the use of cannon and smaller missiles of warfare. I could have learned it very easily and it would not have changed my technique. *I wanted to cover my mother with kisses, and there shouldn't be any dresses there.* She loved me passionately, and kissed me often. I returned her caresses with such fire, that she often found it necessary to leave me. *I despised my father when his arrival interrupted our kisses.* I always wanted to kiss her on the breast. . . . For my part, *I was as criminal as I possibly could be, I was madly in love with her charms."*

It is understandable that this self-confessed intentional incest of the six-year-old caused some controversy among the Stendhal biographers. Most of them drew themselves out of the noose by declaring that they were products of his imagination. They minimized them as cynicism which were not meant to be taken seriously, and even declared that Stendhal, as a joker given to mystification, wished to make fools of the world. Other biographers, on the other hand, believed Stendhal, such as Weigand, Zweig, von Oppeln-Bronikowski. Weigand remarks, for instance, "This confession can be recommended to the adherents of Freudian theory as a perfect example." And Zweig summarizes, "In hardly any other place will psychoanalysis find a better oedipus complex presented in literary form, than in the first pages of Stendhal's autobiography, in Henry Brulard." When one hears that Stendhal always spoke in a disparaging way of his father—bastard was a mild epithet—that he admits that he was in favor of the French revolution because his father preferred the aristocrats and the followers of the Bourbons, that during the terror he desired his father's arrest, all sorts of discomfort, and even his death, and that when he passed away he merely said "I have been informed of a change of circumstance," in short, his dislike of his father was so intense that in his testament he left instructions to be buried as "Arrigo Beyle, Milanese," although actually a native of Grenoble; taking all this into consideration, the intensity of his positive oedipus complex can certainly not be questioned.

Hence the "adherents of Freudian theory," apostrophized by Weigand, can note the existence of the oedipus complex in Stendhal, can refuse to discuss it further by pointing to Stendhal's own confession, they can cut short the dispute of the biographers as to whether the incest was experienced or merely imagined, by tersely calling attention to the identity between inner and outer reality; in short, they can smugly register, catalogue, and rubricate the case Stendhal as a masterly example of the oedipus complex, and hold it up as a paradigm to the unbelievers. Perhaps this description of Stendhal's incest can make an analytic career for itself and achieve the same number of analytic citations as Diderot's statement in his *Nephew of Rameau:* "If the little boy were left alone, if he retained all his characteristic naiveté, and if, to the slight reasoning powers of the infant in the cradle were adjoined the intensity of passion of the thirty-year-old, he would strangle his father and sleep with his mother."

And yet, it is just at this point that the problem begins. The question we pose is: *How did it happen that Stendhal did not repress his oedipus complex, but instead retained his awareness of it?* We are placed in the grotesque situation of not being able to use this rare confession of Stendhal's (or more correctly his self-accusation), and are forced to seek the unconscious motivation which enabled the perception of these subterranean connections. Only then will we perceive how everything fits together.

In other words: Under what conditions will a person become aware of his own oedipus complex, and remain conscious of it? (Exempted here are those lightning flashes of insight, with as rapid repression.) In these days we must eliminate first one source of error, namely, that the individual in question has heard anything about Freud's great contribution, psychoanalysis. It is just for this reason that Stendhal's confession is so important, which was formulated in such exact Freudian terms two generations previous to Freud's. As I understand this problem, the following types of adults can become aware of the oedipus complex under certain exceptional conditions: (1) the psychologic genius; (2) the schizophrenic psychotic; (3) certain types of schizoid personalities (sometimes termed moral insanity); (4) observation of others; the normally functioning repression is lifted for a short time, because of extreme psychic masochism, and the impressions of other persons which the individual obtains are utilized against his own person as a form of punishment.

We have no way of measuring the genius except on the basis

of a rather intuitive judgment. To explain away Stendhal's psyche by saying he was a psychologic genius means to abandon any attempt to unravel his personality, since we are ignorant of the intrapsychologic approach of the genius. The small number of psychologic geniuses of the last one hundred and fifty years have not devoted their time to a study of this problem. The three other types listed can also be excluded as far as Stendhal is concerned. He was neither schizophrenic, nor a schizoid personality, nor did he observe the oedipus complex originally in someone else.

We are exactly as far along as we were before, and at the most we might suspect that masochistic motives play a part in this introspection. However, this will not bring us any farther in the genesis of Stendhal's discovery of the oedipus complex.

Evidently, a *fifth possibility exists,* which could explain a person's own discovery of the oedipus complex, namely, if for instance the *negative oedipal* conflict, that is, the unconscious feminine identification, had been of great intensity, the unconscious ego in this dangerous situation might attempt to effect a compromise by releasing the least unpleasant memory, in order to retain the more unpleasant, which, if conscious, would be still more embarrassing. Hence, the unconscious, feminine tendency in Stendhal must have been one of his strongest drives, if his ego exerted every effort to retain it, even at the price of permitting awareness of other repressed material. This was actually the case, as I have attempted to prove in my book on Stendhal, to which reference may be made for details.[8]

The other example is Sophocles' "King Oedipus," from which Freud took the name of the complex. How are we to explain that Sophocles knew so much about this complex? Why didn't he repress it? The probable answer is that the Greek culture of this time was a homosexual one. Homosexuality is an oral neurosis.[9] As a defense against it, the oedipal wishes become conscious.

In neurosis the Ego suffers constantly because the repressed fantasies, dynamically charged, are counteracted by inner guilt. The Ego is weak, and almost the *entire aggression of the personality is*

---

[8] See the Stendhal study in "Talleyrand—Napoleon—Stendhal—Grabbe." Psychoanalyt. Verlag 1935.

[9] "Eight Prerequisites for the Psychoanalytic Treatment of Homosexuality," Psychoanalyt. Rev., 1944. This paper contains also a section of the extensive literature on that subject.

used by the Super Ego to punish the Ego. The Ego's only defense is "sexualization" of the punishment. Every neurotic is full of *"psychic masochism,"* that is, unconscious "pleasure in pain." By means of "masochization," the punishment meted out by the inner conscience becomes an unconscious pleasure. Of course, the whole "sexualization of punishment" presupposes an abnormal Ego. Normally, pain is avoided and is contradictory to pleasure.

A "normal" man or woman is not the opposite of a neurotic, but is "his brother or sister under the skin" (Kipling), with a quantitative difference. Formulated loosely: A small amount of neurotic tendencies is called normality. Formulated more precisely: A not *too* neurotic person is euphemistically characterized as normal. Everybody has neurotic tendencies, but not in everybody are they increased quantitatively to a degree where *neurosis* results. The problem is one of quantity, not quality, although as Hegel correctly remarked, there is a point where "quantity changes into quality."

The decisive difference between a normal and a neurotic person is that the former has overcome to a greater degree his infantile conflicts and is capable of having a *relatively more objective outlook* on reality, whereas the latter misuses reality for the unconscious repetition of his infantile conflicts. Every neurotic constantly repeats his unconscious patterns acquired in early childhood.

Neurotic people are constantly in conflict with their environment. They are fighting their unconscious battles on two fronts: inside, as visible in their symptoms, signs, and personality difficulties, and outside in their quarrels, obstinacy, provocativeness. Hence the necessity arises to use a yardstick for distinguishing whether specific conflicts with the outer world are normal or neurotic. The differentiation is even more necessary, since a "normal" person can have, *in a specific instance,* a "neurotic" conflict, and a neurotic person a "normal" conflict.

The tabulation at the top of page 27 makes a quick distinction possible.*

I shall discuss now the specific points on the basis of a clinical example.

A patient of mine, a physician, called me one evening to inform me that his friend Dr. X, also a physician, wanted him to arrange an appointment for him to consult me because of "personality diffi-

---

*First published in Quart. Rev. Psych. & Neurol. 1:1, 1946.

Normal Aggression	Neurotic Aggression ("Pseudo-Aggression")
1. Used only in self-defense.	1. Used indiscriminately when an infantile pattern is repeated with an innocent bystander.
2. Object of aggression is a "real" enemy.	2. Object of aggression is a "fantasied" or artificially-created enemy.
3. No accompanying unconscious feeling of guilt.	3. Feeling of guilt always present.
4. Dosis: Amount of aggression discharged corresponds to provocation.	4. Dosis: Slightest provocation — greatest aggression.
5. Aggression always used to harm enemy.	5. Pseudo-aggression often used to provoke "masochistic pleasure" expected from enemy's retaliation.
6. Timing: Ability to wait until enemy is vulnerable.	6. Timing: Inability to wait, since pseudo-aggression used as defense mechanism against inner reproach of psychic masochism.
7. Not easily provoked.	7. Easily provoked.
8. Element of infantile game absent; no combination with masochistic-sadistic feelings; the only feeling is that a necessary though disagreeable job had to be performed.	8. Element of infantile game present, combined with masochistic-sadistic excitement, usually repressed.
9. Success expected.	9. Defeat unconsciously expected.

culties," the nature of which were not specified in the telephone conversation. The appointment was made for the next day. At the appointed time the prospective patient appeared, and after introductions, started to shout in the waiting room: "I haven't the slightest confidence in you." I answered smilingly, "Well, this will be a short visit. Do you want to leave now?" The patient smiled, too. "No, let's have a talk." An observer would have classified the man's behavior—a physician!—as both irrational and aggressive. Irrational because no one forced him to consult me without a minimum of confidence; aggressive because, being a physician himself, he was very sensitive to the upbraidings which physicians receive from patients. Asked why he had no confidence in me, he replied that the preceding evening he had had a theoretical discussion with the physician who recommended him to me, and they could not agree on a specific type of anesthesia. "Well, if an analyzed man talks such nonsense, his analysis can't have been a good one—though I'll admit that my friend has changed for the better in other respects." The senselessness of his argument was augmented when I asked him: "Was your little speech prepared?" The man admitted that it was; in other words, his resistance was impersonal and rather unfair, because he didn't even give me a chance. "What would you have done to a patient who entered *your* office shouting in such a manner?" I asked. "I'd throw him out," was the prompt reply. "That was exactly what *you* wanted. . . ." was my conclusion. In other words, the man used pseudo-aggression to achieve masochistic pleasure. The naive observer would diagnose his behavior as aggression, the analyst, as psychic masochism covered by pseudo-aggression. Superfluous to state, the whole life of this patient was based on that technique.

We see in this example all of the nine points enumerated previously.

1. *Self-defense or prefabricated pattern?* No self-defense was involved for the patient, since the simplest way of defending his precious neurosis was to call off the appointment. His later analysis proved that he acquired the pattern of provoking conflicts in early childhood and repeated it later like a parrot. His technique was always the same. First, he unconsciously provoked a conflict. Not being conscious that he himself provoked the conflict, he saw only the aggressive reaction of the person attacked, who, of course, fought back. With righteous indignation the patient fought back on his side, seemingly in self-defense. As the final act, he pitied himself, reflecting, "Such a thing can happen only to me." In this final self-pity he was, of course, unaware that he was enjoying the "psychic masochistic pleasure" of being mistreated.[10]

2. *Real or self-created enemy?* In our example there was no real enemy involved, since the man wanted help from a physician, and by no stretch of the imagination could the helping physician be construed as an enemy. Therefore the man just used a harmless outsider for his unconscious repetition-repertoire.

3. *Presence or absence of feeling of guilt?* Neurotic aggression is *always* accompanied by unconscious guilt. The reason for this is that the original person against whom the libidinous and aggres-

[10]That triad of the "mechanism of orality" was repeatedly described by me. For details see Chapter VI.

sive wishes in childhood were directed were mother and father. For the more normal person this attachment is practically solved; therefore no guilt appears in "real" aggression, since the enemy is never identified with images from one's own childhood. Moreover, the normal person doesn't pick a fight *per se;* he just defends himself when attacked, thus having the best of inner alibis. The patient described, on the other hand, immediately identified me unconsciously with a person in his childhood—as he revealed in his admission that his speech was prepared, therefore the attack "impersonal." As a result he suffered feelings of guilt, visible in the quick collapse of his aggression when I didn't play his neurotic game, refusing to let myself be provoked.

4. *Discrepancy between provocation and counter-aggression?* Normally one doesn't shoot sparrows with machine guns. Where a normal person teases or uses repartee, a neurotic one strikes. True, he strikes only to be struck back, and harder, for that matter.

5. *Harm the enemy or one's self?* The normal person, if he fights, wants one thing only: to victimize the aggressor. What he abhors most is pain, depression, and guilt. For him that trio is just painful and disagreeable. He has no unconscious strings attached to it. Pain is pain. But for the neurotic, the situation is different. He craves "psychic masochistic pleasure." In other words, he makes out of pain—pleasure. Without knowledge of this fantastic fact, neurosis is incomprehensible.

To give an example from the analysis of a *perverted* masochist: A patient's[11] masturbation consisted of striking his penis forcefully on the edge of the table and the more painful the procedure was, the more pleasurable it was. He brushed aside the objection that to a normal person pain and pleasure were exclusive of each other, and considered the analyst's statement that his way of achieving sexual pleasure might be a punishment in a concentration camp, simply as the expression of "jealousy."

Imagine the same pleasure, consciously rejected but unconsciously approved, and we have a clue to the behavior of the physician of our example. He "hated" being mistreated, played the part of the "he man," but because of his unconscious provocation, was constantly "mistreated." In other words, he was a "psychic maso-

[11]For details see "Working Through in Psychoanalysis." The Psychoanalyt. Rev., No. 32, 4, 1945.

chist" and not a "perverted masochist." Psychic masochism and perversion masochism are different entities.

6. *Waiting for the propitious moment possible or impossible?* There is a clearcut distinction in the timing of aggressive actions. The normal person more often uses the right, the neurotic person the wrong, moment. The reason is that the normal person wants victory, the neurotic unconsciously wants defeat. The normal person strives after the current aim, the neurotic person after the current defense mechanism.[12] Therefore, to furnish his inner alibi—this neurotic cannot wait.

7. *Easy or difficult to provoke?* The normal person has a fair-sized narcissism which protects him from outside criticism; the neurotic is "touchy" to the nth degree. Since the normal person doesn't start fights for the sake of fighting, but fights only in self-defense, he is relatively difficult to provoke. Quite the contrary with neurotics. They see an offense even where a normal person doesn't. In our example the patient felt provoked because of a divergence of opinions on narcosis.

8. *Presence or absence of masochistic-sadistic excitement?* The normal person feels, in acting out his aggression in self-defense, that a necessary though disagreeable job has to be performed—nothing else. The situation is quite different for the neurotic person. He feels a queer excitement, often in the genital region. That feeling is often unclear to him—it is a combination of infantile masochistic and sadistic remnants. The element of infantile game is discernible, so completely absent in such situations in normal people. To be sure, the feeling of neurotic-sexual excitement (pain, tension, shrinking of penis or erection, seldom even involuntary ejaculation) is more or less repressed; the defense against masochistic tendencies with pseudo-aggression is often the only surface reverberation. A patient, for instance, related a newspaper report of rape by colonial soldiers in a captured city as if it were some amusing game. His logic told him that his feeling was shameful, but it was there. Analysis could prove that he identified with the raped women and secondarily warded off this identification with queer pseudo-aggression in thoughts. The element of infantile game was very pronounced in this case. In the evening he felt a strong sexual urge and had inter-

---

[12] See "On the Psychoanalysis of the Ability to Wait and of Impatience." The Psychoanalyt. Rev., Vol. XXVI No. 1. 1939.

course twice with fantasies centering around the rape. Consciously he identified with the raping soldiers; unconsciously with the victims. This can serve as a typical example of the warding off of unconscious feminine-masochistic wishes with pseudo-aggression, intercourse being misused for that alibi.

9. *Success or defeat sought?* The normal person wants victory if he is forced to fight. The neurotic person seeks external defeat, which feeds his unconscious masochism. *His* victory is achievement of masochistic pleasure. These self-constructed defeats are brought about by using arguments which boomerang—for instance, the illogical behavior of the patient in our example.

Neurotics fight their battles only to lose them. The consequences are far-reaching if one takes into consideration their lack of success, which includes also inability to enjoy even transitory success. Those neurotics who are of the criminal variety make use of courts of justice to administer to them their required portion of masochism. The literature on that subject is too extensive to be reported here; it has been dealt with in other papers.[13] In my opinion the criminal is the embodiment, not of aggression, but of exactly the opposite, passivity.

A "not too neurotic" person has the advantage over the neurotic that his Ego is stronger, that is, has *more residual aggression with which to rebuff reproaches of the inner conscience.* Besides the difference in amount of free aggression with which to fight unreasonable reproaches of the conscience, there is a fundamental difference between "normal" and neurotic people in the way they react to aggression.

One could object that neurotic aggressions are not the only tendencies to which the inner conscience (Super Ego) objects. It objects against libidinous drives, too, to be sure. But both are interconnected. A simple example demonstrates this. If the child masturbates, he does so because he wants to achieve a libidinous aim— "sexual" pleasure—but, *at the same time* oversteps aggressively an educational command, that of not touching the penis. The resulting guilt pertains to both elements.

Another distinction between normal and neurotic guilt is that only for the neurotic Super Ego are wish and action fantastically considered to be identical. In other words, a neurotic individual acts *unconsciously* on the erroneous assumption that he is still omnipotent. He pays for that inner assumption with punishment for unconscious wishes, too. As a clinical example I quote the following from the diary of a severe obsessional neurotic.

"Woke up early, parents not up yet. Although I feel wide awake, some magic power keeps me in bed; besides, I reflect that I slept very badly and should have a little more rest because of my bad state of health and my nervousness. I fall into a delicious half-slumber. Waking up again, I hear my parents moving about in the hall outside. The bathroom is occupied; great annoyance at not being able to get up yet—a feeling of captivity. The going to and fro, the opening and closing of the door increase my discontent. I am told that it is half-past eight; annoyance at the time wasted. Yet I stay in bed a little longer, to enjoy the peace which is reigning again after all the disagreeable noises. But I want to get up as soon as possible. Suddenly the question occurs to me, 'What's the good of using the time to work?' A feeling of infinite loathing and wretchedness. My studies seem so dull, so stupid, so hopeless and useless. I shall probably never pass that horrible examination. And even if I do get a position, who knows whether I shall not fail at the very beginning, because of the deep resistance I feel against my presumable profession? Even if things turn out most propitiously, I am going to have a perfectly stupid kind of work, quite unworthy of a thinking human being, mechanical and yet wretchedly paid. Everything I did to procure a good position has failed, and all the plans I'm considering now are doomed to fail, too. (While writing these lines I am becoming terribly afraid that all of these evils are bound to happen, as I employed the present indicative because of the direct form of speech, and that is the *reality* tense.)

" 'But I have to get up anyway to do my work,' I say to myself, and sticking energetically to this thought, I am just about to get off my bed. But stop! If, while thinking of my studies (imagining, for instance, my professor's face), I put my foot on the floor, the stamping involved means destroying the success of my examination. So I stay in bed. (When writing down this diary for the first time, I became afraid that, because I had used the term 'foot' collectively, instead of 'feet,' I might really have only one foot at some time as a punishment for not appreciating my normal physical condition.

Copying this just now I perceive a ghastly mystic connection: On the day of the above-mentioned examination, the son of our caretaker had an accident on his motorcycle and lost a leg and thigh. As to the examination, I have passed it all right, it is true, but I regarded the misfortune that happened on the same day to our caretaker's son, who lives in the same house, as an awful sign of fate, which wants to show how evil clings to me and how my good luck means bad luck to others. To this another anxiety was added. The decisive passage that I was asked about in the examination was on page 113, and yet I passed. An optimist might come to the conclusion that the superstition attached to the number 13 was unfounded. I, however, feared that the 'council of thirteen' had only failed to grasp this opportunity of doing harm by chance, and would make up for it with a vengeance, infuriated by not having obtained its claim.)

"To return to the stages of getting up: The first attempt at rousing myself having failed, I think for a moment that all of these fears are only obsessions, and I see the image of my analyst before me. But now I do not dare to put my feet to the ground at all, as the success of the analysis would be annihilated if I did. As a last means of rousing myself, I think of my girl friend. If I stamp on the floor at this moment, I do not risk anything of much importance, as I believe that I have reached a point where I can replace her quite easily. (I wanted to write, 'I have reached . . .' but was afraid that so pronounced a statement would be punished as a wicked conceit.) In addition, when she is late for an appointment I have repeatedly thrown away smoked cigarettes in my impatience, without losing her love by that. But then it occurs to me that we had intercourse some time ago without using a contraceptive, and that I might be punished by being given illegitimate fatherhood for the presumptuous idea of being safe from that symbolically-determined Power of throwing away and stamping. As thinking of something cheerful has proved of no avail, I try imagining something particularly unpleasant, so I think of the face of a former boss of mine. In this case the annihilating act of stepping on the ground could not have any practical consequence, so it would refer to something I had given up anyhow, my office career. But an unpleasant idea like that does not rouse a man either. At last I try to imagine something innocuous (for instance, the party last night, which bored me horribly), and clinging to this thought up to the critical moment of stamping, I get out of bed."

Anyone who tries to deduce the power of conscience from its outward manifestations is bound to come to false conclusions. The reasons are the following.

First, the effects of the *unconscious conscience are unconscious.* A person can show no guilt, can even brag about his courage and state optimistically that he just takes "reasonable chances," whereas in reality he is embarking at that very moment on a death-or-prison ride. Many neurotics with "personality difficulties" belong in this group.

Second, people converse with themselves and each other on the basis of *rationalizations* only, completely unaware of the inner, unconscious departments of the personality.

Third, one of the techniques of *normal* conscience is, fortunately, to prevent criminal or immoral actions from the start. The *neurotic* conscience works differently: *It lures the victim* by its "small voice" allowing pseudo-optimism *into situations which bring about punishment or self-destruction.*

Fourth, we have to distinguish between the "operative" and the "non-operative" conscience. When the layman says that his conscience has prevented a specific action, he refers only to desired actions *not* performed. He is correct as far as he goes. However, there is a large group of people who perpetrate "impossible" actions and are punished later when caught. These people, too, are under the influence of their inner conscience, though a dichotomy is visible: *Their conscience doesn't prevent the action but insists on punishment post facto.* Even the greatest criminal operates unconsciously on that basis.[14]

The Super Ego, with its constituents, Ego Ideal and Daimonion, is an *unconscious* institution. It has little to do with the conscious department of the conscience. The latter contains a set of rules which are small change compared with the high currency of the Super Ego. If a dollar bill should fall out of your pocket and be picked up by a small undernourished boy, and you rejected the suggestion of a bystander that you report the thief to the police, saying "My conscience wouldn't let me be responsible for sending the

[14]See Chapter XV.

child to a reform school . . ." you would have acted under the influence of the conscious part of your conscience.

The real power of the conscience is based on the *unconscious* part of that strange intrapsychic institution.

Despite all of the safeguards the "normal" person unconsciously takes to escape guilty feelings, he still has to cope with a good many of them. The reason is the insatiable death instinct and its clinical derivatives: guilt, depression and self-punishment. It is practically never possible to achieve fully the demands of one's own Ego Ideal, and every time a discrepancy arises, even in homeopathic doses, the Daimonion uses it as a hitching post for torture. With eternal monotony the self-created Ego Ideal is shown to the Ego like a "silent model" and guilt extracted.

One cannot escape the impression that a great many of the irrational feelings of guilt, depression, expectation of impending doom with which the human being is troubled are connected only secondarily with the reality factors which the individual consciously believes to be their cause. The primary cause of these feelings seems to be quite independent of the happenings to which they are consciously attributed, and the result of an intrinsic self-destructive drive which Freud has called the "death instinct."

Historically speaking, Freud first discovered the repressed libidinous drives of the personality, later described as the principal component of the oedipus complex. During the oedipal stage, from the ages of two to five, the child wants to take the place of the parent of the same sex, to enjoy all the forbidden pleasures of that parent with parent of the opposite sex. The boy, for instance, wants to act the role of his father toward his mother. His wishes in this connection correspond to his distorted fantasy of what constitutes sex, and have little to do with coitus, as the layman erroneously believes they have. These wishes are counteracted by "castration fear," that is, fear that the father will retaliate by hurting the organ executing these wishes in the fantasy culminating in masturbation. In the early years of psychoanalysis, all of the fantastic fears of the child were attributed to phallic castration fear and masturbation fear. The next step was the observation that there was no direct congruity between the real threats administered to the child and his irrational amount of fear; severe education did not automatically produce frightened children, nor a lenient one fearless children. Freud discovered the "anal" castration fear, as the precursor of phallic fear. He found that the child misconstrued the daily loss of stools as castration. Staercke described the precursor of both—phallic and anal-castration fears—as "oral" castration fear. He signalized weaning as the first "castration." Some analysts (for instance Rank) went still further and were of the opinion that Freud's aphoristic remark that birth itself produces strong fears in the child is the real foundation of all fears.[15]

We see a direct retrogressive line in all of these attempts to trace back the origin of fear historically deeper and deeper—birth, weaning, loss of stool, loss of the genitals.

Later Freud discovered the importance of aggression to be equal to that of libidinous tendencies. Since the execution of all libidinous wishes involved at the same time aggression, expressed in going against educational commands, fear became the warning signal of danger stemming from both. Still later, it was stressed that the child projects his own aggression upon the educator, a point brought forward especially by M. Klein and E. Jones. Freud himself pointed out in his last years that every bit of the child's aggression which cannot be executed because of the child's helplessness adds to the aggression of the Super Ego.

Freud's last contribution to the problem was his contention of the duality of death and life instincts. He assumed that there is a force in the human being bent on self-destruction. This force is counteracted by an equally powerful force—Eros—which tries to redirect self-destruction outward. In the interplay of both he finally surmised the process of life. That the individual feeling of guilt leading to unconscious self-punishment is an entity constantly to be reckoned with, is proven in specific techniques by means of which some neurotics strike a bargain with their inner conscience. Freud described such a technique as early as 1914. He called a certain group of individuals "the exceptions"[16] because their inner conscience allowed them to transgress moral laws *because* of their intense suffering. As an example he quoted the Duke of Gloucester in Shakespeare's "Richard III":

[15]Other theories go further and assume residues of old fears of previous generations, dating back thousands of years, as the ultimate basis of irrational fears.
[16]Ges. Schr. X. pp. 288-93.

"But I, that am not shaped for sportive tricks,
Nor made to court an amorous looking-glass,
I that am rudely stamp'd and want love's majesty
To strut before a wanton ambling nymph,
I, that am curtail'd of this fair proportion,
Cheated of feature by dissembling nature,
Deform'd, unfinish'd, sent before my time
Into this breathing world, scarce half made up,
And that so lamely and unfashionable
That dogs bark at me as I halt by them;
And therefore, since I cannot prove a lover
To entertain these fair well-spoken days,
I am determined to prove a villain
And hate the idle pleasures of these days."

Other neurotics who, because of the quantitative amount of inner guilt, cannot be cured, even in analysis, lose their symptoms and signs when they exchange them for some greater danger consuming, like a sponge, all their guilt. Freud mentions in this connection, for instance, severe types of obsessional neurotics, incurable even in psychoanalysis because of the insurmountable quantitative factor, who lose their legion of neurotic symptoms when they have a destructive operation, get cancer, or lose their fortune.

As an example of how the feeling of guilt can be appeased in a sort of bargain with the inner conscience, I quote once more a passage from the diary of a severe obsessional neurotic as mentioned before:

"All of the countless troubles, anxieties and obsessions that haunt me day by day, the painful discrepancy between my wishes and my abilities which manifests itself upon every occasion, my economic inefficiency and my dread of the future, my constant attempts and failures, my horror of death, my bitter self-reproaches for time wasted, the legion of sufferings that persecute me are all checked for a time only if some greater actual grief appears. This I call 'central suffering.' The ideal central suffering has the quality of being, while not injurious to my entire life, strong enough to concentrate all of my forces of suffering in one point, as it were, and to make me forget all other troubles and vexations for the moment. An example is some amorous grief. It results in the happiest condition I know—a dull, even sense of depression, a tight heavy feeling in my chest, which seems to be encircled as if by a hoop, but with all of that, a kind of happiness in comparison to my painful restlessness at other times, to the incessant appearing and disappearing of anxieties and injuries. These are checked a little by the central suffering, but when that has vanished, they shoot up from every corner of my soul like poison snakes and rapacious beasts, and make my life a burden. When I have a central suffering, my obsessions also cease almost completely. If one does appear, I suppress it with the simple admonition, 'Stop; you have a central suffering and are not obliged to have obsessions.' Of course, this consideration, bringing in its wake the desire for some central suffering, rouses anxious apprehensions again that destiny, provoked by such a perverted wish, will send me a grief that will make me suffer enormously throughout all my life."

An important depository of inner guilt is in "worries," which can spring out of almost anything. Life consists mainly of the expectance of things to come. If people have a negative expectation of future events, the depression accompanying it is such a depository. To complicate matters, naive optimism may become in the same way as neurotic pessimism the depository of *future* feelings of guilt. One must distinguish between *normal* refusal to be bothered too much by anticipation of unhappy events and *neurotic* optimism, which bargains for future troubles by oversight of consequences which reasonably must be expected.

The problem of *psychic masochism* is often misunderstood. People having superficial knowledge of psychiatric problems often refer to it as "self-punishment." As a matter of fact, it is far more: It is the most fantastic device of the unconscious Ego to transform the punishment meted out by the Super Ego into inner unconscious pleasure. It is a reduction to absurdity of a punishment. Punishment loses its horror if the victim unconsciously likes it. Basically, it is a triumph of erotic tendencies over the thanatic derivatives accumulated in the Daimonion. One could say that the fact of psychic masochism is the most amazing slave rebellion of the tortured Ego against its chronic torturer—the inner conscience. Undoubtedly not a solution one would recommend—and still from the fantastic "remedy" one can deduce the fantastic severity of the torture!

Chapter IV

A GREAT POET'S OPINION OF THE DEVELOPMENT OF THE CONSCIENCE

Works of great poets often contain remarkable intuitive insight into the dynamics of unconscious processes. Interestingly enough, we have in Calderon's "Life is a Dream" (La vida es sueno) an example of how the poet imagines the development of conscience.[1]

In the following, excerpts are given from a longer study written in collaboration with Dr. Angelo Garma (Buenos Aires), entitled: "On a poetic tendencious presentation of the genesis of inner conscience."

I. Introductory Remarks. In the course of an epistolary exchange of ideas on psychoanalytic problems, Dr. Garma and I came to discuss "La vida es sueno" by Calderon de la Barca, one of the most famous works of Spanish literature, as well as of world literature. Our attention was attracted by this drama because here Calderon presents a creature who, in the beginning of the first act, does not appear to have any conscience at all but who acquires one suddenly in the last act. The question arose: How does a great poet imagine the genesis of the conscience; what happens between the first and the last acts to cause a final triumphant victory of ethics. We are used to finding in poetic writing the instinctive expression of disguised ideas and knowledge which the average person keeps repressed in his unconscious; therefore, at first we thought we were right in assuming that a direct relation might exist between the presentation by Calderon and the findings of analytic research. The fact that the hero of the drama, Sigismund, apparently possesses only a purely formal and not an inner conscience seemed most astonishing to us. We came to the conclusion that our first impression was incorrect and found it improbable that a poet of Calderon's rank would oversimplify the genesis of the conscience. However, this apparent oversimplification reveals a hidden but certain tendency. We found this tendency in the effect Calderon unconsciously wished to produce on the audience, that is, that Sigismund represents the infantile aggres-

---

[1] For the psychology of writers see "A Clinical Approach to Psychoanalysis of Writers," and "Psychoanalysis of Writers and Literary Productivity," in "Psychoanalysis and the Social Sciences," Internat. Univ. Press, N. Y. 1947.

sions which the average man has already overcome. As a contrast
to the "bad" Sigismund there is in the end the tamed "good" Sigismund. In abbreviated form, the audience is shown the development
of his or her own infantile aggressive and libidinous wishes and is
given, by way of identification, the possibility of reconstructing his
or her own conflicting situations of long past. In contradiction to
this assumption—that is, at least to its completeness—the objection
was raised that, apparently, the "bad instincts" of the hero were
neither stopped nor modified, and deviated from their direction, not
by an inner development, but solely by the fear of outside punishment:

> ....I am fearful I may wake,
> And once more a prisoner find me
> In my cell. . . .
>   (Sigismund's final words).

After some pondering we tentatively concluded that the effect of
the drama on the audience did not lie—or lay not only—in the
repetition of infantile aggressions by identification with Sigismund,
but mainly in the tendency to transfer the responsibility for an inner
conflict onto a person of the outside world, namely the father.
Therefore, the playwright and the audience would unconsciously
reason, it is not true that we have unconsciously brought about the
painful process of the genesis of conscience by inner renunciations,
fears, compromises between our inner forces, displacement of affects,
projections and introjections, etc—we can blame the bad father
alone for all of this. This simplification and tendencious distortion
of the genesis of a self-constructed inner restriction (the conscience
being the most excellent example of a mechanism of restriction)
which transfers our responsibility by means of projection, seemed
to explain why the audience unconsciously enjoys Calderon's play.

After more accurate reflections, however, we abandoned the
hypothesis that Sigismund had developed only a formal conscience.
The chief fact that contradicts our original assumption is the depersonalization, which is distinctly expressed in Sigismund and
which presumes a highly complicated inner conscience. Apart from
the shifting of responsibility, the drama must inevitably contain
another unconscious tendency, which we discovered in the playright's
attempt to preserve the infantile megalomania. The development of
an inner conscience is disavowed, in spite of its existence, because

to acknowledge it would destroy the infantile fantasy of omnipotence. We now assumed that the "real" Super Ego-formation is presented as "pseudo"-Super Ego in order to deny the narcissistic grievance that accompanies the development of conscience.

We have finally come to the conclusion that the Super Ego formation of Calderon's hero is a precise description of the real circumstances and at the same time their denial and disavowal.

II. Contents of the drama and characterization of the leading parts. Pedro Calderon de la Barca (Madrid 1600-1681) wrote a drama as well as an "auto sacramental" under the title: "Life is a Dream." Although both works of art reveal analogies as to contents and form, the following refers exclusively to his drama.

The hero of the drama is Prince Sigismund, son of King Basilius of Poland. King Basilius has learned from horoscopy and dream interpretations that his son will kill his mother and victoriously fight his father. Sigismund's mother dies in childbirth and, in order to avoid the gruesome fate he anticipated for himself, King Basilius orders his son to be fettered immediately after birth and kept a prisoner in a remote castle.

Years pass by. Sigismund in prison reaches adolescence while King Basilius in his palace becomes an old man. Tired of reigning, the King wishes to abdicate his throne and name a successor. At once his thoughts turn to his son: Perhaps Sigismund may be able to change his ominous destiny and become a good prince. To find out, the King decides to try his son and orders him to be doped by a sleeping draught and brought to the royal palace. The palace attendants are to show him obedience and humbleness due to a king. If Sigismund "behaves well"—so goes the King's plan—he is to reside at the palace, first as prince and later on as king: if, however, Sigismund fails, he will be put to sleep again and returned to his prison, and will thus believe he has dreamed what really happened.

The King's orders are carried out to the letter. Sigismund awakens at the palace, and after a short period of astonishment he behaves exactly as the oracles foretold. In dealing with his subjects he is brutal and cruel towards the man (for instance, he throws a servant into the sea) and is covetous of the women. Therefore, according to the King's command, he is put to sleep again and returned to the prison.

A few days later there is a revolt aimed to put Sigismund on the throne in place of the foreign prince whom Basilius would force on them. The rioters set Sigismund free, and after some inner conflicts he decides to declare war on his father.

Sigismund's behavior during his second liberation differs greatly from that displayed during his first one. Whereas in the first one he was aggressive and sensuous, in this second liberation he is desirous to behave as becomes a king. Yet he still believes that his life—the past, present and future—is a dream; everything, the reality as well as his own being, seems unreal to him.

Supported by the revolting troops, Sigismund is victorious over his father. But, and this comes as a surprise to everyone, once victorious, Sigismund subjects himself to his father of his own free will. Thus he proves himself a model prince, wanting to devote his life to his subjects' welfare and even renouncing his own desires for their sake.

KING BASILIUS. The main conflict of the drama "Life is a Dream" is the rivalry between the King and his son. Even before the birth of the Prince, this conflict was established, by the King's prophetic sight, which warned him that his son would kill his mother and subdue him. Therefore, he decides to keep his son a prisoner from the time of birth.

From the point of view of psychoanalysis the significance of the King's prophecy is quite clear. It expressed the oedipus complex of the son, e.g. his sexual desires for his mother and his feeling of aggression toward his father. The aggressions toward the father are not distorted in the prophecy: "While his feet on my white hairs as a carpet were imprinted." But the sexual desires for his mother are so described in the prophecy of the King as if they were aggressive desires designed to bring about the death of the mother. (Childlike sadistic misconception of sex.)

This distortion[2] is easily understood through reading the lines in which Basilius describes Sigismund's behavior towards his mother:

> . . . . Many a time his mother saw
> In her dream's delirious dimness
> From her side a monster break
> Fashioned like a man, but sprinkled

[2]Here is shown the effect of the "results of secular repression" (Freud): in the drama by Sophocles the sexual part of the oedipus complex is not yet distorted.

With her blood, who gave her death,
By that human viper bitten.[3]
(Act 1).

In the King's prophecy, the abandonment of the mother's womb brought about by birth has the contrary latent meaning of penetration of her by coitus. The distortion is based on the fact that the birth of the Prince brings about the death of his mother.

The fact that King Basilius wishes to punish his son for "having torn his mother's entrails" ("breaking from her side as a monster") is a proof that this "tearing of the entrails" has a meaning other than that of birth. For it would be unreasonable to punish a person for happenings that have come about without his doing, desire or knowledge. Therefore, the death of the mother occasioned by the son's birth does not arouse normally the wish to punish the son.

The psychologic circumstances which cause the King to make his prophecy may be re-enacted as follows: Some time before his son's birth the King developed a feeling of rivalry towards him. This feeling could be consciously based on the thought that his son would some day "take away" his throne. Unconsciously, the feeling of rivalry originated in his own oedipus complex. He had towards his expected son feelings similar to the ones he had had in childhood towards his parents (Laios complex).

The oedipus complex of King Basilius is rekindled by the birth of his son. But these feelings he projects onto his son and consequently regards the child as having sexual desires for his mother and aggressions towards his father. The unconscious thought of King Basilius is: "My son will have oedipus feelings towards my wife and myself. But it is not true that I expect him to feel thus because once I myself had the same feelings towards my parents."

This thought has to be distorted to permit its appearance on the surface of consciousness. In the distortion aggressive desires are substituted for sexual desires for the mother. Furthermore, the unconscious thought, in the process of becoming acceptable to the con-

---

[3]The translation quoted is that by Denis Florence Mac-Carthy, (The Chief European Dramatists, edited by Brander Matthews, Houghton Mifflin Co. 1916). The translation seems to be a free one and Dr. Garma told me that the following French quotation comes nearer to the Spanish original:

"Il vit, qu'il déchirait
Ses entrailles (de la mère), un monstre
Avec figure humaine
Et que baigné dans son sang
Il la tuait. . . . "

sciousness, must find support in facts of the outside world. For, in order to realize the projection of a thought onto another person, the person projecting must base this projection on a real fact in the outside world. Therefore, for instance when a paranoiac accuses somebody else of homosexual thoughts, he stresses the suspicious behavior of that other person of the outside world, his gestures, movements, words, etc., and bases his accusations on this.[4]

But King Basilius cannot base his projective accusations on such facts as long as his son is not yet born. Therefore, the prophecy is necessary. Supported by outside facts, such as constellations of stars and dreams, which he interprets prophetically, King Basilius is able to project his thoughts onto his son. After a special interpretation of outside events he feels justified in explaining to himself and to his subjects that his son is possessed by cruel instincts which may bring about his own as well as his country's misfortunes, and must therefore be made a prisoner.

Unconsciously, the King may reason as follows: "It is not true that I have prophesied my son's oedipus complex, prompted by my thoughts of rivalry toward him. Prophetic events in the outside world have indicated the future, not my own personality. I have merely collected the prophetic signs and these force me to get rid of my son."

Thus King Basilius realizes his unconscious desires without essential Super Ego reproaches. He comes to the conclusion that his Super Ego forces him to imprison his son. Apparently, Super Ego and unconscious wishes are on the same side of the fence.

The King's ego believes it is right in having Sigismund imprisoned. But his Super Ego, because of its close relation to the Id, is not so easily deceived; it realizes the latent meaning of Sigismund's captivity. This knowledge on the part of the Super Ego is the source of unconscious feelings of guilt which become apparent when the King has advanced in age, that is, many years after he has committed the culpable deed.

The fact that these unconscious feelings of guilt become evident so many years after the culpable deed leads to the assumption that they were present before, that their manifestation, however, was made impossible by an intra-psychic process.

---

[4]The outside facts may be considered a parallel to the "day's residues" in the dream, by which the latent thoughts are expressed.

Here is, presumably, the explanation of this psychical process: The King, young and in full possession of his libido, was able to ward off the aggression of his guilty feelings directed against his own person by turning his aggression toward the outside with the help of his strong libido. In old age, however, when he:

> . . . . doth bow
> 'Neath the weight of years, the doom
> Age imposes, more inclined
> To the studies of the mind
> Than to women. . . .
> (Act 1)

his libido, biologically weaker in intensity, can no longer turn the aggression toward the outside.

There is no doubt that Calderon stresses the fact that it is precisely in old age that the King reproaches himself for his treatment of his son:

> . . . . supposing
> Even my son should be so guilty, (a tyrant)
> That he should not crimes commit
> I myself should first commit them. . . .
> That perhaps I erred in giving
> Too implicit a belief
> To the facts foreseen so dimly; . . .
> (Act 1)

All of this prompts the King to set free the boy he had himself imprisoned and he actually orders his liberation with the aid of a sleeping draught. His conscious motive for the use of a sleeping draught is his desire to spare his son the grief of a possible reimprisonment. For, according to the King, Sigismund would be less unhappy if they succeeded in making him believe that his life at the palace was but a dream. This motivation of the use of a sleeping draught is supported by the King's unconscious wish to enhance by extraordinary means his power over his son and to undermine his son's self-confidence. It is not difficult to imagine that the prince transferred to the palace and back to prison without awareness of what went on, would feel lost and utterly helpless and quite subordinate to the persons who possessed such secret powers over him.

The use of sleeping draughts, etc., which Sigismund was bound to consider the doings of secret powers, may be compared to the puberty rites of the primitive people. These people try by magic and symbolic sets, to subordinate the youths to their elders before granting them sexual or social liberties. Perhaps there is a similar significance to the drugging of the prince and transporting of him forth and back.

To appease his conscience, King Basilius decides to set his son free under certain conditions and to make him his heir. But the manner of his liberation points to the presence of neurotic motives. The King's actions are based upon the demands of the Super Ego as well as on the rivalry of the ego under pressure of the Id. Sigismund is to leave prison, where he has lived for many years incarcerated like a "wild beast," is to be brought, without any transition period whatsoever, to the royal palace, where everybody shall obey him. The contrast between life in prison and that in the palace is too great for Sigismund to accustom himself to overnight. No wonder he loses control of himself when, all of a sudden, he sees so many things he has longed for for so long. He wants to satisfy, recklessly, his longing desires.[5] Anyone who had lived in such wretched conditions and suddenly found his position ameliorated greatly would behave at first, perhaps, in as unruly a fashion. Also, the average person tames his instincts and builds the respective defense mechanisms only after a long period of inner adaptation and education.

The Prince at the palace behaves, therefore, as is to be expected. And the King must have anticipated, more or less consciously, that his son would behave "badly" and that his demeanor would, of necessity, cause his reimprisonment. In spite of this knowledge, the King does not refrain from trying the Prince in the above-mentioned way; for in consequence of his feelings of rivalry, he, unconsciously, wants the Prince to fail, so that he can send him back to prison without inner conflicts.

The King's Super Ego and Id are satisfied by this meaningless trial, the result of which was, a priori, manifest. We conclude that the same psychical forces which have led to the prophecy, here once more play a decisive role.

CLOTALDO. The main inner conflict of Sigismund is whether he should rebel against his father or submit to him with or without renouncing the satisfaction of heterosexual instincts. The very same

---

[5]The further development of the drama proves that Sigismund's bad behavior does not originate in a deficiency of moral capacities, but rather in the incapability of immediate adaptation.

conflict harasses another personage of the drama; or rather has harassed him in the past and has now been aroused anew; this personage is King Basilius' faithful servant, Clotaldo.

As a youth Clotaldo lived in a town far from the royal palace. There he fell in love with a beautiful woman, Violanta, and the fruit of their love was Rosaura. But as the King's vassal, Clotaldo's duty was to return to the palace and leave his beloved wife and daughter. Clotaldo's soul was torn between love and duty, and he settled his conflict by abandoning wife and daughter and returning to the palace, where he submitted himself completely to the King. In taking leave of his beloved wife he gave her his sword. This action may be interpreted as symbolizing renunciation of sexuality. The King to whom he submitted himself symbolizes the father.

In Clotaldo, Calderon illustrates the conflict between heterosexuality and femininity and the solution of this conflict by subordination to the father. In the course of the drama the conflict is reactivated by the appearance of Rosaura, Clotaldo's daughter, who comes to the palace in search of the man who seduced and left her. Rosaura then returns to her father the symbolic sword.

Through the arrival of his daughter, Clotaldo is forced once more to choose between heterosexuality (defense of his daughter's love) and unconscious femininity (submission to the King). The poor Clotaldo, in doubt and uncertainty, finally solves the situation as before, by submitting himself to the King. He renounces his desire to help his daughter. He even advises her to forsake her love and enter a convent:

> . . . .I, Rosaura, will to thee
> All my property present;
> In a convent live; by me
> Has the plan been weighed some time, . . .[6]
> (Act 3).

[6] As we intend to show mainly the genesis of conscience in the drama by Calderon, we must refrain from discussing in detail the subordinate parts of the drama although they are interesting. Rosaura, for instance, although endowed with the traits of a sister-mother-image, appears to be, in a way, Sigismund's feminine double. The undeveloped part of the mother in the drama is stressed by the fact that Rosaura appears twice disguised as a man, rather, a knight, and that she once even calls herself a hermaphrodite. It is also interesting to note several parapraxies in Calderon's drama, which distinctly refer to incest. First of all, the planned marriage of Estrella and Astolf is a marriage of kin; their respective mothers were sisters. It is also significant that this marriage, apparently because of unconscious feelings of guilt, does not take place. Furthermore, Sigismund originally loves Rosaura but in the end renounces her (sister?) and weds Estrella. Still further, Basilius says his wife's

Certain passages of Clotaldo's monologues remind us of a compulsion neurotic who, also undecided between heterosexuality and unconscious femininity, is brooding all the time, and incapable of finding a solution for his conflicts. The sexualization of thinking is evident in several passages.

It is Clotaldo who was ordered by the King to imprison and guard his son. Sigismund recognizes in Clotaldo, in contrast to his own rebellious conduct, the faithful and willing way of carrying out the commands of the king-father. Therefore, after subduing his father, Sigismund submits to his former jailer. He expresses clearly that he wants Clotaldo to be his "north and leader"; he chooses an advisor who, when compelled to act, loses himself in endless doubts and is unable to find a simple solution for his own conflicts. His newly developed Super Ego forces Sigismund to make resolutions that may hardly be considered reasonable.[7]

Reproduction of childhood scenes. The infantile situation which is the basis of the drama "Life is a Dream" may easily be traced. Calderon describes the situation of the child who has to subordinate himself to paternal authority. King Basilius stands for the father; the Prince, for the child himself; the men and women in the drama, for the objects of the negative and positive oedipus complex; the soldiers who set the Prince free symbolize the child's aggressive wishes against his father; and finally, the imprisonment of the victorious leader of the soldiers after Sigismund's submission to the King, represents the repression of aggressive desires after the formation of the Super Ego.

In dreams an abstract conception of the latent desires is expressed by a concrete image from the dream contents; the dream manifests itself in image, not in abstracts. Let us assume that Sigismund is a patient under psychoanalytic treatment and as such relates a dream: He has seen himself fettered in prison where he had been

---

name is Clorilene, but "forgets" that this is his sister's name. There is another example for the continuous doubling of the same person in order to be exonerated from the feeling of guilt: The names Estrella and Astrea (Rosaura's fictitious name) mean one and the same thing.

[7] Choosing Clotaldo as advisor may constitute at the same time an unconscious ironization of the father, implying: "This is the kind of subjects you have." One of the authors of this study has shown in an earlier work that the choice of the representatives of the Super Ego may contain a hidden aggression against the Super Ego: often persons are used that are held in contempt. (See Bergler, "Remarks on a compulsion neurosis in ultimis," Section II. "Degradation of the Super Ego," Internat. Ztschr. f. Psychoanalyse. 1935.)

brought by his father. One interpretation of this dream would be that Sigismund thereby wanted to express that his father kept him "chained" and did not permit him any sexual liberty. Thus the prison in the drama "Life in a Dream" might be interpreted, and therefore we might indeed assume that the chains had a psychical reality only.

During the phase of his oedipus complex, the child—as English authors have shown—projects his innate, as well as his reactive aggressions onto his father.[8] As a consequence of these projections the child fancies his father to be a cruel person, for instance, the sadistic interpretation of the "primary scene," even where such cruelty does not really exist. In connection with this we may assume that King Basilius is not as cruel as his son describes him to be. However, the son attributes by projection his own aggressions to his father.

The drama, "Life is a Dream," appears to be much more human when, in summing up these interpretations, we consider that chains and prison are not based on reality and that King Basilius is not as cruel as his son describes him to be. In spite of the intensity of his rivalry with his son, the King may be considered almost a normal man.

III. Sigismund's depersonalization. In a short essay[9] one of the authors has pointed out that Sigismund, after being imprisoned for the second time, produces symptoms which are typically those of depersonalization. Calderon rationalizes as follows: Everything must necessarily seem a dream to Sigismund because when brought to the palace, as well as when returned to prison, the hero was under the influence of a sleeping draught. This well-devised rationalization covers up a complete depersonalization. In Calderon's words:

> . . . .Nor is this a great mistake;
> Since if dreams could phantoms make
> Things of actual substance seen,
> I things seen may phantoms deem.
> Thus a double harvest reaping,
> I can see when I am sleeping,
> And when waking I can dream. . . .
> Dreams he too who rank would hold,

[8] Likewise, in the preceding pre-oedipal phase aggressions are projected onto the phallic mother.

[9] Garma, "Sigismund or the triumph of ethics" (Psychoanalytic sketch of "Life is a Dream"). Bull. hispanique (Bordeaux) 1937.

Dreams who bears toil's rough-ribbed hands,
Dreams who wrong for wrong demands,
And in fine, throughout the earth,
All men dream, whate'er their birth,
And yet no one understands.
'Tis a dream that I in sadness
Here am bound, the scorn of fate;
'T was a dream that once a state
I enjoyed of light and gladness.
What is life? 'Tis but a madness.
What is life? A thing that seems
A mirage that falsely gleams,
Phantom joy, delusive rest,
Since is life a dream at best,
And even dreams themselves are dreams.
                    (End of Act 2).

The problem of depersonalization has repeatedly been the subject of analytic writing. (Schilder, Hartmann, Nunberg, Reik, Federn,
Sadger, Oberndorf, Bergler-Eidelberg, Searl.) We assume with Bergler and Eidelberg that in the neurotic depersonalization an originally
exhibitionistic desire is transformed into a voyeuristic one.[10] According to this conception the following takes place:

"Basing our observation on cured cases, we may say that the
specific mechanism of depersonalization is a mechanism captivating
the Super Ego. The libidinous instinctive desire of the Id is, primarily, anal exhibition. The Ego rejects this desire, whereby fear
and denial are developed in the form of a feeling of unreality, defects
of perception, doubts, intellectual uncertainty, outbursts of despair,
etc. By some sort of autotomy, the Ego to a great extent lends its
services as 'auxiliary police' to the Super Ego in the form of over-
emphasized self-observation, since all depersonalized people are constantly observing the minutiae of their feelings or, more precisely,
'lack' of them. The normal function of the Ego, which is self-observation in the service of the Super Ego, is enormously increased, and
the Ego is defeated by its own weapons. The rejected instinctive
claim takes the Ego by surprise in undergoing a change from exhibitionism to voyeurism and is subsequently accepted by the Ego
as self-observation which rejects the Id-desires. Under the pretext
of a police report to the Super Ego, this narcissistic self-observation

[10]"The Mechanism of Depersonalization." Internat. Ztschr. f. Psychoanalyse.
1935.

is smuggled into the process and the inwardly directed sexualized destruction connected therewith is thoroughly enjoyed. In analogy to the other defense mechanisms, such as conversion, projection, etc., the 'mechanism of depersonalization' is a compromise in the formation of which all three parts of the unconscious personality participate. The Ego is not conscious of the pleasure resulting from satisfying the voyeurism."

Let us consider in the light of this conception Sigismund's condition after his second imprisonment. He has been kept imprisoned for years, and his first experience in the outside world resembles an exhibitionistic orgy. The rejection of this exhibition—Sigismund, as we know, considers his return to the prison a punishment—brings about the exchange of the active part of the scopophiliac instinct (exhibitionism) into the passive one, namely voyeurism, hence causes the most intensive self-scrutiny. According to Reik, depersonalized people change into "psychic observatories." Behind this very detailed self-observation, however, pleasure of voyeurism is concealed. Since the Super Ego forbids this pleasure, too, the latter remains unconscious and is perceived as masochistic suffering: "I do not enjoy myself, I suffer." Thus the depersonalization reveals itself as masochistic voyeurism.

Yet it would be wrong to call Sigismund's feelings "that all life is a dream" merely depersonalization. What else does he wish to express? Primarily, that all which we consider materially real, all which "exists," is only illusion. And therefore, life with its false realities should not be taken too seriously.

Sigismund's condition after his stay at the royal palace may be compared to that of a traveller who is lost in the desert and suffers from thirst and hunger. He has appealing illusions of possibly satisfying his desires, but later he learns that they are but a mirage. Such delusions are, in Sigismund's case, the power, wealth, and the women he meets at the palace. Sigismund longs for them, yet in the end, when reawakening in prison, must realize that all of them were but a mirage:

> . . . .Now I know ye (the reality)—know ye all,
> And I know the same false glimmer
> Cheats the eyes of all who sleep.
> Me false shows no more bewilder; . . . .

"Dreaming" has for Sigismund another meaning, that is, the op-

posite of life and fulfillment of desires. Therefore, he leads the rebellious soldiers who freed him, against his father saying:

> . . . .But supposing the bright vision
> Even were true, since life is short,
> Let us dream, my soul, a little,
> Once again, ...

In Sigismund's mind, "not to dream" or "to awaken" signifies lack
of desires, disillusion and death.

There is a third conception of Sigismund's dreams which we are
inclined to call unconscious. According to this conception, sub-
jecting his father and himself to the dream is identical with submitting to his father. The connection between the psychic conceptions of dream and father is based on the fact that the dream Sigismund mentions was caused by the father's sleeping draught. This
third meaning is explained in his words:

> Why this wonder, these surprises,
> If my teacher was a dream, ...
> (Act 3).

In other words: "Why are you surprised? You know that my
teacher was my father." The dream refers, not only to the real
father, but also to the father who had been introjected into the
Super Ego and who has the power to punish again:

> . . . .I am fearful I may wake,
> And once more a prisoner find me
> In my cell. But should I not,
> Even to dream it is sufficient. . . .

IV. Why do playwright and audience enjoy the tendencious presentation of the genesis of the conscience? The problem of the
genesis of the inner conscience (Super Ego) in the boy is, analytically, not yet settled and fully explained. At present, there are three
theories concerning this problem: We find one in the writings of
Freud; in addition there is the English theory (Jones, Melanie Klein,
etc.) ; and finally we have the theory of Jekels and Bergler, which
is based on Freud's Eros-Thanatos-theory. All three theories have,
among other features, this one in common: They do not find a
direct relation between the sternness of education and the sternness
of the Super Ego. On the contrary, each contends that it is always
one's own aggression which, instead of being directed toward the

outside world, is turned further inside and becomes the basis for the strictness of the unconscious conscience. Freud's words, "Every impulse of aggression which we omit to gratify is taken over by the Super Ego and goes to heighten its aggressiveness"[11] (against the Ego), have by now been more or less accepted among psychoanalysts, whatever differences of opinion may exist regarding the genesis of the Super Ego. We must agree as to the practical effect of the sternness of the conscience, though, whether we believe that it results from projecting of aggression toward the outside and secondary introjection by identification with the infantile image (this image being considered especially "evil" because of the falsification of reality in the process of projecting one's own aggression), or that it results from a simpler process, in which projection and introjection have a smaller scope.

Whatever the facts may be, the unconscious part of the conscience is by no means a direct, stereotyped image of the real sternness of the persons who reared the child during his pre-oepidal and oedipal phases.

How shall we explain the fact that a great poet apparently juggles the truth and maintains that the parent was sterner than the son's Super Ego? Sigismund's "being good," he states, is exclusively the consequence of his fear of outside punishment. Why does Sigismund forgive the King, his jailer, his other enemies and torturers? Why does the hero renounce the women he loves, as well as his vengeance? According to Calderon, the only explanation is fear of outside punishment.

> A soldier: If thou honorest those who serve thee,
> Thus, to me the first beginner
> Of the tumult through the land,
> Who from out the tower, thy prison,
> Drew thee forth, what wilt thou give?
>
> Sigismund: Just that tower: and that you issue
> Never from it until death,
> I will have you guarded strictly;
> For the traitor is not needed
> Once the treason is committed.
>
> Basilius: So much wisdom makes one wonder.
>
> Astolfo: What a change in his condition!

[11]"Civilization and its Discontents" p. 114; translation by Joan Riviere. The Internat. Psychoanalyt. Lib. No. 17.

Rosaura: How discreet! how calm! how prudent!
Sigismund: Why this wonder, these surprises,
          If my teacher was a dream,
          And amid my new aspirings
          I am fearful I may wake,
          And once more a prisoner find me
          In my cell?[12] But should I not,
          Even to dream it is sufficient:
          For I thus have come to know
          That at last all human blisses
          Pass and vanish as a dream,
          And the time that may be given me
          I henceforth would turn to gain:
          Asking for our faults forgiveness,
          Since to generous, noble hearts
          It is natural to forgive them.

Sigismund's fear of outside punishment, after being freed from prison the second time, is quite unjustified, as the force that might punish him—his royal father—has just been dethroned by the rebellious soldiers and Sigismund is already king himself. His fear of being reimprisoned is furthermore unfounded, as he has already decided to imprison his liberator, the leader of the rebellious soldiers to whom he owes his being enthroned; and so definitely realizes his own capacity of punishing.

At first we were inclined to assume that it was wrong to consider Calderon a great psychologist among poets, as he seemed to oversimplify the complicated inner processes. This explanation, however, was not satisfactory, because it was too simple and obvious; an underestimation of the object being examined always arouses suspicion in a psychologically experienced person. Several facts in the drama are contradictory to a conception of ethics as being based purely on external reasons, as Calderon emphasizes that Sigismund's are. This made us suspect that Calderon unconsciously knew all about the real mechanisms but had an unconscious reason for denying them.

In the last act, for instance, Sigismund's conduct does not seem to make sense. On the one hand, he has already established a normal Super Ego and has identified himself to a great extent with his

[12]These words prove that the simple explanation often offered, that Calderon was afraid of the Inquisition and therefore made Sigismund send the leader of the rebellion to prison, is not sufficient to explain this strange action.

father; on the other hand, Sigismund speaks as if he had only a formal conscience although he acts like a person with an inner conscience. The explanation for this contradiction between words and action may lie in an attempt to deny the inner facts, to preserve the infantile megalomania, which was injured in establishing the conscience.

The infantile megalomania of Sigismund is "justified" by a number of apparently contradictory factors: (1) Sigismund's father is to be blamed for whatever is wrong with him. (2) His father is subdued by him during a fight. (3) The focus of importance is transferred from the father-son conflict to the conception of life as a dream, which annuls the value of reality and makes all humiliating compromises seem of no avail. (4) An attempt is made to transfer the inner punishment to the outside in some sort of "devaluating projection" after establishing his conscience.[13] (5) The father is included in, as well as excluded from, the subsequent "devaluating projection": On the one hand, the bad father is blamed for everything; on the other hand, the father is nullified and an impersonal outside world is called upon to inflict punishment. To be punished by an impersonal outside world is less humiliating than to be chastised by the real father.

All five mechanisms just enumerated, by which Calderon attempts to save Sigismund's narcissistic face during the genesis of his conscience, contradict one another.

This extraordinary oscillation between the establishment of an inner conscience and denial of the same by means of the above described "devaluating projection post factum," yields an explanation for several apparent contradictions in the conduct of Calderon's hero. Why, for instance, does Sigismund condemn to life imprisonment his liberator, the leader of the rebellious soldiers, as a reward for assisting him to gain the royal crown? Whence this odd ingratitude? The phrase

"For the traitor is not needed
Once the treason is committed"

[13] In order to avoid misunderstandings, we would like to point out that the "devaluating subsequent projection" has nothing to do with the projection which plays so large and decisive a part in forming the Super Ego. This "devaluating projection" is secondary; it tries to depreciate something already perfected and irreparably completed—the inner Super Ego formation. This intrapsychic "I wish it had not happened" may be compared to a "battle of retreat."

is a superficial rationalization. It is understood that Sigismund, in identification with the father-King, punishes the rebels the way the former ruler would have. This very action is proof of his inner identification with his father, and of an inner conscience. On the other hand, in this act we find traces of the hatred he had for his father before establishing his Super Ego. It seems that Sigismund's first queer official duty on accession to the throne contains some sort of mocking irony directed against his father: "Remember the way you treated the man who saves you now." (Sigismund spares the life of the old defeated King and saves him from the angered revolutionists.) In this action Sigismund plays his father's part and the soldier, Sigismund's at the time of his imprisonment.[14] This, however, does not explain everything. It is true that the leader of the soldiers has freed Sigismund, but he has also forced him, indirectly, to give up part of his infantile aggressions toward his father, since the free Sigismund identifies himself with his father. This he cannot forgive, and for taking away this pleasure of aggression, he makes the leader pay with lifelong incarceration. This very action of Sigismund seems to reflect the counteracting, partly contradictory unconscious tendencies which brought about the formation of his Super Ego.

This "last" aggression of Sigismund before his "fortissimo of good behavior" which concludes the drama by Calderon, is still further superimposed. We know that children before giving up a certain "naughtiness" indulge in it once more—"for the last time." This conduct, a sort of obstinacy, was described by Freud (in "Wolfsmann") and was repeatedly interpreted: It may be the child's infantile megalomania making believe that renouncing a forbidden deed is not caused by prohibition (and later introjection), but is a voluntary resignment (Reik, Jekels, Bergler, etc.).

The desperate attempt to preserve the infantile megalomania, which is injured during the genesis of conscience, is strung like a red thread through the entire drama by Calderon.[15] Yet, Calderon

[14]Sigismund partly shifts his hatred from his father to the soldier whom he condemns to a fate identical with the one his father forced on him for years. The unconscious impulse of repetition plays a role here too: what was passively experienced is actively repeated in order to heal the narcissistic injury (Freud). As to the ingratitude toward his liberator, it is important to remember that the soldier is "innocent": Sigismund, too, was innocent.

[15]Jekels and Bergler have stressed this feature in describing the Super Ego formation in "Transference and Love." Imago 1934. No. 1.

is not satisfied with the usual attempts at repairing the injured infantile megalomania, which are automatically included in the formation of the Super Ego. He also tries to demonstrate the above-disclosed mechanism of the subsequently devaluating projection at a time when the inner conscience has already been established and cannot be undone any more.

Here it seems possible to try to outline the effect of Calderon's drama on the audience. Why does the audience leave the theater so contented? Because the playwright tells the audience unconsciously, to be understood unconsciously: "Don't mind the infantile megalomania being injured during the genesis of conscience." He extends this consolation to the audience by different methods which we have tried to outline above and which have as a common denominator the denial of inner processes. The absence of the entire pre-history of the father's influence upon the child—the phase of pre-oedipal attachment to the mother—is proof for the complicated process of repression and the secondary disavowal in Calderon's drama. The mechanism of disavowal[16] appears all throughout the drama. The father disavows his son (Basilius-Sigismund), the father his daughter (Clotaldo-Rosaura), the bridegroom the bride (Astolfo-Rosaura), etc. Due to this enormous mechanism of disavowal, the important phase of mother-dependence is denied too.

[16]Calderon's drama might be summed up as presenting the idea of disavowal.

CHAPTER V

A FEW TYPICAL EXAMPLES OF NEUROTIC GUILT, INCLUDING SUICIDE

The manifestations of neurotic guilt in neurosis are hundredfold,[1] and cannot be schematized. Individualism is trump. In the following pages a few typical examples are collected. The common denominator is irrational and self-damaging action under the influence of unconscious guilt referring to repressed wishes and defense mechanisms.

CASE I.[2] Agoraphobia is a neurosis of relatively frequent occurrence, which may be recognized by the following complex of symptoms: the patient suffers from an invincible dread of going out into the street alone. To step out into the street becomes a nightmare, the very thought of which arouses fear of the expected fear. This fear increases with every unsuccessful attempt to go out, and continues, accompanied not only by successive fits of depression but by palpitations, trembling, and sometimes breaking out into perspiration. The intensity of the fear is very great, and (as all psychoanalysts confirm) bears all the characteristic marks of a real fear of death. If we ask such a patient just what danger they stand in dread of, they draw upon all sorts of well rationalized possibilities: the fear of sudden death, of being stricken with apoplexy, of fainting, and being run over. Often these patients offer statistical proofs of the dangers of the street; some take careful note of every traffic accident, of every collision between streetcars or automobiles. All methods of suggestion which persons of the patient's environment may use to combat such arguments are useless, and roll off him without effect. The fear of the agoraphobe may be banished under two conditions only: if the patient does not go into the street at all, or if he goes out accompanied by a protecting escort. There are certain conditions attached to the choice of this escort. Noticeably often it is a member of the family (father, mother, brother, sister, husband, or fiancé). If, for any cause, such patients are forced to a compromise in the choice of their escort, they make a fine dis-

---

[1] A textbook of neuroses must be consulted for completeness. In a deliberate one-sidedness some typical mechanisms are isolated in this book, which has a purpose completely different from that of textbooks on neuroses.
[2] First published in Psychoanalyt. Rev., 22:392-408, 1935.

tinction in the degree of fear which they experience when in the street, and secure at last, by dint of endless complaining, the companion of their choice. The despotism of these patients (they are typical tormenting, unconsciously aggressive spirits—the more so as their fear in untreated cases may persist for years, and even for a lifetime) hiding behind their tearful lamentations, beggars description, as well as the obstinacy and iron-willed persistence with which they make their habitual announcement: "I cannot go out into the street alone." If one does not know this type of patient, one may at first be surprised at this amount of "energy" in a seemingly helpless invalid. The patients who whine and weep most when describing their condition, are absolutely unshakable in their refusal, when the people of their environment try to force them to step onto the street, or walk a little way alone.

Agoraphobia is further characterized by its endurance. The illness, which begins[3] with occasional attacks of anxiety and a reluctance to go out of the house, increases up to a certain point and remains there for a very long time, sometimes with occasional fluctuations, until the death of the patients. Ability to work is disturbed in various degrees. Often a "pressure in the head" is the motivation for inaction. One characteristic in the treatment of agoraphobia is the noticeable difficulty one has in keeping these patients in analysis. The number of "runaways" among agoraphobes is especially great. These patients often refuse to wait for the cure to take effect, and the first signs of success may not appear until many months after the beginning of treatment. They run from one doctor to another, "give up" with remarkable ease, and seem peculiarly ready to resign themselves to their fate. This does not mean that they bear this fate in silence. On the contrary, they complain a great deal, are typical martyrs with all the martyr's airs, but frequently try to avoid a cure. To express this in the language of the unconscious: the compromise between the unconscious pleasure-gain and the unconscious desire for punishment, which expresses itself in the neurotic illness, has a particularly great carrying power—the wish for health, despite outward assurances to the contrary, is an extremely small one. The prognosis for a psychoanalytic cure is favorable, but the treatment lasts for a period from a half-year to

[3]A frequent variation is the fear that harm may come to the relatives on the street, so that the patients try to hold them back whenever they wish to go out.

two years—and it is typical for many months to go by before the first signs of improvement appear.

The following is a description of a completely analyzed, cured case of agoraphobia which, despite certain individual traits, may be counted a typical one.

A thirty-two year old female patient had been suffering from agoraphobia for the past two years. The attacks of anxiety were at first mild in character, consisting of a "slight feeling of dizziness" which came on in the street. The patient was "afraid of falling," and felt herself constantly "drawn" toward the left. She felt as though everything about her were swaying and turning around, the ground seemed made of rubber. Sometimes she had the sensation of being aboard a steamer upon stormy seas. "I reel about as though I were drunk." If the patient closed her eyes, the condition seemed more bearable, but the sensation of falling continually increased,[4] slight feelings of depersonalization made their appearance, in short, the condition became so much worse that as long as six months before the beginning of the analysis, the patient was no longer able to go out alone. At this time, a deep depression became noticeable, which became worse when a country doctor made a diagnosis of tumor cerebri. The patient was repeatedly examined, both neurologically and by X-ray, with negative results—until a general practitioner with some understanding of psychology, diagnosed neurosis, and advised the patient to be analyzed. For some months before the beginning of the cure the patient had been unable to work, no longer went to the office (she was an employee in a big concern), and sat continually at home as she felt better there, while the mere thought of going out into the street brought on feelings of fear. To go out alone was impossible. The patient clung to her companion (either her fiancé or a sister twenty years her senior), like a person in imminent danger of death. The patient's mother, an eccentric old woman seventy years of age, was quite out of the question as an escort — for this mentally senile, quarrelsome, and otherwise peculiar old woman, complaining of "neuralgic" pains, never went out in winter, and seldom in summer.

The patient was quite a pretty woman, somewhat colorless and indifferent in appearance, who faced her condition fatalistically, but

[4]When questioned as to whether she ever really had fallen, the patient answered that she "certainly" would have fallen, if she had not clung to her companion.

without despair. She had no exaggeratedly high hopes of what analysis could do for her. She had a whole series of false diagnoses and unsuccessful treatments to look back on, and had an extremely poor opinion of medicine and its representatives. According to her way of thinking, each doctor made a different diagnosis, but these were all alike in two respects. First, the diagnosis proved (after a very short time) to be wrong; and second, with the same absolute certainty with which the false diagnosis had just been made, it was then replaced by a new one. She made an exception only for the last doctor, who had said he considered the cause of her trouble a psychic one. This doctor had made an impression upon her "all the same." Perhaps just because of the "new idea," as she added sarcastically. At first the patient came to the analyst in a quite rejective mood, yet was able to accord him a minimum amount of confidence; perhaps just because he stood ready to begin a cure which many people had advised her not to take. As her faith in medicine was shaken, the rejection of analysis by several physicians whom she had questioned acted paradoxically as a recommendation.

Either the sister or the fiancé of the patient accompanied her. This fiancé was a gloomy person of dark looks, whose face clearly showed his dissatisfaction with everything and everybody. He gave the impression of continual inner fury and whimpering at the same time.

From the curriculum vitae of the patient we note: the patient's father died when she was ten years old, but the patient lived with her father until her seventh year only, as the parents were divorced at this time. The patient describes her father as an amiable man, although only one scene remains in her memory: she is taken to her father's funeral, but does not cry. Later came further memories which, connected with much that her mother had told her, gave us the following picture. During about his fiftieth year (the patient was then between five and six years old) the father (until that time industrious and disinclined to alcohol) underwent a change of character. He began to drink, became noisy at home, and *exhibited* himself when drunk. Once, in his drunken state, the father stripped himself naked before the children, and this, after twenty-five years of married life, acted on the mother as a signal to leave her husband, and to take the children with her. The father lived three years longer, took another wife, and saw the patient only a few times more.

Evidently in order to paralyze the influence of the father, the patient
was sent to a convent school, to have "good morals" knocked into
her. This year—from her seventh to her eighth—the patient describes as the unhappiest of her life. She lived in a constant condition of fear, scarcely daring to go to the toilet—the nuns (evidently
working against masturbation among the children) had said the
devil was in there. In short, in the course of a few months, the
patient was turned into a fearful, intimidated child. After desperate
pleading on the part of the patient, her mother took her away from
the convent, but the patient still kept up a slight connection with
the institution, and attended the sewing lessons there.

The further outward developments of her life are described by
the patient as colorless. She was good at her studies, and later
became a functionary in a large concern, and had been employed
there for twelve years. There she is regarded as a person who does
not allow herself to be imposed upon, and who often comes into
conflict with her employer, whom she despises, etc. The patient
cannot recall masturbating as a child, and claimed to have no childhood remembrances whatsoever up to the age of eight. The patient
owns to having masturbated during puberty. In her twentieth year
she became acquainted with a man considerably older than herself,
who was suffering from a serious case of tuberculosis, and was at
times incapacitated for work. With this "first fiancé" the patient
had a sexual relationship for seven years. The patient describes this
bond as a very close one, in which she enjoyed complete orgasm.
The mother of the patient had in the last few years become dissatisfied with the choice of this man as fiancé, and continually
harped on the fact that he could not possibly be taken into consideration as a husband because of the advanced stage of his illness.
Conflicts with the mother followed, with the result that the patient
no longer met the man in her own home (which she shared with
her mother), but arranged their meetings elsewhere. This relationship remained a good one—the patient took care of her invalid
fiancé with great self-sacrifice, but *abandoned him suddenly* (seemingly a psychologic enigma) *at the very moment the man was
cured.* According to the official explanation of the patient, she had
realized, as time went on, that her mother had been right when she
tried to "talk her out of" this man because of his illness.

Now one might believe that the patient, who had broken off her first "engagement" just because of the man's tubercular condition, might be more careful in the choice of a second fiancé. A curious "coincidence" occurred, however, for the second betrothed also suffered from a severe case of tuberculosis.

The first symptoms of agoraphobia appeared during the last months of the relationship with the first fiancé. The patient began the affair with the second man in a state accompanied by rather strong symptoms, and felt, even after the first sexual contact with the second man, that he was "not the right one for her." All tenderness was lacking, the patient said, and complained of the causeless and pathologic jealousy of this man. This jealousy had certain peculiarities: On the one hand, he tortured her with accusations of faithlessness, yet demanded that she be unfaithful to him, in the realm of fantasy. The conditions under which this man was able to have sexual intercourse were as follows: he demanded that his love-partner describe to him, *during intercourse,* her intercourse with other men: (as the patient could only oblige with *one,* the man had to content himself with stories of imaginary love-affairs) just how the man conducted himself on those occasions, what expressions he made use of, just how she reacted, etc. All this his love-partner had to describe in an extremely realistic manner. If she did not, the man was impotent, or was not able to reach ejaculation during coitus. He demanded that, in telling the stories, she make use of "the popular designations"—that is to say, obscene words. The patient indignantly refused to gratify these wishes of her betrothed. Since the agoraphobia had set in more strongly, the sexual desires of the patient had almost completely disappeared; intercourse between the pair became most infrequent, and every coitus (in spite of orgasms) brought the patient a stronger feeling of antipathy.

The analysis took the following course. The patient, as we have noted, came to the treatment in a spirit of grim humor, and was very skeptical. After telling me the story of her life, she communicated her dreams from the first days of the analysis, and these might be divided into three groups.

(A) The mother of the patient is murdered in the doctor's office. A young girl bursts into the waiting room, and, despairingly, proclaims her innocence. The patient stands by without taking part. Strangely enough, in this dream the patient's mother has the figure and the facial characteristics of the analyst, and is a kind of inter-mediate thing between the doctor and the real mother.

(B) An unknown woman is cutting meat, while the patient looks on with a feeling of disgust.

(C) The patient is sitting on the toilet. A man is looking at her. The front door of the water closet is missing. This dream shows certain variations concerning the man: once he falls into a ditch, another time his eyes are injured, etc.

The dream type described under (A) is of especial importance. It shows all the stigmata of the transference, and proves the right-ness of the Freudian claim (doubted again and again in the outside world), that the transference represents nothing else than the emo-tions which the patient felt in his childhood toward the psychically unmastered people of his environment to whom he was attached—which emotions he now repeats toward the person of the doctor, *whoever this may happen to be.* This chance doctor becomes un-consciously identified with the people of the patient's childhood, and is, for the changing positive and negative emotions brought to bear upon him (according to a telling simile of Anna Freud's), like a cinema screen for the film projected upon it. In the case of our patient, the lack of dependence of the transference upon the real person of the doctor is particularly noticeable, for it simply passes over the sex of the doctor, and this analysis—with a male analyst—opens with a negative mother-transference. The cause of this atypi-cal beginning evidently lies in the fact that the main psychic con-flict had to do with the mother.

This negative mother-transference made it possible to show the patient that many hateful, negative elements of emotion directed against the mother must be present in the unconscious. As may well be imagined, the first main resistance set in at the discussion of the ambivalent attitude toward the mother. The patient politely but firmly declines to accept the interpretation and, as time goes on, displays neither violence nor anger in the expression of her resist-ance. She opposes quietly, politely, rather cautiously, a little sneakily, and is at time downright hypocritical.

The patient counters the interpretation of her unconscious nega-tive attitude to the mother with the following arguments: she loves her mother intensely, supports her, etc. After a time the patient adds a new note to the description of her attitude, and admits that the mother "gets on her nerves." But from this point in her feelings to the unconscious thoughts of murder (for the patient is also the young girl who committed the murder in the dream) there is, as the patient expressed it, "a long way to go."

And now, whence springs this hatred toward the mother? It carries us far back into the history of the patient's childhood, to the time between her fifth and her seventh year. This was the time when her father used to return home in a drunken state. The patient suddenly remembers that she was the only one who could "tame," that is, restrain, her father. Completing reports of her mother on these events, the patient adds that she, herself, was her father's favorite child, and that the mother, who did not know what to do with the raving, drunken father, used to send her right into his room. When the father came home, the mother and sister would withdraw, and leave the child alone with the drunken man. What then took place between father and daughter was, at first, not clear. There is no proof of the supposition that the father sexually misused the child. Probably the father exhibited himself and urinated before the child. However, we know that for the unconscious, wish and reality have the same psychic valency. *The fact remains that the child, when in the first blossoming of her oedipus complex, found an opportunity just at this critical time to take over the role of her mother—indeed was actually pushed into this role by her own mother.* The patient, however, acquired a truly murderous sense of guilt, with the consequent desire for punishment—for as may be imagined, the permission of the mother went only as far as the child's taking care of the father, but not to the extent of the realization of the oedipus fantasies. The fact that the mother left the father, and placed the patient in a convent school was unconsciously interpreted by the patient as a punishment. Then came added feelings of guilt because of masturbation. All this led to an increased feeling of aggression against the mother-rival, to repression of this hatred, and to a *reactive love.* Further, we must consider that the patient, unconsciously fleeing toward her mother from those unconscious wishes which drew her to her father, and after the great "day of judgment" when the father was abandoned by the mother, lived in constant dread of *meeting her father on the street.*[5] At this point we begin to gain insight, through the patient, into the riddle of the part played

---

[5] Of course this fear was also the defense-reaction against the unconscious wish to meet her father, and, as well, the Ego's warning signal of the threatening emotional urges.

by her first fiancé. The patient identified this man unconsciously
with her father, and *the violent effort of the mother to get her to give
up this man, was the signal for the neurosis, which had been present
since her childhood, to become manifest.* I believe that this conduct
of the mother was the *actual* cause of the neurosis becoming apparent, and played somewhat the part of agent provocateur. The advice
to give up the man *mobilized the entire repressed sense of guilt and
need of punishment in the patient,* and to do penance for this, she
gives the man up, as her mother renounced her father—which quite
corresponds to the identification with the mother in childhood. The
grotesque fact that the patient gives up the first fiancé, whom she
loves, just as he becomes cured, in order to take up her part of nurse
with the second, who is also tubercular, may be explained as follows:
*to the patient, the illness of the man is a necessary condition for
every sexual relationship,* as in her childhood the unconscious oedipus
wishes were only permitted when accompanied by the thought: "I
am taking care of my sick (drunken) father"—thus relieving her of
the feeling of guilt. So the patient leaves the first fiancé, *not in spite
of, but because of, his return to health*—for the guilt-relieving fact
of his illness exists no longer—and again becomes attached to a man
who fulfills her condition, that is to say, is ill. The patient sticks
to this second man, in spite of her feeling that he is "not the right
one for her," and the fact that he "nags" and torments her, because
at this stage of the patient's neurosis he takes over the part of the
executor of her desire for punishment—this extremely neurotic man
being at the time well suited to the role of jailer.

The analysis of the relationship to the mother took a long time,
and was accompanied by great resistance on the part of the patient.
Again and again the dream material of this very intelligent patient
gave proof of the connections claimed by the analyst. It was possible
to analyze the *castration dream* reported under (B), where the "unknown woman," cutting meat, was finally recognized as the mother.
At the same time, the patient began to show more interest in an
hysterical conversion-symptom which she had hitherto not noticed
and therefore not mentioned: this was a *disgust for meat,* which on
some days increased to a point where it became impossible for her
to eat meat at all. We find here a combination of defense-reactions
against fellatio-fantasies and genital fantasies of loss-of-the-penis,
for the patient, in her childhood, had built up the typical conception

that she had really had a penis, but that her mother had cut it off on account of her masturbation. Parallel to this runs another fantasy in which, as well, we hear a reproach against the mother: to the effect that the mother (by means of the "omnipotence of thought") had caused her clitoris (that is, her penis) to wither away, as a punishment for masturbation and the oedipus fantasies. This neurotic conception of the "omnipotence of thought" also caused the patient to punish herself for the death fantasies against her mother, which had been carried out in the unconscious wishes only, as though she had really murdered her mother. This led, even in the early stages of the cure, to a discussion of the patient's *fear of the street* which, when schematized, showed the following unconscious contents, representing an unconscious repetition of the childhood situation:

(1). The patient's childhood conception of death was apoplexy (to "have a stroke")—from descriptions of her mother whom she used to question at an early age, she knew of the following prodromal symptoms: falling, fainting, feeling of dizziness, etc. Now the patient unconsciously wished death to her mother, because of the rivalry with the father. The *infantile* conception of "having a stroke" was carried out by the patient *on herself (because of the unconscious desire for punishment) as a turning-inward of her aggression upon her own person under the pressure of the power of her own conscience (the Super Ego).* This presupposes an unconscious identification with the mother, which we find to be abundantly present in the case of this patient.

(2). This turning-inward of her aggression partly explains the patient's fear of death, but as yet gives us no clue to why death is feared just on the street, while the house is looked upon as a protection. (The patient feels much better at home.) Now we know from Freud that the house carries the unconscious meaning of the protecting mother. On the other hand, the street is looked upon by the patient as a place of temptation (rendezvous, sight of prostitutes, dogs mating, etc.). Above all, the street came to typify temptation to the patient because (after the divorce of the mother from the father) she "feared" she might "by chance" meet her father on the street (that is, she wished to meet him). So we may explain the patient's fear of "falling" in the sexual-symbolic sense.[6] So from

---

[6] That the patient feared precisely falling "to the left" also has a symbolical sense: for "the left," as is well known, is to the unconscious a symbol of the forbidden.

this cause the street is avoided, and in the symptom of the street-fear the situation of the seventh to the tenth year of the patient's life repeats itself.

(3). But the street is also avoided because the patient plays "*watchman*" *to her mother*, and would like to remain with her constantly in order to prevent the sexual union of her parents.

(4). On the other hand, *the mother must constantly keep watch on the patient at home*, so that a reunion of the child with the father (so much desired by the unconscious of the patient) should not take place—that is, in the only possible way the patient can imagine it—if she should meet her father (whom the mother has forbidden her to see) on the street.

(5). As the patient, however, also continually harbors death-wishes against the mother, to go out at any time without the mother or the sister (identified with the mother) becomes impossible, because only *the constant presence of the threatened person proves that the death-wishes are without effect*. In this way, as Helene Deutsch expresses it, the protector becomes the "protected protector."[7]

(6). The fiancé is accepted by the patient as an escort because, as a result of his whole gloomy, misanthropic, and jealous outlook on life, he seems to the patient a sufficient defense against the men whom she identifies with her father. For, to the patient he is mainly (for her unconscious) *the executor of her need of punishment*.

(7). In this way the patient builds up a *complete and constant alibi for herself*.[8] The presence of the mother proves: (a) that the mother has not been murdered by the patient, (b) that the mother is not sexually united with the father, (c) that the mother does not wish to punish her, but to protect her.

---

[7] H. Deutsch. "On the Origin of Agoraphobia" Internat. Ztschr. f. Psychoanalyse. 1928: "I hold the identification with the object (conditioned by the oedipus relationship), at whom the inimical tendencies are aimed, to be a characteristic of agoraphobia. The sense of guilt may be appeased by the fact that the Ego is made to suffer under the threat of death by turning this threat against itself. The tension between the Ego and the threatening principle of conscience (the Super Ego) is relieved only when the presence of the protecting object confirms that the latter is not in mortal danger and has not abandoned the frightened Ego. . . . The circumstance that the object of the identification, against whom the aggression is directed, is present in the world of reality, and makes his guardianship felt, not as a threatening, but as a loving principle, can cause the mortal anxiety to disappear." My cases confirm the statements of H. Deutsch.

[8] Another agoraphobe (after I had made clear to him his constant seeking for an alibi) wittily spoke of his trouble as an "alibi-illness."

But that "tireless pleasure-seeker, Man" cannot be psychically satisfied by the mere negative proof of his "goodness" with reference to the Super Ego. *Unconscious sources of pleasure must be hidden in the symptom itself.* This we find to be the case. For the patient proves to herself—as we have seen under (3)—that the mother cannot be sexually united with the father. At the same time, the patient, on the street, constantly plays with the thought of "falling." But as this happens in the presence of the representative of the Super Ego, there exists only the intention of "falling," but it is constantly inhibited, and made harmless. The "return of the repressed material" also explains why the thought of "falling"[9] is connected with the feeling that "the ground is made of rubber." In the analysis, this "rubber" proved to be the pillows on which the child lay beside her father. Here, too, we may mention the feeling that the patient frequently had when on the street; that the ground not only was swaying but that it rose up and came toward her. This was an indirect description of the erection of the father.

(8). The repugnance for the street is at the same time an affirmation of the feeling of being safe at home. Then, when at home, the patient repeats her childhood situation in so far as she is *constantly waiting for her father to return.* In this way she makes the separation of her parents and the two and a half decades which had elapsed since then, as though they had never been.

((9). The statement of the patient, *"I reel about as though I were drunk,"* takes on the following significance in the analysis: *the drunken father* used to reel about in the old days, so the patient in her "reeling about" imagines the condition that was prerequisite to her childhood pleasures with the father.

(10). On the other hand, we find in this "reeling about" an identification with the father, which seems to act as a means of relieving the guilt-feelings, somewhat according to the formula: "Not I, but my father, is drunk." Now we know that the cause of the separation of the parents was the *exhibitionism* of the father before the children. In this way the patient placed the responsibility for her own exhibitionism on her father. The patient had strong unconscious exhibitionistic tendencies. We have several proofs of this.

---

[9]It is superfluous to note that the idea of "falling" points to certain unconscious *prostitute-fantasies.* Also, for the religiously brought-up patient, "falling" meant "falling into sin."

In the analysis, there were two reasons for the exhibitionism coming under discussion. The patient had a series of dreams in which she exhibited herself while urinating or defecating. The dream-type we have described under (c) was repeated regularly. On the other hand, the patient had frequent conflicts with her fiancé because of her exhibitionism. A typical example: the patient and the fiancé were employed in the same office. One day, while they both were going up in the elevator in the office building, she opened her coat and noticed that she had "forgotten" to put on a blouse. The reactions to this were an outbreak of rage on the part of the fiancé, and hearty laughter from the patient. Or, the patient injures her knee, and displays it quite freely at the office, etc., etc.

So we find the patient's fear of the street to be also *a defense against her unconscious exhibitionistic desires*—for the exhibitionism is sternly forbidden by her conscience (Super Ego) because of its connection with the forbidden relationship to the father. In dream-type (c) it is the watching man who is punished (falling into a ditch, injury to his eyes, etc.). Beside the sexual-symbolic sense of these punishments, punishment as such is clearly intended here. Then, the dream also shows a turning around of the childhood situation—not the patient, but the father exhibited—so the man to be punished in the dream is the patient herself; again a male identification. On the other hand, during her exhibitionistic acts, the patient identifies herself with the spectator and narcissistically observes herself. It is well known that there is no exhibitionist who is not at the same time unconsciously a voyeur, and *vice versa*.

Furthermore, there exists a connection between exhibitionistic tendencies, masturbation, and anal birth fantasies. At the convent the patient was not allowed to remain a long time in the toilet for the nuns used to say the devil was in there. Now the patient used to masturbate in the toilet, so that her fear of the convent was intensified by her increased guilt-feelings while there.

(11). From what we have seen of the defense-reactions against the unconscious exhibitionistic tendencies on the one hand, and the voyeur-wishes on the other, we now understand why the patient feels safer on the street when she shuts her eyes. She both keeps herself from seeing, and at the same time symbolically punishes herself with blindness. Then, also she may safely exhibit, on the strength of that old child's saying: "Shut your eyes, and then no one will see you."

But these voyeur-wishes of the patient lead to excited conflicts with the fiancé. For instance, he notices that when in the streetcar, the patient stares fixedly at the men opposite her, then slowly lowers her gaze to the genitals, and as the fiancé says, allows it to "stick there." The patient denies this vehemently at first, but is gradually forced to give in and retires to the more correct statement that she does this "without conscious intention." For behind the voyeur-wishes we find the repressed infantile pleasure-situation—to look at the exhibiting father.

(12). We have observed that the patient had a *strong desire to be a man*, and at times unconsciously identified herself with her father. This identification served various ends: first of all, it was the fulfillment of the infantile wish for manhood, which dominates the unconscious of every girl. Second, this identification served to relieve the sense of guilt: "Not I, but my father, exhibits himself." (See point 9.) Third, in her reeling she pictures the drunken state of the father, which was the necessary condition preceding her childish pleasures. (Point 8.) So this identification is servant to the unconscious wishes. Fourth, she uses it to undo her imagined castration, thus rendering void the smallness of the female penis, the clitoris. Fifth, in this identification with the male, we find part of a "masculine" bond to the mother to whom the patient plays the role of the father. This identification is later reactively strengthened when the patient flees to the mother out of fear of the father. Sixth, we find in this identification a certain amount of active castration-wish—and indeed in a double sense: on the one hand, as the expression of an infantile sadistic coitus-fantasy ("the man does something terrible to the woman"); on the other hand, in a definitely revengeful attitude against the castrating man, with also a feeling of revenge out of envy for the liberties allowed to the man in contrast to the woman; for instance, the exhibition of the penis during urination, etc. Let us note further that the patient twice chose for herself men who were seriously ill (which means for the unconscious, castrated). Otherwise, as we have already explained, the illness of the men was the condition set by the conscience-principle (Super Ego) as the necessary prerequisite for sexual relations.

(13). Lastly, let us remember the part the *constitutional factor* plays with the agoraphobes, to which Abraham pointed more than

two decades ago.[10] We are referring to the constitutionally height-
ened *"pleasure in motion"* to be found in these patients. (Muscle-
erotism according to Sadger.) It is Abraham's opinion that in
neurotics suffering from locomotory fear, there existed at first a
constitutional over-strong pleasure in motion and out of the unsuccessful repression of this tendency grew certain neurotic inhibitions of bodily movements. "I have often observed in neurotics,
when walking, the fear of getting into too rapid motion. Here we
are dealing with the repression of pleasurable emotional urges, which
might 'run away' with these people." The "fear of fear" is enjoyed
by these neurotics like a clinging to a prolonged (sexual) fore-
pleasure; and there are many persons among them who are incapable of the normal sexual pleasure-satisfaction. "Fear prevents
patients with topophobia from becoming freed from themselves and
the love-objects of their childhood, as well as from finding the way
to objects in the outer world." "Every path which takes them out
of the magic circle of those persons on whom they are fixated is
forbidden. The sufferers may enjoy their pleasure in motion only
when accompanied by these very persons." Lastly, we find a deter-
minant in the sexual significance of walking.

In these statements of Abraham we miss the motive of the unconscious sense of guilt, but his assumption of the constitutionally
exaggerated and inhibited pleasure in movement still proves to be
right today. So, for instance, my patient, when the analysis had
brought her to the point where she was able to go out socially, had a
more than normal *pleasure in dancing,* and at such times felt no
dizziness, which seemed very remarkable to the patient, and greatly
helped to fortify her opinion of the psychic origin of her trouble.[11]

Case II. A young lawyer entering psychoanalysis because of
potency disturbance told me, in relating his life history, that in 1918
at the age of nineteen he had inherited, through the death of his
parents, a large fortune which was "eaten up" by inflation. The
patient was an Austrian, and the money was deposited in Austrian
money in Viennese banks. In order to avoid inheritance taxes and

[10]"On the Constitutional Basis of Locomotory Fear," Clinical Contributions
to Psychoanalysis, pages 159, etc.
[11]The patient had a like experience with alcoholic beverages, which she had
feared because of the intoxication, that is, "dizziness" they might bring. The
facts proved that a moderate consumption of alcohol caused her *no* dizziness
—which at first seemed very strange to the patient.

foreseeing the devaluation of Austrian currency (quite a foresight in 1918!), he protracted, by constant protests and legal procedures, the final settlement. "Cleverly" speculating on inflation in order to pay taxes in worthless money, he "forgot," seemingly "idiotically," as he later put it, that his money, since it was deposited in the bank, would depreciate too. The result was that after a few years of legal fighting, he achieved partly his aim of cheating the government, but received his inheritance in worthless money. Until now one might say that the man acted stupidly; he "overlooked" a decisive factor. On the other hand, as he related to me, he was earning his livelihood at that time by teaching foreign languages. Every penny he could save he converted into American dollars and Swiss francs. Considering this, his behavior becomes even more incomprehensible, since he foresaw inflation and counteracted its danger as far as the money he earned was concerned. His "oversight" was concentrated exclusively on his inheritance.

The solution of the riddle lies in his unconscious feeling of guilt. His father was sixty when he married, his mother thirty-five. In the patient's recollections, his father was always a "very old, sick man." The relationship between the parents was strange. The old man complained constantly of pains in practically every organ of his body. The mother discarded all of these complaints as hypochondria, and would not call a physician. In the course of their many quarrels concerning the man's "imaginary diseases," the mother would frequently exclaim: "If you would only die finally so that my son and I could live in peace." The patient always sided with his mother, being unsympathetic to the old man's complaints. One day the father could not leave his bed. The frightened son called a physician, for the first time in his life, who suspected cancer of the stomach. The father was taken to the hospital, the diagnosis confirmed, and he died there a few days later. The mother "caught a cold" during the funeral and died shortly thereafter of pneumonia.

The psychic situation of the patient was one of despair over the death of his mother. His father's death bothered him little. Still, feeling of guilt concerning his father explains his irrational behavior in handling the inheritance. His Super Ego accused him of having killed the father. "Didn't you wish him dead often enough?" The patient behaved inwardly as if his "bad wishes" and not cancer had killed his father. In inner penitence for that guilt, he could not accept his father's money. Therefore, the irrational behavior resulted in final loss of the money. The patient paid for his inner guilt!

III. Neurotic suicide, the outcome of an inner guilt conflict, is rarely found without psychotic admixtures. The candidate for suicide usually has a depressive psychosis which has remained undetected; or hysteric manifestations which occasionally succeed without real inner decision to end life. One has to take into account that sometimes even hysteric suicide succeeds. For example: in a woman's not too seriously intended opening of the gas jet with the expectation that the husband will be home in a few minutes. If the husband is late and the gas makes the woman unconscious, even this not too seriously intended dramatization may have a fatal outcome.

Psychoanalytic theories concerning suicide are replete with contradiction.[12] These contradictions are partly explainable from the "historic" viewpoint: earlier conceptions have not been co-ordinated with later discoveries. Other contradictions petrify the fact that Freud discovered first the repressed libidinous wishes in the unconscious to complement them only much later with repressed aggressive tendencies. Still other incongruities are based on lack of theoretic precision in the formulation: some authors stress a variety of types, some with, some without acknowledgment of a predominant type. Last, but not least, some writers in this specific field deny the applicability of the clinical approach altogether, reducing the genetic problem in suicide to an "archaic form of man's response to his various inner conflicts," which allegedly only ethnologic science can solve.

In the first decades of existence of Freudian psychoanalysis the accent in studies on suicide was placed on a libidinous gain derived from the symbolic connotation of the suicide method chosen by the specific person. Only later feelings of guilt because of inner aggression were added. Paradigmatic is Freud's explanation in "Psychogenesis of a case of female homosexuality" (1920).[13] The girl described, commits suicide because of "self-punishment and wish-fulfillment." The unconscious wish consists of the symbolically achieved giving birth to a child conceived in an incestuous relation: the girl unconsciously identified jumping from a height with giving birth. The self-punishment pertains to death-wishes directed toward

---

[12]"Problems of Suicide," first published in The Psychiat. Quart. 1946.
[13]Ges. Schr. V. 312-343.

the mother, who was pregnant at that time, and with whom the girl identified herself, since she herself wanted to take her place. Freud adds, however, "In the identification with the mother who should die during childbirth of this child, denied to the girl, the punishment itself is once more a wish-fulfillment." This dichotomy between libidinous wishes and later superimposed feelings of guilt because of aggressive wishes, was never clearly solved in our literature. Since both, the libidinous wishes and the guilt problem stemming from aggression, were pointed out by Freud at different times, both can be quoted with Freud's authority. How unclarified the interconnection really is, is best proven by Freud's explanation quoted above. If we ask: did Freud's patient attempt suicide because (a) she hated her mother and therefore felt guilty, (b) she wanted to give birth to the child with which the mother was pregnant and therefore felt guilty, (c) she permitted herself only on condition of death the identification with the mother comprising the inner right of giving birth to an incestually conceived child, and therefore felt guilty, the answer is all three reasons are valid, as far as Freud's description goes. Freud stresses specifically: "The punishment becomes once more wish-fulfillment." One gets the impression that Freud himself followed at that time only reluctantly the path he himself discovered: feeling of guilt because of unconscious aggression. He stresses precisely the libidinous components embedded in the method chosen for suicide: "These interpretations of the methods of suicide through sexual wish-fulfillments are known to analysts for a long time (to poison oneself—get pregnant, to drown oneself—to give birth. to jump from a height—give birth)."

Freud described in 1918 in his paper "Mourning and Melancholia" the "introjection"-type of suicide. After a deep disappointment this type does not cast off the disappointer, but identifies himself with him. The so-called self-reproaches of the depressive psychotic pertain in psychic reality to the introjected disappointer; the suicide is unconsciously a murder of the disappointer. Practically every analytic author who investigated the problem of suicide (f.i.: Federn, Menninger, Zilboorg, Garma, Friedman), confirmed Freud's "introjection" type. The question arises whether or not this type represents the typical or predominant one in suicide.

I propose to subdivide the whole problem into three categories: the introjection type, the hysteric type and a miscellaneous group.

I. The Introjection Type. There is an incongruity between the earlier and later statements of Freud concerning suicide. In 1920 he stated: "It is possible that nobody has the psychic energy to kill himself who, first, does not at the same time kill another object, with whom he identifies himself, and, second, in doing so turns a death wish against himself which was originally directed against another person."[14]

In 1923 Freud explained once more that two basic instincts, life and death instincts, are operative in every human being. Of course, what we see clinically is never life or death instinct *per se*, nor even their original mixtures, but only the derivatives of these mixtures. In this sense we can speak of "libido" and "destrudo" (aggression), assuming that each contains mixtures of both drives, libido more of the derivates of Eros, destrudo more thanatic elements, but both admixtures of erotic and thanatic elements. Normally, the life instinct redirects toward outside objects the death instinct which is originally directed toward the Ego. Under specific conditions a de-fusion of both instincts takes place and the death instinct rages against the Ego. To quote Freud: "Let's turn to depressive psychosis. We find that the over-powerful Super Ego (inner conscience) . . . rages against the Ego with merciless violence, as if it had taken possession of all the sadism the person has at his disposal. According to our viewpoint of sadism, we would say that the destructive component has placed itself in the Super Ego and is directed against the Ego. What now reigns in the Super Ego is like a pure mixture of death instinct, and often enough it does succeed in driving the Ego to death, unless the Ego unburdens itself of its tyrant by turning into mania."

Freud explains also that the more a person restricts his inner aggression, the more severe does his Super Ego become.

How can we reconcile the two approaches? In the first, stress is laid on the fact that the Ego can be driven to self-destruction by the inner illusion of killing the tormenting disappointer. In the second, the decisive factor is the de-fusion of instincts, with the result that the Super Ego usurps the whole energy of the death instinct, actually driving the Ego to death. True, both approaches assume inner guilt to be the motor which starts the procedure.

I am personally of the opinion that the decisive element in suicide

[14]See Chapter II.

is the predominance of death instinct, *changing the afflicted person into an exquisite seeker of self destruction.* I believe further that the overdimensional feeling of guilt, because of death wishes toward the introjected disappointer, is the *covering cloak of pseudo-aggression disguising this inner passivity.* In other words, what really drives the suicide to death is not his inner guilt but the de-fusion of instincts, leaving the death-instinct no longer attenuated by life-instinct. But even then the *illusion of pseudo-aggression* must be maintained—therefore the unconscious fantasy of killing the disappointer. One could say that the suicide must convince himself, even in death, that he is capable of aggression.

In a short story by the French writer, Villiers d'Isle Adam, an aristocratic French family of the time of Richelieu is confronted with the fact that a young member of the family has taken part in a rebellion against the King and Cardinal, has been arrested, found guilty, and condemned to die on the scaffold. The honor of the family is at stake should the condemned not die proudly and defiantly. To bolster the morale of the unfortunate man, he is sent word by his family that an attempt will be made to save him, and that he is to look for a sign from a certain window visible from the place of execution. He is told that the attempt will be made in the last few seconds, and not to lose courage. The hoax works, and the man dies proudly. *Mutatis mutandis,* the suicide fools himself with his pseudo-aggression toward the introjected object similarly. Instead of hope, aggression is the prop.

Another set of facts indicates the same psychologic picture of suicide. It has been repeatedly observed that the choice of form of suicide has an unconscious libidinous meaning. As an example a case of Mary Chadwick can be adduced. A woman, who, as a little child, was raped by a friend of her father's, repeatedly tried suicide. She always chose a method which involved falling—being run over by a car, falling down stairs, etc. She was symbolizing the "fallen woman." A great many examples have been amassed by different authors stressing that libidinous symbolic motive in suicide. All of these elements seem to me unimportant[15] in the suicide—

---

[15]Many libidinous tendencies projected upon suicide belong in this—as I believe, dynamically unimportant—category. They are often overstressed. Zilboorg pointed out that in some cases of suicide an identification with a person already dead takes place and the actual suicide expressed unconsciously the wish to be reunited with the dead person (I.Z.f. Psychoan. 21:102, 1935). B.

they are the bait the inner conscience gives to lure the victim into self-destruction.

K. Menninger[16] distinguishes three elements in suicide: the wish to kill, the wish to be killed and the wish to die. He states: "We have presented the thesis that suicide is a gratification of self-destructive tendencies which upon analysis appear to be composed of at least two elements—an aggressive element, the wish to kill—and a submission element, the wish to be killed. In addition, it is postulated that a wish to die may be present to a variable degree for which, however, no definite psychological evidence can be offered."

To sum up: The suicide of the introjection type is a person laboring under deepest feeling of guilt because of his over-dimensional *psychic masochism*. To counteract this reproach, *pseudo-aggression is mobilized*—the fantasy of killing the disappointer. The disappointment is always self-provoked, by choice of and attachment to the disappointing person. The feeling of guilt is *shifted* from the masochistic act to a pseudo-aggressive one.[17]

II. The Hysteric "Dramatization" Type. Clinical experience proves that the majority of suicides are depressive psychotics, whose

---

Warburg described a case of a deformed and gonorrhoic girl in whom suicide meant also to be reborn and emerge unblemished; besides feeling of guilt this "suicidal attempt not only gratified her heterosexual but also her aggressive homosexual wishes." ("Suicide, Pregnancy, Rebirth," The Psychoanalyt. Quart. 7:490, 1938).

[16]"Psychoanalytic Aspects of Suicide." The Internat. J. Psycho-Analysis. 14: 381, 1933.

[17]"I am not quite sure but I have the impression from some not too clear passages in K. Menninger's "Psychoanalytic Aspects of Suicide" (l.c.) that Menninger, too, came close to the assumption that the unconscious erotic gratifications in suicide which he stresses specifically (masochism, erogenized submission, symbolic erotic gratification in choice of technique) are compensatory. He does not say so *expressis verbis* and states only: "We know also, however, the curious propensity of the erotic elements, the sexual element of the life instinct for making the best of a bad situation and endowing every object relationship with some of its saving grace. Hence in any attack upon an enemy, however strong the wish to kill, we must expect in varying quantities erotic satisfactions." (p 379, l.c.) This gives more the impression that because of the chronic duality of destructive and libidinous tendencies, the latter must appear too. In any case, if one goes one step further, the compensatory character is obvious. Another passage of Menninger's paper (p384) points in this direction: In discussing a patient's unconscious wish to be homosexually attacked, he uses projection as defense in the reconstruction: "Thus, it is not I who play tricks upon the analyst, it is he who plays tricks upon me. He attacks me. Therefore I hate him, I want to kill him, I do kill him. But for killing him, I also feel guilty and must suffer like fate for myself." Here the Freudian explanation of paranoiac projection in "The Schreber Case" (Coll. Pap. III. p. 388) is referred to.

illness is detected during lifetime, or, more often, has remained undi-
agnosed. The question arises as to whether all suicides belong in this
category. There seems to be agreement in the view that other types
are possible. (Freud, Federn, Menninger, Zilboorg.)

The most important group among these other types is the hysteric. In my personal opinion, the hysteric suicide is based on a specific type of "magic gesture." There are different types of "magic gestures"[18]; the one important in suicide is one which I have called the
"negative magic gesture." The term denotes an *unconscious* dramatization of how one does *not* want to be treated. It constitutes a
bitter unconscious irony directed against an authoritative person
in early childhood. An example of this type: A patient while waiting for her appointment made movements with her mouth reminiscent of a wild animal snatching at its victim. I asked her: "Do
you imitate the lion in Metro-Goldwyn-Mayer's pictures?" Analysis
showed that in this gesture she was playing the role of her own
"devouring" mother, thereby showing up her mother, whom she
accused of all possible crimes, in a caricature.

"Magic gestures" of this type presuppose a three-layer structure:
1. unconscious masochistic attachment toward the person in childhood, as the end-result of the infantile conflict; 2. objection by the
inner conscience (Super Ego) to this enjoyment of inner passivity,
forcing the unconscious Ego to furnish a defense mechanism in the
form of the pseudo-aggressive alibi, "I hate my mother (father)";
3. objection by the Super Ego to this defense, too, with the result
that even the defensive pseudo-aggression is modified into: "I'm
just showing them how mean they acted." The whole process is,
of course, *unconscious*.

The hysteric suicide makes use of this technique. Coupled with
the "magic gesture" is the infantile unconscious misconception of
death, which, for the child, lacks finality. This is easily observable
in children to whom "death" is often represented as "going away,"
"taking a long journey," etc. (Freud). Children's play bears this
out. One patient as a child played with his brother the game of
"being dead." He would command, "Now you are dead!" and his
brother would stretch out motionless, holding his breath. After a
few seconds would come the counterorder, "Now you are alive

---

[18]See my paper "The Problem of Magic Gestures." The Psychiat. Quart.
19:295, 1945. See also Chapter VI.

again!" It is obvious that the play had—at least superficially—
an aggressive connotation: death wishes against the brother.

All of this indicates that hysteric suicide—provided the hysteric
superstructure does not cover an "introjection" mechanism—is not
too seriously intended. There is no doubt that a severe inner guilt
conflict is involved, too. In such cases there are discernible death
wishes or incest fantasies which, because of the inner "poena talionis" boomerang in the form of self-punishment. Let us take two
clinical examples.

Case I. Mr. A., a young man of 24, had for many years a severe
conflict with his father, a wealthy and tyrannical individual who
wanted to force his son into a commercial career. The boy refused,
left home, became attached to a radical party, thus mildly compromising his father but infuriating him beyond every logical reason.
To complicate matters, the boy married, against his father's wishes,
a girl "beneath his own station." This resulted in a complete sever-
ance of relations between father and son. When the young man
became ill with an acute tuberculous condition, the father refused
to help him as long as he did not renounce his wife. The couple
agreed to an official separation to enable the boy's transfer to a
sanitarium. After long months his condition improved, and he
started once more his contact with his wife. The father discovered
this and refused even to see him. A few days later the son went
to a hotel and swallowed an overdose of sleeping pills. Immediately
afterward he started frantic telephone calls to his wife and family
physician. His father still said "To hell with him! Why doesn't
he commit suicide more successfully?" and refused to pay the
doctor's bill.

The analysis of the young man started after his release from the
hospital a few weeks after his suicide attempt. It showed that his
hatred for his father was the covering cloak for his deep attachment
to him. The boy was a typical example of regression to the "negative oedipus," which consists of feminine identification. Unconsciously he identified with his mother and wanted to be sexually
"mistreated" by his father, since, as a child, he believed that parental
congress consisted of sadistic attacks on the part of the father upon
the mother. After a short-lived "positive oedipus," he renounced his
libidinous wishes toward his mother and hatred of his father because
of an overdimensional "castration fear," and took refuge in passivity
by identifying with his mother.

This inner passivity was counteracted by a strong feeling of guilt, which forced him to establish an inner defense: pseudo-aggression. This explains his acts of "aggression" toward his father (refusal to take up a commercial career, escape from home, political activity and marriage against his father's wishes, etc.). All of these actions had a double meaning unconsciously. They gave him the illusion of being aggressive as a defense against his masochistic submission *and*, at the same time, provided the masochistic pleasure of being "mistreated" (with its above-mentioned sexual connotation) by his father —a perfect neurotic setup.

It also became clear that the patient was inwardly uninterested in his wife, that he was just using her as a tool against his father and for the inner defense of being a "he man."

The conscious motivation of his suicide was: "Father will feel sorry after my death." In other words, consciously it was an act directed against his father. Unconsciously the situation was quite different. The suicide represented, first, a masochistic "magic gesture": "The only thing you can get from father is rejection. He lets you starve and drives you to suicide. True, he would perhaps provide poison." In attempting suicide he demonstrated in an ironic accusation his father's "meanness." That he himself was the victim and not his father did not occur to him.

The suicide in this case was an unconscious wooing of the father. It was an attempt to make him understand that the son was willing to give up everything to get the old man's forgiveness and "love." Asked why he had made the telephone calls immediately after taking the poison, he replied that new hope came over him when it occurred to him "in a flash" that his father would see the "seriousness of the situation." Asked whether that included acceptance of the daughter-in-law, the patient said that he doubted that, even at that moment. In other words, the young man was willing to sacrifice the girl.

Once more, we see, under the disguise of pseudo-aggression, masochistic submission. The question as to whether simulation was involved can be answered in the negative. A deep inner conflict was involved.

Case II. A woman of forty, a widow, had an affair with a somewhat younger man. One day the lady's eighteen-year-old daughter declared that she intended to marry her mother's lover. Excited quarrels between the two women, in the course of which the daughter demanded that her mother separate from her lover, culminated in a suicide attempt on the part of the daughter. Her mother was afterward on the verge of suicide, too. The analysis of the mother, which followed, yielded the fact that a photographic reproduction of her own childhood had taken place. Many years previously, it developed, she had found herself in an unusual situation of conflict. Her mother(the grandmother of the girl who attempted suicide) had a lover, of whom the patient was very jealous. The energetic and unscrupulous grandmother apparently wished to get rid of her lover, and suggested to her daughter that she should marry him. The daughter was indignant and at the same time overjoyed. Although it was never officially admitted that it was her mother's lover whom she was to marry, it can be understood that she found the proposal unsuitable. But since this marriage represented a realization of infantile oedipus wishes (it was clear that her jealousy of her mother's lover was in itself a repetition of the jealousy of her father), she agreed, without of course, suspecting her unconscious motive. The marriage was very brief and unhappy. The husband was brutal, infected the young woman with gonorrhea, had relations with other women, and died, deeply mourned by the patient, shortly after the birth of her daughter. The patient clung to this child with a remarkable combination of hate and love. As the girl grew up, she brought her indirectly into contact with her own lover. This took place unconsciously, but none the less effectively. She constantly brought the "young people" together, although she was consciously very jealous. A certain scene bears this out. While the "young people" played duets on the piano in the music room, the mother put on her glasses and darned stockings. She thus enacted the old lady chaperoning the "children." She was not conscious of this, for when the daughter "to her astonishment" fell in love with her lover, she was indignant. The behavior of this woman is incomprehensible without the assumption of unconscious guilt feelings. "You snatched away your mother's lover, and as punishment your daughter will do the same to you." It was certainly no accident that the daughter fell in love with her mother's lover. This oedipus relation continuing through three generations is a classic example of the operation of these unconscious attitudes.

The suicidal ideas of the mother could be analyzed. The guilt pertained to the oedipal period, when she had wanted to take her father away from her mother. Interestingly enough, the guilt was not relieved through her mother's invitation to marry her lover; the guilt was already established. The reproachful "magic gesture" was discernible, directed toward the mother: "You forced me into a marriage, and now my child takes revenge on me." Behind this pseudo-aggression self-destructive masochistic tendencies were clearly visible.

K. Menninger was the first to point out the paradox that many a suicide does not want to die.[19] "Anyone who has sat by the bedside of a patient dying from a self-inflicted wound and listened to pleading that the physician save his life which only a few hours or minutes before the patient had attempted to destroy, must be impressed by the paradox that one who had wished to kill himself does not wish to die . . . . One gets the impression that for such people the suicide act is sometimes a sort of insincere play-acting and that their capacity for dealing with reality is so poorly developed that they proceed as if they could actually kill themselves and not die. We have reason to believe that a child has such a conception of death: that it is a going away and that for such going away there is often a returning . . . ."

III. Miscellaneous Types. Not all persons who commit suicide are depressive psychotics or neurotics of the hysteric type. And still, the majority of all suicides are depressive psychotics. In general, A. A. Brill's statement is analytically universally accepted: "I do not think I am exaggerating when I assert that probably *eighty-five to ninety percent* of all suicides belong to the depressive type of this disease (manic-depressive insanity.")[20]

P. Federn[21] stressed in 1928 that in his opinion two groups are especially prone to suicide: manic depressives and addicts, whether they are, in addition, hysterics, obsessional neurotics, psychoasthenics, or do not show any clear-cut neurosis. Federn is of the opinion that suicide may be the final destiny of a completely normal person.

In a paper[22] read at the Thirteenth International Psychoanalytic Convention in Luzerne (1934), G. Zilboorg stated: 1. "Not all depressive psychotics tend to commit suicide; 2. not only depressive

---

[19] l. c. 387.
[20] "Fundamental Concepts of Psychoanalysis," Harcourt-Brace & Co., 1921, p. 262.
[21] "Suicide-Prophylaxis in Psychoanalysis," Ztschr. f. Psychoanalyt., Paedagogik, 3:379, 1928-29.
[22] Summary published in Internat. Ztschr. f. Psychoanalyse., 21:101, 1935.

psychotics tend to commit suicide, since one finds suicide also in cases of schizophrenia, obsessional neurosis, hysteria; 3. a series of suicides has the precise stigma of practically uncontrollable instinctual impulses,[23] without reference to what nosologic group they belong, even in so-called normal individuals." Zilboorg claims further, that not all suicides can be subsumed under Freud's classic formula of the introjection type, and that some suicides are the pathologically dramatized expression of repetition of a form of mourning which in its turn stems from the primitive killing at funerals. Suicide was originally a ritual, a ritual-murder—killing of the old, later suicide of the old and sick; killing, later suicide, of the wives and slaves of a deceased chief of a clan.

In a later paper[24] Zilboorg advocates "an entirely different, non-clinical approach" based on ethnologic studies:

> "One may state, therefore, that a suicidal drive is not dependent on or derived from any traditional clinical entity found in present-day psychiatric nosology; it is to be viewed rather as a reaction of a developmental nature, which is universal and common to the mentally sick of all types and probably also to many so-called normal persons. The very universality of the reaction, and particularly of some of its outstanding characteristics, such as oral incorporation, spite, and identification with the dead, leads one to suspect that one may be dealing with an archaic form of men's response to his various inner conflicts, and it would prompt one to seek an answer to the problem in the study of primitive races and their reaction leading to suicide."

There is no doubt in my mind that the great majority of suicides belong to the introjection and hysteric types. True, though, an infinitesimal percentage has a different etiology. For instance, there are schizophrenics of the paranoid type who project their Super Ego outwardly and hear voices commanding them to kill themselves. I have observed a patient of this type who repeatedly attempted suicide while in a psychiatric sanitarium. In moments of discernment the patient claimed that he understood that these voices were a symptom and sign of his disease, since "they never give me advice as to where

[23]Zilboorg mentions that the active suicidal impulse is especially strong in individuals who identify unconsciously with a person who, at the time of completion of this identification, is already dead. In these cases the wish to die corresponds to the desire to be reunited with the dead person.

[24]"Differential Diagnostic Types of Suicide," Arch. Neurol. Psychiat., 270, 1936.

to get the knife to cut my throat. If the voices were real, they would have provided a knife."

In obsessional cases suicide is an extreme rarity. Freud was of the opinion that obsessional (compulsive) neurosis was practically immune against suicide.[25] Zilboorg[26] believes that some severe cases of compulsive neurosis and some addicts are capable of committing suicide in a momentary impulse of spite. This is paralleled by Zilboorg to the behavior of Indians of North and South America, who before or immediately after being taken prisoner by white soldiers killed themselves by the hundreds and thousands.

In any case, obsessional neurotics are not the typical material for suicide,[27] and Freud is undoubtedly clinically correct in his opinion that these neurotics are more or less immune against it.

That addicts are endangered by suicide is clinically provable. The reason is obvious. They are orally regressed and are generally near to depressive psychotics.[28]

I very much doubt whether suicide occurs in normal people. The statement to the contrary is not borne out by clinical facts.

Further studies will have to find a connecting link with problems of criminality, especially murder.[29] Studies of suicide of the introjection type will further increase our knowledge of the manic phase of cyclothymia. I believe that we shall get more information about motives for suicide when we shall have more opportunity of studying depressive psychotics *also* in the manic phase. Here is an example:

The following case was brought to my attention in a circuitous way. A young man met, at a social gathering, a young girl who, in the course of the evening, directly offered herself to him. He slept with her. She was frigid and did not allow any petting or preliminary acts, was uninterested in the sexual act, but kept repeating in a flighty manner during the act how much she was admired and sexually

---

[25]"The Ego and the Id," Ges. Schr., VI 399.
[26]l.c., 101.
[27]The problem of obsessional neurosis has, in my opinion, a more complicated substructure that is generally assumed. See my paper "Two Forms of Aggression in Obsessional Neurosis," The Psychoanalyt. Rev. 29:188, 1942, and "The Leading and Misleading Basic Identification," Ibid, 32:323, 1945.
[28]For a compilation of analytic literature and my personal opinion on the subject of alcoholic addiction, see "Clinical Contributions to the Psychogenesis of Alcohol Addiction," Quart. J. Stud. on Alcohol, 5:434, 1944.
[29]See my paper "Suppositions About the Mechanism of Criminosis," J. Crim. Psychopath., 1943.

desired. The man could not understand her behavior, especially her objection to "petting," since he believed that morally petting was less objectionable than intercourse. When he learned, a few days later, that his so suddenly acquired friend was to be found in a psychiatric sanatarium where she had been committed because of manic psychosis, he severely reproached and blamed himself for it. The irony of the situation was that he did not understand the psychotic condition and yet felt responsible for it. A year later I had the opportunity to observe the psychotic girl in a pre-depressive phase in which she tried to commit suicide. At that time she accused herself of being "good for nothing" since she had masturbated as a child. Interestingly enough, she accused herself only of masturbation, not of promiscuity. According to her, this masturbation was responsible for everything. Especially she had alienated her "innocent cousin" through it. The real inner facts were, as is so often true, the reversal of the conscious reverberations. The patient had an orphan cousin two years her senior, who was brought up with her. The two children were deeply attached to each other. When the patient was five, the girls masturbated mutually, the cousin taking the initiative. The mother discovered them and ordered that they sleep in separate rooms. The hypocritical cousin convinced the mother that the younger girl was the seducer. The mother believed this because some of her daughter's friends had a poor reputation. The patient's hatred was overdimensional. She remembered later having condemned her cousin to death in her mind. What she did amounted practically to "detaching" herself from her cousin, only to be drawn time and again back to the girl. The cousin, obviously a psychopathic personality, was a parasite who later took advantage of the younger girl's adoration. At the age of eighteen the cousin married a masochistically-tinged Hungarian aristocrat and left the country. A few months later the patient had her first depressive phase.

All of the reproaches which she heaped upon herself were inwardly directed toward her cousin. The introjected cousin was accused of having spoiled the patient's chances in life with the masturbation. The patient believed that she herself did not marry because of the masturbation. Of course, she was unconsciously blaming not masturbation but the underlying oedipal and homosexual connotations and fantasies.

The case was interesting because it showed that the transition between the manic and the depressive phase of cyclothymia did not change the basic conflict. Freud pointed out that the mania is the stage of triumph, in which the humiliated Ego revolts against the cruel inner conscience (Super Ego), nullifies it temporarily, throws off its chains in a sort of slave revolt and ecstasy of freedom. In other words, it is an attempt of the Ego to free itself of the tyranny of the conscience. The accent lies on *attempt,* because the hypomanic mood just covers depression. (H. Deutsch, Schilder.) In the case in question, even the manic phase did not remove the old fear of masturbation. (The girl refused petting and clitoridian preparatory acts, shifting her compensatory aggression toward the family by permitting intercourse, the adult outlet for sex.)

Despite some attempts to revise[30] Freud's findings on suicide, the majority of analysts believe—as the previously quoted statement of Brill illustrates—that "eighty-five to ninety percent of all suicides belong to the depressive type."

This does not exclude the fact that further studies are necessary. The main problem that remains is whether aggression leading to inner guilt is the basic principle involved in suicide. I doubt this assumption and believe that inner passivity, masochistically tinged—the end-result of the death-instinct—is the decisive element.

Fear of death is one of the typical depositories of unconscious guilt. Normally the thought of death is suppressed,[31] shoved aside; we don't want to think about it. In specific conditions it predominates in neurotic thinking. In one neurotic disease, obsessional (compulsive) neurosis, it is the focus of attention. These neurotics think in a form of obsession constantly of their impending doom. Here are the words of an obsessional neurotic patient:

"I think constantly about my death. Every minute passed reminds me that I am nearer to death. I don't dare look at my

[30]See Zilboog's "Suicide Among Civilized and Primitive Races," Am. J. Psychiat. 92:1347, 1936: "If we turn now to purely clinical observations we find that the old point of view, according to which depressive psychoses have more or less monopolized the clinical right to commit suicide, requires substantial revision." (p. 1356).

[31]The difference between repression and suppression is that the former is an *unconscious* mechanism, while the latter is a conscious one. If a person is unaware of his hatred for another person and produces in consciousness a defense mechanism of pseudo-kindness and pseudo-love toward that person, all this without conscious reasoning, he "represses." If, on the other hand, he is fully aware of his hatred for that person, but chooses consciously not to express it, he "suppresses" his hatred, or, more precisely, the verbal expression of that feeling.

watch anymore. Every time I start something, I am tortured with the idea: 'This is your last deed.' Yesterday I entered a restaurant, and while waiting for my food, I was obsessed with the thought: 'You will die in this restaurant.' "

Many compulsions are inner defenses against these inner tendencies. For instance, when a compulsive neurotic, before going to sleep, must look twenty times to be sure that the gas jet is closed, so that the lives about him are not endangered, he is unconsciously warding off aggression with hyper-meticulousness.[32] Because of feeling of guilt, the defense sets in.

Now, no relatively healthy person is capable of living with the constant thought of death. The typical defense is suppression of the thought.[33] The defense is a relative one, and does not prevent the disturbing thought from creeping in. There is no doubt that a good deal of inner guilt is concentrated and absorbed in that thought.

One can observe the fight between the derivatives of death and life instinct in the orbit of fear of death. Neurotics who constantly think of death—especially obsessionals and hypochondriacs—acquire, after a period of torture, the ability to sexualize that fear, to enjoy psychic masochism.

Unconscious neurotic feeling of guilt leading to self-punishment may invade every province of human action and reaction. The pupil may fail his examination, the husband become impotent, the business man reveal himself as a failure, the actor get stage fright, the driver of a car kill a passer-by "accidentally," and the criminal commit a crime, etc. The feeling of guilt is always one participant in every neurosis. It does not cause the neurosis *per se*, but every neurotic symptom and sign is a compromise between repressed wishes and unconscious guilt. To use a simile, it is like one half of a dollar bill. It is not the whole bill, but without it, the bill is incomplete and not even imaginable.

---

[32]There are two theories concerning hyper-aggression of obsessional (compulsive) neurotics. The older assumes that these neurotics ward off an original aggression; the newer claims that a three-layer structure is involved: Strong passivity warded off with a pseudo-aggression, which in turn is warded off with pseudo-kindness. For a discussion of the problem, see my papers "Two Forms of Aggression in Obsessional Neurosis," Psychoanalyt. Rev., 1942, and "The Leading and the Misleading Basic Identifications," Psychoanalyt. Rev., No. 3, 1945.

[33]Freud stated that everybody considers himself unconsciously immortal.

CHAPTER VI

THE "INJUSTICE COLLECTOR"

There are neurotics who constantly construct unconsciously situations in which they are disappointed and "mistreated." It consists of the following triad:

1. "I shall repeat the masochistic wish of being deprived by my mother, by creating situations in which some substitute of my mother-image shall refuse my wishes."
2. "I shall not be conscious of my wish to be refused and initial provocation of refusal, and shall see only that I am justified in righteous indignation and aggression because of the refusal."
3. "Afterward I shall pity myself because such an injustice 'can happen only to me,' and enjoy once more psychic masochistic pleasure."

This triad, which I have repeatedly described as the "mechanism of orality,"[1] induces the Ego-strengthening mirage of aggression, while in unconscious reality, the wish to be refused, deprived, and mistreated is foremost. Under the disguise of pseudo-aggression the oral neurotic unconsciously enjoys masochistic self-pity and the pleasure of being refused.

The discrepancy between the real situation in the psyche of the oral neurotic and that attributed to his psyche by the outer world is striking. The naive opinion generally current is that "oral" people are parasites and want to get, get, and *get*. In my opinion, what they really want is to be refused, refused, and *refused*. The wish to get is, in these cases, a palimpsest for the wish to be refused, as is evidenced by their reaction when they do get—they always feel that they are not getting enough, in other words, are still being refused.

These oral neurotics constantly identify harmless people in the outer world with their introjected image of the "bad," refusing mother of their babyhood. This *external* identification via projection is necessary to permit them to play their repetitive neurotic game:

[1] A summary of this mechanism can be found in my monograph, "Psychic Impotence in Men," Med. Edition, Huber, Berne, 1937, and "A Clinical Approach to the Psychoanalysis of Writers," Psychoanalyt. Rev. Vol. 31, No. 1, Jan. 1944.

"Someone is unjust toward me." We see therefore that *two sets of identification* have taken place. The image of the fantastic monster of a mother is first introjected and secondarily projected upon other people. The *inner* identification comes first; the projection, later.

The question arises as to how such an identification could be established in the first place. Such a monster of a devouring, depriving mother simply does not exist. And yet, such an identification is intrapsychically created. To understand this phenomenon, we have to recall that the child projects his own aggression onto his parents. The devouring witch of fairy tales,[2] that is, the distorted image of the pre-oedipal mother, is the picture of the child's own projected and later introjected aggression. A few examples of the queer mechanism of masochistic self-damagement:

A patient coming for treatment because of ejaculatio praecox, told me the story of his life. Filled with rage and hatred, he said that he had continually met with bad luck in all his plans for marriage. The last attempt had failed because of the "malice" of his presumptive father- and mother-in-law, and a "lack of love" in the girl. He, a man of thirty-two years, had fallen in love with a girl of eighteen. When the girl's parents made inquiries concerning his financial status, he represented his income as eighty per cent lower than it really was. Alarmed at the prospect of such a "misalliance," the parents, who were calculating business people, rich, and rather purse-proud, and who wanted their daughter to marry only for money, opposed the engagement and influenced their daughter in accordance with their views. When the patient's relatives heard about this "awkward behavior" of his, in reference to his income, they were horrified. They had impressed upon him, that in this connection "it is better to say too much than too little." When I asked the patient why he had not simply told the truth about his circumstances, he answered that he had wanted to "test" his parents-in-law. Unconsciously he had wanted to drive the girl and her parents into the role of "giving" persons *ad absurdum*, as if to say, "Nobody loves me, therefore I may be aggressive and enjoy my unhappiness." I was able to show that the failure of previous marriage plans had been brought about in a similar manner.

Another patient in treatment because of impotence, was continually complaining about his wife. Above all, he reproached her

[2]For instance, Grimm's "Hansel and Gretel."

with "malicious refusal in sexuality." When I asked him what this malicious refusal consisted of, he said that his wife "was completely passive" as to sex. The patient had married a virgin with a repugnance to everything sexual, who theoretically assented to coitus only because, as she said, one had to be "normal." Besides, she wanted to play the woman's part, be passive, and be forced by the man. The patient, on the other hand, expected his wife to take the initiative in coitus, to "seduce" him.

When I tried to explain to him that the wish to be forced was typical in virgins, I met with complete absence of understanding. "What do you mean! I am to take the initiative? Ridiculous!" was his repeated reply. When I protested that if he wanted to be seduced he should have chosen an older and more experienced woman for his partner, he replied in an injured tone, "Oh, if the woman enjoyed it, the whole affair would give me no pleasure." Analysis showed that the patient did not really want intercourse. He only wanted to drive the woman, the dispenser, *ad absurdum*. In this he succeeded by means of a simple unconscious trick. Since both partners wanted to be seduced, a complete inactivity lasting for years resulted. The patient's wife was still almost untouched when he came to me after seven years of marriage. Unconsciously the patient identified the sexually inexperienced woman with the "maliciously refusing mother" who denied him pleasure, toward whom, therefore, he could behave aggressively without feelings of guilt. He refused to have intercourse, did not even talk to his wife about sexual matters for years, and pitied himself masochistically because of the "bad luck" which he had unconsciously brought upon himself.

Another patient had conflicts with his wife over golf, his favorite pastime and one she despised. His wife's "lack of understanding" on this subject was a constant source of "injustice" to the man. They finally compromised on the understanding that he would play golf only when it did not interfere with her plans, for instance, on Sunday morning while she slept. One day his wife arranged to meet him in town for dinner after a doctor's appointment. In the early afternoon the patient felt disinclined to work, so left his office to play golf on Long Island, near his home. He felt very happy over being able to arrive home earlier than usual, and rang up his wife at 6 p. m. to tell her he was coming. At that moment he remembered his appointment with his wife in town . . . . The result was a row, since his wife could not be persuaded that his appointment with her had "completely slipped his mind," and accused him of lack of interest in her. His happiness during the afternoon could be interpreted as anticipation of the self-provoked "injustice-conflict" which was to befall him in the evening. That he provoked the scene was not conscious to him. By the same token, he could not understand how he could consider his wife—"even unconsciously"—a denying and refusing person, since she was "rather nice." The answer was that in his unconscious fantasy he converted even a "nice" person (even this conception was an illusion; she was not a kind person) into a malicious denier.

A female patient constantly complained in larmoyant tones about her "complete isolation" and lack of friends. She claimed that in company she was "the life of the party"; still she had no friends. Asked what her technique in amusing people was, she replied that it was very simple. She told everyone the truth—"but in a teasing way." She did not understand why everyone rejected her after laughing at her jests. Naively she asserted that everyone should be able to "take it." At the same time, she herself reacted with fury when "put on the spot," even with attenuated truth. By using the simple trick of telling the truth—"You know, my mother told me always to tell the truth"—she achieved complete rejection by her environment and as a result could enjoy the feeling of being unjustly treated. That she herself provoked and wanted this situation was not conscious to her.

As a literary example for this attitude of oral neurotics I shall cite an episode from the life of the poet Grabbe. Grabbe had been a military judge, and unresistingly allowed himself to be dismissed without a pension—he had neglected his duty in a most provoking manner—and then expected his rich wife to support him. Though Grabbe was aware of the pathologic miserliness of his wife, he let himself come to this state of dependence. His wife refused him all support; this caused Grabbe to flee to Frankfurt and Duesseldorf; later on, after he had been taken seriously ill, the police compelled her to take him into her home. The unconscious meaning of this action was: to drive the woman into the part of the denier, so that he might be aggressive without feeling of guilt and enjoy self-pity (masochistic pleasure).

The "mechanism of orality," which I described first, is not

understandable without taking into account the overdimensional unconscious guilt because of the masochistic solution. This feeling of guilt forces the individual to create his pseudo-aggressive defense.

Another type of "injustice collector" is provided by the neurotic performing *"magic gestures."* A magic gesture denotes the *unconscious dramatization* of the following thought: "I shall show you by my behavior how kindly I would have liked to be treated." That dramatization corresponds to a defense mechanism, and is not quite understandable without taking into account a complicated inner development.[3]

The history of the magic gesture in psychoanalytic literature is unclear. The reason for this is primarily that the term is used, if at all, in different and often contradictory ways. The first to use it was Ferenczi, in 1913, in "Development of the Sense of Reality,"[4] where he applied the description, "magic gesture" to one part of the baby's attempt to grasp reality via omnipotence. According to him, the magic gesture represents the third of the infant's four stages in achieving the sense of reality—the stage in which the child gives signs (for instance, sucking movements of his mouth, stretching of his hands toward objects, etc.), and misconceives the response of the environment to be the result of his own omnipotence. Since Ferenczi's authority is acknowledged among analysts and that paper widely read, many analysts still associate the term "magic gesture" with the meaning designated for it in that paper.[5]

A few months after Ferenczi's paper, Freud's "Totem and Tabu" was published (1913). In this, Freud does not use the term magic gesture directly, although he describes different techniques of magic. Analysts, strangely enough, have often mistaken that basic book of Freud for a purely anthropologic work. The result, as far as the magic gesture is concerned, has been to increase the involuntary confusion in the minds of many colleagues (of course, through nobody's fault), since these colleagues have regarded anthropology rather as a hobby than as an obligatory part of knowledge.

Years later, in 1924, Hans Liebermann presented at the Eighth International Psychoanalytic Congress in Salzburg a paper entitled

[3]First published in the Psychiat. Quart. 19:295-310, 1945.
[4]Internat. Ztschr. f. Psychoanalyse., I, 124-138, 1913.
[5]A critical review of Ferenczi's paper is found in my article "Thirty Years After Ferenczi's 'States in the Development of the Sense of Reality.' " Psychoanalyt. Rev. 1945.

"On Monosymptomatic Neuroses."[6] In this, Liebermann uses the term magic gesture in an entirely different sense. He believes that it is possible to recognize unconscious omnipotence in certain symptoms: ".... That type of neurotic uses his symptom in the meaning of a magic gesture *with the purpose of demonstrating to the person against whom he directs his neurosis how that person should suffer or perish.*" Liebermann speaks primarily of hysteriform "bodily symptoms" which, until the time of his paper, had been exclusively in the domain of the internist, but concedes that magic gestures may be encountered in every neurosis. He suggests that, in cases in which analysis is impossible (hospitals, clinics, etc.), the unconscious ideas of omnipotence should be isolated in psychotherapy by concentrating exclusively on analysis of magic gestures. Liebermann even believed that the explanation of his magic gesture to the patient could thus be used as a short cut in therapy. He seemed to have the naive view that simply repeated naming of the unconscious technique embedded in the magic gesture could eliminate the neurotic symptom automatically, and he bolstered that assumption with claims of clinical successes achieved in that way. He was obviously mistaken, and his suggestion was passed over and forgotten. Unfortunately, his excellent clinical observation was forgotten, too.

Since then the term "magic gesture" has seldom been used in our literature. When it is employed, it is with Liebermann's definition in mind, and even then with modifications.

In an attempt to clarify the meaning of the term, I would like to subdivide magic gestures into four groups.

Type I. Liebermann's magic gesture is obviously a result of unconscious feeling of guilt because of inner aggression. It is seldom observable in its pure form. Experience has proven that, provided it is applied for some time, it takes on a more complicated structure. Then the masochistic complication comes to the fore, automatically making the quick destruction of the symptom impossible. In my opinion, Liebermann correctly described the surface reverberation of a deeper conflict. His observation itself, although incomplete, is of the highest merit, and secures for Liebermann, who unfortunately died young, an eminent place in psychoanalytic science.

Type II. Analysts are faced with magic gestures of another type in practically every analysis. The magic gesture of this type expresses the dramatization of the following unconscious thought: "I shall show you, my bad mother (father), how I would have liked to be treated."[7] The accidental beneficiary of this behavior is impressed with the "niceness" of the person performing it. He sees only the gift or kindness displayed, not the aggression hidden behind it. If one is not familiar with this unconscious technique of masochistically-tinged aggression, one can only conclude that there is a contradiction in the usually malicious or aggressive behavior of the specific person, and optimists about human nature can triumphantly conclude that everyone is, at bottom, kind. Clinical experience, however, proves that the person performing the magic gesture of this type accuses without conscious knowledge his bad mother (father) of being unkind, and demonstrates to her (him) *ad oculos* how he allegedly wanted to be treated. For example, I would like to mention a case of a patient of mine, a business woman, known in her environment as a "slave driver," a hard, bitter, and sometimes rather cruel person. One of her girl friends said of her: "That woman hasn't a kind spot in her makeup, even if you look for it with a magnifying glass." Yet this woman was always showering some little girl with presents, kindness and invitations. The few persons who knew about it found her behavior so strange and unusual that even those who were her so-called friends suspected her of homosexual relations with the beneficiaries of her magic gesture. Analysis could prove that the patient used the magic gesture to express an inner accusation against her father, whom she considered cold and neglectful. That she identified with the girl whom she treated kindly was obvious; on the other hand, at the same time, she also played the role of the kindly "corrected" father.

So far, one could say that the magic gesture of Type II is but a modification of Liebermann's original Type I. True, the person making it does not directly express aggression turned upon his own person because of unconscious guilt feelings, but acts out an inner accusation via dramatized kindness. In both types, however, hidden aggression seems to be the basic element. This apparent similarity between the two types is proven by clinical experience to be super-

---

[7] Owing to the confusion surrounding the magic gesture in analytic literature, Type II is sometimes also attributed to Liebermann, for instance, by Reich, despite the fact that Liebermann's publication, at least, describes something similar but not identical. It is not clear who first described the magic gesture of Type II. Psychoanalytic literature does not contain, however, any deeper analysis of the magic gesture.

ficial and false. It is evidenced time and again clinically that the weak aggression displayed in the magic gesture of Type II is but a covering cloak for a deeper layer, which is genetically psychic masochism. In other words, a three-layer structure is involved in neurotics who make use of this type of magic gesture. The dynamically-decisive first layer consists of an unconscious wish to be mistreated. This wish is warded off by a severe Super Ego reproach leading to the second layer, pseudo-aggression toward the disappointing mother (later, father). This defense, too, is forbidden by the severe inner conscience, with the result that a form of kind giving is established. This third layer is expressed in the magic gesture, which contains elements of aggression in a sort of weak repartee. Our skepticism in encounters with a magic gesture in analysis must be directed, first against the superficial kindness, and then, against the deeper aggression. The neurotic who makes use of magic gestures is deeply masochistic and is trying frantically to deny this by means of a three-layer unconscious dramatization. In other words, magic gestures represent a complicated inner defense mechanism.

Interestingly enough, the pseudo-aggression displayed in layer two, which is hidden and must be analytically deciphered, is often so strong that it prevents the application of the third layer (pseudo-kindness) toward living persons. In such cases, the material chosen for dramatization is an inanimate object, not because it has any importance in itself, but because it is more suitable for the purpose. In a previous paper[8] I have described such a case. A schizoid patient suffered from, among other things, reckless spending. This brought him into serious conflict with his penurious mother, toward whom he used this method of showing aggression. In addition to unconscious motives of revenge, self-injury, and "mechanism of orality,"[9] a further curious incapacity to make a decision in the selection of objects for purchase came into play. Wishing to order three shirts, the patient went to an expensive shop, where he saw hundreds of samples. Very definitely and without hesitation, he narrowed down the choice, selecting perhaps thirty samples. Although he could readily separate the ones he liked from those he considered in bad taste, he was incapable of making a further choice among those which appealed to him, and, according to his statement, there was

[8]Four types of neurotic undecisiveness. Psychoanalyt. Quart., IX, 4, 1940.
[9]Details can be found in my monograph, "Psychic Impotence in Men," Medical Edition, Huber, Berne, 1937.

no way out of his indecision but to order the entire thirty. On another occasion, he went to a book store to buy a certain recently published book. The salesman showed him several dozen publications which had appeared within recent months. The patient rejected a number on the ground that they did not interest him. About fifteen remained, and the patient, unable to come to a decision, bought all fifteen.

From the history of this patient one could learn that his mother paid more attention to some of her six children, neglecting the others. The patient felt that he had been discriminated against. By means of his extravagance and indecision, he acted out a magic gesture. Unconsciously he performed a symbolic act, clearly, in the superficial layer, an act of aggression toward his mother and one designed to show her how he would really have liked to be treated. His unconscious formula was: "You, mother, have discriminated against some of your own children; at any rate, you have played favorites. I, however, cannot even choose between indifferent objects—shirts, books, etc. How much less would I be capable of doing so among my own children!" Behind this tearful aggression, deep masochism was hidden. That defense-aggression was not the real reason for his actions was also proved by the fact that, by being a spendthrift, he also showed conscious aggression toward his mother, who paid the bills. His pseudo-aggression was a palimpsest only, covering his deep masochistic attachment to his mother.

In place of inanimate objects, some neurotics choose animals as the recipients of their magic gestures. One of my schizoid patients was an enthusiastic "pigeon feeder." He collected crumbs incessantly and spent hours watching the pigeons eat from his hand, with tears in his eyes. He did not wish to be put in the same category as "ordinary animal-loving humanitarians riding their ridiculous pigeon-horse," as he, strangely enough, called his competitors, paraphrasing Lawrence Sterne's "hobby-horse" ("Tristram Shandy"). Correctly enough, he placed the emphasis, not on the pigeons, but on his tears, although he was incapable of explaining their cause. Unconsciously, his tears meant: "You treated me badly, bad mother. Look how I wanted to be treated—kindly." The previously described three-layer structure was fully visible under the analytic microscope, as was the specific determining factor in the symbolic use of pigeons.

Whether the neurotic uses the mechanism of magic gestures

on living persons, inanimate objects, or animals, the fact remains that he always expresses in it an aggressive reproach, hidden behind the disguise of the superficial layer: unconscious identification with the "beneficiary" and idealized mother (father).[10] Hidden still further, behind this reproach, is the real, dynamically-effective, psychic masochism, which is warded off by pseudo-aggression.

Some neurotics place the emphasis, in their magic gestures, on the irony which they execute in the pseudo-aggression of layer two. One patient, for instance, chose as her "beneficiaries"—exclusively millionaires. This female patient was a physician and had many members of the social register as patients. These patients constantly took advantage of her, claiming poverty, and she, seemingly believing them, made their fees ridiculously low, even lower than those of less wealthy patients. For the sake of discretion, details cannot be given. They were so ludicrous, however, that one observer remarked: "The millionaires should erect a monument to you with the inscription: 'To the only person who has pity on the financial worries of millionaires.' "

The fact of psychic masochism in magic gestures is observable particularly in neurotics of two types: alcoholics and gamblers. We know that in the initial stages of inebriation there is an hilarious and jocose mood, which later gives way to a depressive, bellicose tendency. Only the former mood, the jocose one, is important for our understanding of the magic gesture. Without going into details given elsewhere,[11] I will point out that chronic alcoholism is, in my opinion, one of the specific masochistic techniques used in repetition of the situation of oral disappointment, complicated by pharmacodynamic factors. I do not mean that the neurotic uses alcohol, as some observers naively assume, simply to get in symbolic substitution what was refused him in childhood (milk). He uses it for exactly the opposite purpose: to repeat masochistically the oral refusal allegedly experienced at the hands of the pre-oedipal mother.

The next questions are: Whence come these tendencies? when are they acquired? And why are they repeated? These questions lead

[10]There is double identification in every magic gesture. The patient acts both parts.

[11]The problem of the oral pessimist. Chap. III. Talleyrand-Napoleon-Stendhal-Grabbe. Int. Psycho. Verlag. Vienna. 1935.—The Psychologic Interrelation between Alcoholism and Genital Sexuality. J. Crim. Psychopath. IV, 1, 1942. —Contributions to the Psychogenesis of Alcoholism. Quart. J. Stud. on Alcohol, December, 1944.

us back to a view of early childhood. Every human being is, in his
first months of extrauterine life, dependent on his mother's breast
or the milk bottle. The first approach of the baby to reality is an oral
one. Some people never outgrow intrapsychically this dependence.
Even the unpsychologic outer world often jokingly compares the dependence of the drinker upon his whiskey bottle to that of a baby
upon his milk bottle. For instance, the brother of one of my drinking
patients sent the man, years before the latter entered analysis, an
ironic gift on his twenty-fifth birthday, a milk bottle with a note asking, "Why not switch to this once more; it harms you less." The
brother did not even know how near to the truth he was. Of course,
the idea of simple substitution of milk for whiskey was naive; yet
there are psychologic connections between the milk bottle and the
whiskey bottle. It has struck a number of analytic observers—the
first of this long series being Freud, forty years ago—that what the
alcoholic really does is to bring up to a higher psychic level of
development the unconscious recollections of the early days of
infancy, when to drink from the breast or bottle was not only a
caloric necessity but a pleasure, too. The alcoholic apparently unconsciously returns to this oral phase, and his regression is supposed
to explain his addiction. So far so good. The question remains
whether there exists a "pleasant," direct return to old desires on
the oral level. Do alcoholics really desire, in a form of unconscious
substitution, merely to "get" what was once denied them? In that
case, why do they consume alcohol instead of milk? How can we
account for the self-damaging and self-destructive tendencies associated with heavy drinking?

I personally doubt whether the contents of the oral regression of
neurotics can be summarized in the simple formula, "I want to get."
Quite the contrary, these neurotics want to take masochistic revenge
for oral disappointments under self-damaging conditions. I have
mentioned repeatedly in previous years the triad of the "mechanism of
orality."[12] It represents, not at all the reactivation of the wish to get,
but a means of indulging in chronic disappointment through being
refused. Once the refusal is established via unconscious provocation,
the vicious circle of aggression in self-defense and self-pity is brought
into action.

[12]This mechanism consists of self-constructed defeats, repression of the provocation, conflict with the self-created enemy seemingly in self-defense, and finally,
self-pity with unconscious masochistic enjoyment.

"What type of people are these?" one could object. What reasonable person will repeat a disappointment to the point of self-destruction? If a child is refused candy, for instance, he can buy as much candy as he likes when he grows up. Why, as an adult, should he repeat, without knowing it, the situation of the child being refused candy? From the viewpoint of logic, the reaction of these neurotics is incomprehensible. Unfortunately, the unconscious part of the personality is not in the least governed by logic. Seemingly, the wish to show up the mother as a refuser is of greater importance to these sick people than the original wish to get. Their psychology is that of the boy who cries, "It serves my mother right that I've frozen my fingers; why didn't she buy me gloves?" In this philosophy of the boy, one sees some aggression and spite toward his mother, which corresponds to a denial of the masochistic wish to be refused, but executed in self-damaging conditions, because of an unconscious feeling of guilt, since every aggression toward the mother or her successive representatives is inwardly forbidden.

We have, in the formulation, unconscious aggression in self-damaging conditions used as defense against deeper repressed masochistic attachment, one of the clues to the understanding of the alcoholic addict. His basic mood is depression, apathy, or affective instability until he gets his drink. Let us quote a patient, a society woman. "To avoid depression I drink. Whenever I drink I am happy at first, then feel a deep depression coming on. I keep on drinking in order to recapture my initial happiness, unfortunately, in vain." We can understand neither the patient's pre-potus depression nor her initial happiness in potu unless we take into account the unconscious reasons mentioned here. All alcoholics are depressed because they labor under the unconscious fantasy that they were not loved enough by their mother in childhood. This fantasy has no reference to the later, oedipal wishes. It refers to the pre-oedipal, oral stage of childlike megalomania, in which the child identifies love with being given milk. Basically, the harmless and necessary act of weaning is perceived by the infant as a terrible injustice and an act of malice.[13] Every child experiences this early feeling of injustice and lack of love; the oral neurotics are those people who are unable to overcome it. Of course, the conscious rationalizations of alcoholics for their

[13]Bergler and Eidelberg: The Breast Complex in the Male. Internat. Ztschr. f. Psychoanalyse., 1933.

respective depressions are different. They drink, if we want to be naive and believe them, because of disappointment or disillusionment, weakness of will, weariness, inability to cope with a situation, or inner emptiness. No matter how sincerely they believe this consciously, it is a mirage. For many of these "misfortunes" and "blows of fate" are unconsciously brought about deliberately by the patients themselves. In some cases, of course, the misfortunes are real enough, but the patient unconsciously perceives them, not as obstacles to be overcome or adapted to, but as maternal punishment which is to be answered with oral aggression, possible only in self-damaging conditions which alleviate the inner guilt feelings. Again and again, with eternal monotony, the triad described is reenacted, "I am treated unjustly; therefore I may be aggressive and pity myself as well," with the monotonous drinking revenge that follows.

Here we meet, seemingly, with an impasse. If our assumption is correct, that the alcoholic addict repeats unconsciously the situation of the bad mother refusing and orally frustrating him, why then, does he allow himself to be served drinks? Why not repeat the situation of scarcity and refusal directly? To understand his reasoning, we must take into account two facts. First, drinking in itself is in the beginning an attempt at self-cure and reparation, based on the idea, "Mother refused me; now I will give myself everything she refused. I am independent and autarchic." This element of reparation accounts for the initial happiness when drinking. In other words, drinking is at first a triumph over the refusing mother. The second fact to be taken into account is even more complicated. It refers to the inner identification of the drinker with his mother.[14]

To clarify this fact of identification, I might point out an incident which happened to a patient of mine years before he entered analysis because of alcoholism. This man once had a violent conflict with his mother, whom he accused of being instrumental in obtaining what he considered an unfair share of his father's estate. His mother defended herself against these—by the way, unjustified—accusations. During their argument, the man drank one brandy after another. His mother asked him reproachfully; "Why do you drink so heavily?" "What's that to you?" was the son's brusque retort. His mother objected with the sober and rather melancholic statement:

[14] A similar conclusion was reached, though through a different trend of reasoning, by English analysts.

"Everything which harms you harms me, too." The patient responded by taking two brandies at once. In evaluating the scene, we have to assume that the man, in identification with his mother, wanted to harm her. He was filling her, so to speak, with poison. Actually, he harmed himself; in doing this, his self-damaging or psychic masochistic tendencies had their expression.

In other words, the initial jocose mood of the drinker springs from the attempt to repair the original oral trauma by establishing an autarchy and state of independence from the allegedly refusing mother and also from the attempt to retaliate on the mother in unconscious identification with her. This jocose phase also reflects irony, achieved through making fun of authority in general, and at the same time, kindness toward the environment. Everyone is familiar with the transitory initial mood of the drinker: "You are my friend; everybody is my friend." This mood shows the ambivalence of the conflict: aggression toward the intrapsychic mother-image coupled with denial of loss of love. It also expresses propaganda for one's own kindness, based on the theme: "You see how good I am though mother was so bad to me."[15]

The tendency toward logorrhoea[16] often observable in drinkers in the jocose phase gives us an indirect hint as to the genetic basis of the illness. The superabundance of words—giving of words—is an indirect reproach toward the denying mother. It is a magic gesture, an unconscious aggressive device designed "to show the mother up" by giving freely of the very thing which she denied, based on the reasoning, "I shall show you through my behavior how I wanted to be treated originally by you." Behind this aggression, a deep masochistic attachment is hidden. The potus-logorrhoea demonstrates in an unconscious innuendo that the child in the drinker wants allegedly to be given kindness (words = milk, love) by the mother. Magic gestures must always be scrutinized for the unconscious aggression hidden behind their apparently gracious facade. They must also always be scrutinized for the defense mechanism they represent. The drinker makes use of magic gesture to give an exaggerated impression of his desire to be "given," and thereby to disguise his real aim, that of being unjustly treated. The masochistic enjoyment of being refused, not pleasure in being given, is his real object in life.

[15]Later, in the "morose" stage, the defense collapses, after it was taken up in the "bellicose" phase once more.
[16]Bergler: Logorrhoea. Psychiat. Quart., 18:1, January, 1944.

An excellent example of the magic gesture in drinking is found in Charles Jackson's "The Lost Weekend."[17] The hero in this, drinking in a bar, starts a conversation with an entertainer, a girl, who asks him why he is so depressed. The man immediately fabricates a sad tale. According to him he is disappointed over his wife's frigidity. (In reality, he is not even married.) In the next breath, he invites the girl to spend an evening with him visiting high class night clubs, which she joyfully agrees to do. Of course, he disappoints her by completely "forgetting" their date. In this incident, we see unconscious aggression in the complaints about being unjustly treated (and not by chance by a woman) and the simultaneous attempt to show the treatment desired, exemplified in the kind gesture toward the girl of no importance. The repressed aggression comes to the fore, however, in the eventual disappointment of the girl, reflecting the disappointment experienced originally through the mother.

Another example of the magic gesture, this time a clinical one, is offered by a well-to-do patient who, in the initial stages of inebriation, would promise people who happened to be at his table aid in getting jobs. Seemingly full of kindness, a trait really foreign to him, he would promise them recommendations to various important acquaintances. Confronted by the applicants on the following day, he always denied ever having made such promises. Only once did he keep his word; however, on this occasion he wrote the promised introduction in such ambiguous terms that it gave the man to whom it was addressed the impression that its bearer was an impostor, to be disposed of quickly.

In gamblers, magic gestures are often associated with, in addition to the factors just sketched, a deep superstition. Without going into the psychology of gamblers[18] one can assume that these people are deeply masochistic. They use a specific device of the "mechanism of orality," wanting unconsciously to lose in order to place their opponent, be he an individual or a bank, in the position of the orally refusing pre-oedipal mother. The gambler wishes to reduce this mother to absurdity as a giving person. On the other hand, when gambling, he consistently reduces to absurdity also the "reality principle" (Freud); for, in the game, chance alone dominates, and

---

[17]Farrar & Rinehart. New York. 1944.
[18]Bergler: On the psychology of the gambler. Imago, 1936.
————: The gambler—a misunderstood neurotic. J. Crim. Psychopath., Vol. IV, 1943.

he tries to direct it, via "omnipotence of thoughts." In other words, the old rebellion against the logic governing the "reality principle" is renewed. The gambler insists on the "pleasure principle," that is, on childish megalomania.

A patient of mine related that once in Monte Carlo, during a period of winning, she was approached by a casual woman acquaintance, who told her a hard luck story and asked for a loan of 100,000 francs. The patient's finances were in a bad state, as usual; her whole fortune consisted at that moment of her winnings, exactly 110,000 francs. Without hesitation she gave the money to the woman, without asking for a receipt, without inquiring into the background of the woman, and without even ascertaining the truth of her story. From that moment on, her luck changed, since she had to win now to live. She lost and lost. Many years later, in analysis, it became clear that this patient habitually performed magic gestures with the three-layer structure described before. The case was interesting because of the amount of money involved and because the patient complicated and increased the usual element of masochism involved in every magic gesture—by losing consistently after performing the magic gesture. Unconsciously she expressed in this conduct: "My bad mother (casino, bank) takes everything away from me; after robbing me she lets me starve!" Needless to say, the casual acquaintance in the instance mentioned never did pay back the money. The patient did not even resent this. ("What can you expect from the bad mother (casual acquaintance)?")

Type III. There is still another magic gesture, which I have called, in previous publications, the "negative magic gesture."[19] It constitutes an unconscious irony directed against the educator, the unconsicous formula being, "I shall show you in my behavior how I did *not* want to be treated."

An example of the magic gesture of type three sometimes produces great technical difficulties in clinical analysis. I refer to the use of silence as a main weapon of resistance in analysis. This silence may have very different reasons, which have been discussed elsewhere.[20] One of the possibilities is the indirect demonstration of

[19]Previously I subdivided magic gestures into two groups, "positive" and "negative." They correspond to Types II and III respectively. I have since abandoned my former nomenclature.

[20]Bergler: On the resistance situation: the patient is silent. Psychoanalyt. Rev., 25:2, 182, 1938.

"being refused." The patient misunderstands the analyst's silence as oral refusal and retaliates masochistically. Such a patient habitually answers the question, "Why don't you talk?" with the observation, "You are silent too." Unconsciously he means, "I will show you by my behavior how I don't want to be treated." If silence involving the magic gesture of type three is not understood, a stalemate lasting for years may result.

The magic gesture of type three has some connection with a mechanism first described by Aichhorn, who did not associate it with magic gestures. Aichhorn observed a boy, who, without knowing it, made facial grimaces while being scolded by his teacher. Unconsciously the boy was overcoming his fear through identification with the scolder. His grimace was, I might add, a caricature of his teacher's scolding, a form of unconscious reducing to absurdity.

Interesting parallels can be found between the magic gesture of type three and the mechanism described by Anna Freud as "identification with the aggressor."[21]

Combination of Types II and III. In one exceptional case, I have observed a queer combination of the mechanism of types two and three. This patient, a well-to-do society woman, twice married ne'er-do-wells. At first she lived out with them magic gestures of type three; in other words, she caricatured her mother's (father's) alleged neglect of her. She was disappointed in her incompetent husbands, completely overlooking the fact that she had created the situation of being refused, having picked out these men herself. In each case after a short time, she was "through" with the man, but could not get rid of him. Then she would start, to her surprise, to act the role of the giver; in other words, she switched to magic gestures of type two. In this phase, she was helpless against the current husband, who behaved "as no gentleman should."

Type IV. In rare external conditions, a specific type of magic gesture can develop. The required situation is the pronounced outward coldness of the mother toward the child. One patient, a woman of forty, was brought up in a milieu in which it was believed that cold and detached behavior toward the child was the best educational medium. Her mother pronounced the theory; her father followed, though reluctantly. The patient herself was a deeply maso-

[21]Freud, A.: The Ego and the Defense Mechanisms. P. 126 ff. Psycho. Verlag. Vienna.

chistic person, who consistently spoiled her opportunities in life. She was brought into analysis by one of her many husbands because of constant "rows." According to him, though she was ordinarily cold and detached, she could rave "like mad." He himself was a "cold person," who hated a display of feelings. It was obvious that the woman's choice of such a "cold" personality for a husband was based on narcissism (he was a copy of herself) and on her masochistic repetition of her mother-child situation. She had some knowledge of analysis. Eighteen years before, she had entered analysis in another country, only to interrupt it after eight months "because she could not talk" and because the analyst kept repeating in general terms that her behavior was based on "resistance" without being able to change that behavior. She suspected that she repeated in her "rows" her conflict with her mother, overlooking, of course, that all of her reproaches against her "cold" husband were unjustified since she herself had chosen him, unconsciously, because of his coldness. Deeper analysis showed that her explanation was not sufficient. She was not only repeating her fruitless attempts to get some effective reaction (even hatred!) from her cold mother; she was acting, in her own rows, the role of the angry mother, her unconscious reasoning being, "I can't stand that coldness; even your anger and hatred would be more pleasant!" One can see that she was acting neither a magic gesture of type two ("I show you how I wanted to be treated") nor one of type three ("I show you how I did not want to be treated"), but seemingly something different.

Magic gestures of the various types do not constitute symptoms *per se*. They represent part of the personality makeup, are encountered on every genetic level of libidinous-aggressive development, and must be analyzed in every attempt to take the "whole personality" into account. These personality "difficulties" are extremely resistant, especially those of type two; strangely enough, those of type three are sometimes easy to change. No analysis is, in my opinion, complete, which does not change the craving for neurotic magic gestures. These gestures are embedded so deeply that patient and analyst overlook them only too easily.

Ironically enough, one could ask one's self whether it makes sense to destroy the mechanism of magic gestures (especially of type two) in analysis. The friend of the patient mentioned as an example of Type II, who sent that patient into analysis, showed skepticism about the advisability of destroying this mechanism in the patient, after pronouncing her harsh but correct judgment of her friend, "That woman hasn't a kind spot in her makeup, even if you look for it with a magnifying glass." This woman, who herself excelled in magic gestures, asked, "If you destroy that in her, what will be left but her mean and cruel personality?" This woman was wrong, since the pseudo-kindness of magic gestures is paralleled by the bitterness of other character traits. Since the personality is a unit, no eclectic selection of symptoms from the viewpoint of "nice" and "not nice" is possible.

To what degree in general magic gestures, even in persons who are not too neurotic and are sometimes euphemistically described as "normal," are one of the bases of what is called decent behavior, is difficult to determine quantitatively.

Other people cash in on their chronic tendency to be unjustly treated via ingratitude.

Expectation of gratitude is one of the best examples of psychologic naiveté, based on oversight of unconscious factors. The basis of gratitude is the idea that a good turn should be rewarded by something similar. That logical conclusion is "mathematically" correct. Unfortunately, it comes into conflict with unconscious factors and evaporates in the collision.

The feeling of gratitude is clinically not observable in the very young child and has to be taught. The child has a peculiar feeling of omnipotence, the outerworld "owes" him everything the child desires. And if the outerworld denies or refuses a specific wish? Fury, anger, and disappointment, are the child's responses.

If one thinks through the fallacy of omnipotence which every child harbors, it becomes clear that the child does not feel gratitude. Only secondarily, the child finds out that gratitude is expected from him. The situation is tragicomic: imagine that you buy for yourself with your own money a ticket for a round-trip around the world. Imagine that another person who has no connection whatsoever with the whole procedure, asks you to feel gratitude for giving you the possibility of buying that ticket. You will feel that the request is— to be polite—unjustified.

One could, of course, object that the example does not fit: the parents are the providers of everything for the child. Without their loving care, the small child would die of hunger and exposure. True enough, these are the facts, but facts just don't count with the immature child.

The next objection is obvious: the child corrects his misconceptions of reality, as years go by. To say this is to say that this really happens on an *emotional* basis with normal people, on a *logical* basis, with neurotics. That lack of congruity between logical and emotional digestion of facts, accounts for lack of gratitude in neurotics. Neurotics suffer from an anachronistic disease: they never inwardly give up their megalomania.

To go one step further: not only do neurotic people not feel any debts of gratitude, it intervenes unfavorably with their neurotic repetitiveness. I once analyzed a neurotic woman, a writer. In analyzing a writer, one is forced to read everything the writer wrote previously: it contains a great deal of valuable material. In this specific case, I spent 80 hours of my spare time, reading her books, memoirs, autobiographic notes, etc., and thinking through the psychologic connections. That woman repeated in her transference neurosis the situation of projecting the "bad," "cruel," "refusing" mother upon the innocent physician. She accused me constantly of lack of interest, greed for money, coldness, and what not. During one of her repetitive outbursts, I interrupted her and explained patiently what she repeated. This did not make the slightest impression on her, she just continued to abuse me. The next objection presented to her made her very uncomfortable. I told her that I had spent 80 hours for which I was not paid in reading her literary productions. I proved to her that—counting the time on the basis of her fee—I invested more in her analysis than she did. (The whole scene took place after approximately four weeks of treatment.) I reminded her further that had I been as uninterested in her case as she claimed, I could have either refused to read her works during my spare time, or could have asked her to read her "stuff," as she called it, during her appointments. "How do you reconcile these undeniable facts with your accusations of my exclusive interest in money?" The patient felt ashamed and admitted: "That was very decent of you." After a few minutes, however, the old lamento started again: "You are cruel, and only interested in money. . . ."

In evaluating that scene, we have to take into account that the patient would have lost her mortgage on constant complaining, had she accepted the objective facts. The whole neurosis is based on that, and exactly that, specific misconception of reality. Neurotics misuse real people as hitching posts for their bygone conflicts.

The simple but impressive fact remains that neurotics don't feel *emotionally* any gratitude. To count on gratitude from a neurotic, is sheer fantasy. Not only are neurotics not grateful, they often repay a kind action with some "mean" trick. One gets the impression that they take revenge for every kind deed.

The explanation for that enigmatic tendency, is to be found in the fact that every neurotic is full of psychic masochism. Psychic masochists have a very peculiar approach to reality; they want their "daily dose of injustice." They achieve their quota in the following way: they provoke mercilessly, till they get the rebuff asked for. To get the full dose, they must unconsciously choose "stronger" people. Therefore, they provoke that type and afterwards complain bitterly, since the whole process is unconscious. On the other hand, the poor psychic masochist is under constant reproach of his severe inner conscience reproaching him with enjoyment of hidden masochistic pleasures. An alibi is needed. That alibi is provided by being aggressive toward "weaker" people. Now, every person who does a neurotic a good turn, is automatically classified by the latter as "weak." Decency, commiseration, even "magic gestures," don't count with the neurotic—emotionally. His formula is simple: kindness = weakness. Hence, the innocent benefactor is used as intrapsychic alibi, and not gratitude, but exactly the opposite, appears in consciousness.

You cannot appease a neurotic with kindness, gifts, help. Nothing will deter him from his masochistic schedule.

Another element enters the picture: by being ungrateful, the beneficiary makes it impossible for the benefactor to repeat his kind action. Therefore, ingratitude is the preparation for the next—self-provoked—"injustice."

It is, from the logical viewpoint, really fantastic that people who repay some kind deed of a benefactor with a mean trick, choose so often exactly the same victims—for a renewed demand. Without understanding the unconscious aim of being refused, the whole action is simply idiotic.

People have, of course, no idea why ingratitude is so often encountered. They just see the facts, and get bitter and hard. On the other hand, ingratitude is a typical neurotic technique. A typical and banal technique, one must add.[22]

---

[22]For other aspects of the problem of ingratitude see "Psychopathology of Ingratitude." Dis. Nerv. System, VI. 7, 1945.

CHAPTER VII

TENDER LOVE—THE CLASSICAL ANTIDOTE FOR GUILT

Normal· people use a strange antidote for guilt—tender love. The connection between love and unconscious feeling of guilt is consciously so far-fetched that when I, in collaboration with L. Jekels, Freud's oldest pupil, presented this theory to a competent scientific forum,[1] we met with even more surprise than disapproval. Still, I fully maintain that theory.

What is love? There are eight symptoms and signs of being in love:[2]

1) Subjective feeling of happiness.
2) Self-torture.
3) Overvaluation of the loved object.
4) Undervaluation of reality.
5) Exclusiveness.
6) Psychic dependence on the loved object.
7) Sentimental behavior.
8) Dominance of fantasy.

In the "Baths of Lucca," the poet H. Heine contended that there is always an instinctive defense against any attempt to solve the riddle of love:

> "We know what blows are, but what love is, has never yet been discovered. . . . What is love? Has no one fathomed its nature? Has no one solved the riddle? Perhaps the answer would bring greater misery than the question itself, and one's frightened heart stands still before it in horror, as at sight of the Medusa. Serpeants writhe about the dreadful words that solve the riddle. Oh, I wish never to hear these words, for the burning misery in my heart is easier to bear than such petrifaction."

We shall understand the reason for this defense only when we have clarified the nature of tender love.

[1] Psychoanalytic Society in Vienna, Nov. 8, 1933. Published in Imago, 1934, No. 1, pp. 5-32.
[2] For more extensive presentation, see my books, "Unhappy Marriage and Divorce," Int. Univ. Press, New York, 1946; and "Futility of Divorce," Harper & Bros., N. Y., 1948.

Let us begin with what seems obvious. In his beloved, the lover sees his ideal. Ideals are, nor can this be disputed, products of fantasy. So the whole process of love is based primarily upon a fantasy.

Secondly, the lover seeks in reality for a material objectification of his ideal. It is not entirely due to the "trickery" of the chosen love object that mistakes are so often made. Popper-Lynkeus illustrates this in a short story, "How Long Must I Pretend to be Your Ideal?"

"One evening, when the street lamps in the city had just been lighted, a very young man ambled through the streets gazing at the busy or idle people who passed him.

"Full of the joy and vigor of youth, he stared instinctively at the women and girls, and, still a virgin, he regarded them with a sort of awestruck shyness.

"In the course of his wanderings, he entered a narrow street, and there he noticed, standing under a lantern, an attractively gotten up girl, who beckoned to him in a very friendly manner. Her face, shaded by a large hat, seemed so interesting to him, that after gazing at her for a while, drawing gradually closer, his heart beating, he believed that he had found the ideal which would fulfill his desires. He felt a great, vague, undefined joy at the thought of being alone with her. When he came up to her, and she invited him, whispering sweetly, to visit her, he immediately went with her, filled with desire, to her nearby home. When they arrived at her apartment, where a lamp burned dimly and a child could be heard crying from time to time, she invited him to sit down, took off her hat and coat, examined herself briefly in the mirror and sat down beside the youth on a couch. She looked at him quietly, and her face with its natural unconstrained expression seemed to him to resemble hardly at all the face she had revealed to him on the street. The longer the young man looked at her, the more disappointed he became. He raised his eyebrows inquiringly, and the girl, noticing, said, 'What's wrong?' The youth answered, 'Forgive me for speaking so openly. When I first saw you on the street, I thought you were surpassingly beautiful. I thought I had found in you the realization of my ideal. Now that I see you more clearly I hardly know whether to believe that you are the same person that I saw under the lantern.'

"'Of all the nerve!' the girl answered excitedly. 'How long do you think I should pretend to be your ideal? I had to play up to you for five minutes or more before you spoke to me, and you still complain! Five minutes is a long time, much too long for one man! The evening is short, and I need bread for my child and for me. Do you understand, you ninny, what that means?'

"Just at that moment the child in the next room began to cry again. The girl jumped up quickly, and went to look after it. During the few moments that she stayed with the child, the youth could hear her try to quiet it and put it to sleep. Then she sat down again with obvious impatience beside the young man, who remained where she had left him, completely disconcerted.

"It took him some time to straighten all this out for himself: his ideal, her misery, her two faces, her child. He neither spoke nor moved, but continued to gaze at her and read in her features ever more clearly the whole misery of her existence. Consequently his face assumed an expression so sad that the girl understood what was going on in him. She too became serious, but when she saw that this scene would continue indefinitely, she kissed the young man on the forehead, and said, 'You must be a good man. . . . But I have no more time for you,' and tears came to her eyes, 'for I have to go back on the street!' With these words she put his cap into his hand and gently shoved him out the door. The young man crept away as though he shared the guilt for the girl's unhappiness, and feeling like a poor sinner—he himself did not know why— he slipped out of the house."

How are we to explain the "two faces" which the young man of the story sees in the girl? The first face clearly has little relation to the object as such; it has been artificially transferred to the object by the lover. Every lover seeks the realization of his fantasy in the object: "the fulfilment of his ideal." Disappointment sets in when the object shows too clearly that it is not the sought after materalization of the fantasy, but leads an independent life of its own.

In other words, the more closely the mask of the fantasy resembles the face of the object, the closer the conformity of the "two faces," the more impetuous and gratifying is the love.

Let us compare the popular conception of love with the conclusions we have reached so far. The world says of a man, "He has fallen in love with the girl," apparently meaning that he loves the girl herself. This requires amplification as follows: he unconsciously believes that the girl corresponds to his fantasied image, and therefore he loves her. This apparently slight difference in formulation is significant, since in the popular view, the center of gravity lies in the real object ("he loves the girl"), while in our view it lies in the fantasied object, which is only secondarily merged with the real object.

The real love object thus becomes the personification of a fantasy, and this is what gives it power over the lover. To be sure, the process is unconscious, since the lover is subjectively convinced of the virtues of his beloved. He does not know why he has fallen in love. Suddenly love is there. Behind the curtains of the psyche something has happened. The lover does not know what forces are driving him—he is happy and that suffices him. Psychologic explanations are far from his mind.

Our next question is: If, then, the lover sees his ideal in the love object, on what model is this ideal based? To find the answer to this problem we must look for it in the nursery. Freud's psychology has shown that the psyche is formed by an unconscious elaboration of infantile fantasies and experiences, resting on a biologic base.

The child lives for a long time in a sort of hallucinatory omnipotence. He has but one standard of measurement: his own ego. The conduct of adults contributes to this misapprehension. All the child's wishes for food and care are automatically fulfilled in the civilized family, so that the child, misinterpreting the causality, considers the fulfillment of its wishes to be, not the result of the kindness of its nurses, but a consequence of its own omnipotence. Experience of reality breaks down this fiction bit by bit, and probably this breaking down is one of the most painful experiences of childhood.

It is this overwhelming self-confidence of children that, among other things, we love in them. Children, in their naive refusal to recognize reality, represent that state of omnipotence which apparently we have all gone through, and which we have all been forced to give up. Comparison with the young Narcissus of the Greek myth, who fell in love with his own image, inevitably comes to mind. In his "Eclectic Affinities," Goethe says:

"... but man is a true Narcissus, who likes to find his own reflection everywhere, and offers himself as a mirror to the whole world. . . . Indeed, he treats everything he comes across in this way. His wisdom as well as his folly, his will as well as his whim he attributes to animals, plants, the elements, and the gods."

The child's delusions of grandeur are constantly threatened and humiliated by reality. To maintain whatever can be rescued, the child builds up the Ego Ideal, by internalizing the educators. This

Ego Ideal consists of the child's indestructible narcissismus plus educators. The whole process was described at length in Chapter One.

The idea, a good one, works, however, only partially, because the "Daimonion" takes possession of the Ego Ideal, using it for his antilibidinous purposes. The Ego Ideal, originally created to safeguard the child's narcissism, becomes thus a weapon against the individual's narcissism.

The technique of torture is simple: The self-created Ego Ideal is shown intrapsychically like a silent model—and when a discrepancy can be proven, guilt is felt. What can the victim, caught in his own net, do? He can ask for a moratorium, can plead, can promise. All that in vain. You cannot argue with a monster. One of the most fantastic devices which the tortured Ego "invents," to combat the inner enemy, is—paradoxically—*tender love.*

How does that happen? The unconscious victim argues something like this: "I wanted originally to become the world's most famous chemist. I am now tortured with the fact that I'm only a clerk in a pharmaceutical concern, and shall, perhaps, become junior partner in a few years. If I could find somebody who attests to me that I *am* the famous chemist of my childhood dreams, though the bad and cruel outerworld doesn't give me a chance—well, I could beat my tormenter with his own formalism. I could tell him: 'You wanted the attest of my Ego Ideal that I'm successful and the big shot I promised myself to become—here it is.' "

Expressed scientifically: *the lover projects his own Ego Ideal on the beloved, in so doing gets rid of a torturing inner conflict—simply by checkmating the Daimonion. He takes away from the Daimonion the instrument of torture—the Ego Ideal.* The latter is transformed once more into its original benevolent state.

As a result, the lover dwells upon his original narcissism. Since the Ego Ideal is composed mainly of self-love, *the lover enjoys in his projection*—as long as love lasts—*an orgy of selflove without the slightest feeling of guilt.*

This fantastic way out explains what Mencken meant in his "Prejudices":

"To be in love is merely to be in a state of perceptual anesthesia—to mistake an ordinary young man for a Greek god and an ordinary young woman for a goddess."

The 'mistake' is not so senseless, if we take into consideration the fact that the lover means himself in his over-valuation of the beloved.

This projection, self-love, and lack of inner guilt, explain the eight symptoms and signs of being in love:

Subjective Feeling of Happiness. The manic elation of the lover arises from the fact that all tension between Ego and Ego Ideal has disappeared: *"If my Ego Ideal* (projected on the object) *loves me, the world is mine,"* runs the unconscious argument of a happy lover. For only when an appreciable tension exists between Ego and Ego Ideal can guilt feelings trouble the Ego. We have already said that the state of relatively greatest happiness occurs when there are no unpaid accounts due the conscience. In happy, that is, reciprocated love, there is an absence of tension between Ego and Ego Ideal. That "instrument of torture," the Ego Ideal, is rendered ineffectual, and is transformed into its original benevolent state.

Self-torture. The happy mood of the lover is accompanied by self-torture, superficially concerning doubts as to the correctness of the choice of object. What is really going on unconsciously, is far more complicated. The unconscious Ego doubts whether or not the "trick" of projecting the Ego Ideal—thus wresting from the Daimonion the instrument of torture—will be effective.

Overvaluation of the Loved Object. Since the loved object represents one's own projected Ego Ideal, the typical overvaluation of the object is equivalent to self-love, to narcissism, and everybody loves himself with an intensity bordering on the ludicrous.

Undervaluation of Reality. Normally reality is represented in the personality by the Ego Ideal. It was just because of "unpleasant" reality that the educators were taken into the Ego Ideal. If, then, the Ego Ideal confirms the lover ("reciprocated love"), the world becomes a matter of indifference. Thus it happens that the very parents who were taken into the Ego Ideal in childhood, can protest without success against the choice of an object. For the lover already has his approval in the consent of the same parents—narcissistically assimilated, to be sure—in the projected Ego Ideal.

Exclusiveness. The exclusive interest of the lover for the love object is explained by his boundless self-love. We possess no instrument with which to measure the proportions of narcissism in the

Ego Ideal, and our estimate of nine-tenths is of course inexact, yet it conforms to the actual behavior of the lover.

Psychic Dependence on the Love Object. Since the object represents a projection of the Ego Ideal, it is comprehensible that the Ego wishes to avoid tension. The more often the loved one voices approval, the happier is the lover, since this is practically an orgy of self-love without the slightest feeling of guilt. The paradisiacal infantile delusion of grandeur seems to be realized.

Sentimental Behavior. This corresponds to self-worship, a mirroring of the I in the You.

Predominance of Fantasy. The rampant growth of fantasy, that is to say, the comparatively flimsy relation to the real object, is one of the strongest supports to the theory of projection in love. "Happy alone is the soul that loves" means that the central infantile wish fantasy has been realized. Basically this says: I want to be fondled and praised by my parents; that is, loved by them. The lover experiences in the intoxication of love the realization of the deepest yearning of every human being—the wish for tenderness from the persons who originally took care of him, above all, from his mother. Thus it happens that so many elements are included which, one might almost say, are non-sexual in the popular sense, and which are reducible to the common denominator of tenderness[3], rather than of sex: stroking, fondling, pressing close to one another, holding hands, gazing into each other's eyes, etc. In the healthy individual these tendencies are later bound up with crude sexual desires, but the character of tenderness as such is not eliminated. Although both parents are represented in the Ego Ideal, a certain "division of labor" is brought about by means of complicated psychic changes, which we shall not discuss here. In the boy the father is rather the model of duty in the Ego Ideal, and the mother the representative of love. The reverse is true of girls. As a result the object choice of the healthy individual tends to lean toward the infantile image of the opposite sex, even though crude sexual wishes relating to these highly valued persons of childhood are comprehensibly not present in consciousness.

The great happiness of love, then, lies in the realization of three early infantile wish fantasies: 1) the paradisiacal state of childhood omnipotence and of early infantile delusions of grandeur seem to

---

[3]Analytically viewed, the preliminary stages of sexuality.

be realized; 2) tender parental love is attested; 3) parental approval is achieved and inner guilt eliminated.

All this leads to a magnificent narcissistic "Ego inflation," concretely visible in the manic elation of the lover.

We see that *tender*[4] love is the most powerful antidote against inner guilt. It is therefore, not surprising that only relatively *healthy* people are able to solve an inner conflict of guilt through love. Neurotics are, in my opinion, capable of *"transference"* only. The latter term denotes the *unconscious* repetition of patterns built up in early childhood. The two mechanisms—love and transference—are different although the person concerned does not feel this.

The reason leading neurotics to their inability of loving tenderly is this: their unconscious fantasies always center around oedipal and pre-oedipal persons. Hence their inner feelings of guilt are the neurotic "fee" they pay to the Super Ego for maintenance of these fantasies.

Some neurotics make out of their inability of loving tenderly a virtue, proclaiming proudly that tender love is "romantic nonsense." To give an amusing example: The husband of a patient of mine, a severe neurotic and enemy of analysis, read in my book, "Unhappy Marriage and Divorce" the sentence, "Not everyone who feels sexual desire is 'overwhelmed' by tender emotions . . . ." (p. 16). "At least one statement I can accept," exclaimed the man triumphantly. "Why don't you read a few sentences further?" retorted his wife ironically. On the next page you can find:

> "Those who doubt the existence of tender love will point out that there is a large group of men and women who never have shown signs of being truly in love. This must be admitted. But we must add at once that *these people are psychically ill, so-called neurotics, in whom the inability to love is a well known symptom.*"

"I don't like that sentence, I rather stick to the first one," was the husband's undisturbed reply.

[4]Normally tender love is combined with sexual desires. That duality in love is indispensable and cannot be broken arbitrarily.

CHAPTER VIII

OTHER NORMAL ANTIDOTES: WORK, SUBLIMATION, RATIONALIZATION, AND "PATHOS"

A. Work and Sublimation

Work is generally viewed as the simple necessity of earning a living. The psychologic implications are far more involved, and have been explored analytically repeatedly.

To start with, work is a successful attempt to redirect aggression away from one's self. The material worked upon, the problem "attacked," uses energy. That energy is directed outwardly and productively in sublimated form and not inwardly, which would be very dangerous to the personality.

At the same time, work, since it is tiring and often unpleasant, *absorbs a great deal of inner guilt*, in a normal person. If this seems fantastic, just remember that people have known it intuitively from time immemorial. In Genesis, Adam and Eve, expelled from Paradise, had to work as *punishment*.[1]

Both beneficial factors—redirection of sublimated aggression and deposition of inner guilt—account for the fact that people who retire in their fifties or sixties often die soon after, without having been able to enjoy the leisure of which they dreamed.[2]

Now, not all work is punishment. Freud stated his views on the subject succinctly:

> "It is not possible to discuss the significance of work for the economics of the libido adequately within the limits of a short survey. Laying stress upon importance of work has a greater effect than any other technique of living in the direction of binding the individual more closely to reality; in his work he is at least securely attached to a part of reality, the human community. Work is no less valuable for the opportunity it and the human relations connected with it provide for a very considerable discharge of libidinal component impulses, narcissistic, aggressive, and even erotic, than because it is indispensable for subsistence and justifies existence in society. The daily work of earning a livelihood affords particular satisfaction when it has

[1] The first to draw attention to that connection was T. Reik.
[2] See Bergler-Knopf, "A Test for the Differential Diagnosis between Retirement Neurosis and Accident Neurosis," J. Nerv. Ment. Dis. 1944. No. 4.

been selected by free choice, i.e., when through sublimation it enables use to be made of existing inclinations, of instinctual impulses that have retained their strength or are more intense than usual for constitutional reasons. And yet as a path to happiness work is not valued very highly by men. They do not run after it as they do after other opportunities for gratification. The majority work only when faced by necessity, and this natural human aversion to work gives rise to the most difficult social problems."

The problem of work is psychologically difficult to evaluate without taking into account the problem of sublimation. Sublimation—a term coined by Freud—denotes transformation and desexualization of repressed phallic and pregenital libidinous wishes, into functions approved by the respective society.

Sublimation is one of the bases of cultural development and an indispensable part of our daily life. In the words of Freud, who introduced the term, "Sublimation of instinct is an especially conspicuous feature of cultural evolution; that it is that makes it possible for the higher mental operations, scientific, artistic, ideological activities to play such an important part in civilized lives."

A great deal has been written about sublimation, and still the problem is replete with unsolved riddles.[3] The latest paper on sublimation is one of G. Roheim,[4] who comes to the following conclusions:

". . . . the fundamental situation (in neurosis) is always that the Super Ego represses the Id strivings. In sublimation, however, Id strivings reconquer the ground in a disguised form, and if they are not again subjugated by the Super Ego, neurosis is avoided. In contrast to the prevailing view, this would mean that in sublimation we have no ground wrested from the Id by the Super Ego, but quite the contrary, what we have is Super Ego or Ego territory inundated by the Id . . . . The Ego allied with the Id is victorious and ousts the Super Ego. In neurosis the depressive state dominates, in sublimation the manic."

In applying his newer formulation of magic to sublimation, Roheim states:

"This is just what magic means: the emphasis on the autoerotic aspect of pleasure, the denial of object-relationship, and the

[3]First published under the title, "On a Five Layer Structure in Sublimation," Psychoanalyt. Quart. XIV, 1, 1945.
[4]"Sublimation." Psychoanalyt. Quart. VII, 3, 1943.

withdrawing of libido from the mother, i.e., the child emerging from the dual-unity situation."

Although I agree with Roheim in many respects, I believe the problem to be far more complicated. Let us enumerate a few unsolved contradictions in the generally prevailing views on sublimation.

1. At the time Freud formulated his views on the subject, only the repressed phallic and pregenital wishes and their contributaries were considered to be the contents of the Id. Later, Freud put at least equal stress on repressed aggressive trends. However, no revision of the problem of sublimation was undertaken on the basis of this inclusion of aggressive trends, with the result that even today the roots of sublimation are held to be "always in an erotic activity, either pregenital or genital."

2. The psychologic method through which sublimation takes place has never been analytically clarified. Freud assumed that even the tendency toward sublimation had a biologic basis.[5]

3. There is no uniformity of view on what is to be considered sublimation. Many inconspicuous neurotic symptoms are classed as sublimations.

4. Sublimation implies, with but few exceptions, a freedom from psychic masochism in the act of redirecting instincts—a fact never stressed. For instance, Freud, in his paper on Dostoevski, says that a certain type of gambling can be a substitute for masturbation. If a gambler of another type "sublimates" part of his masochistic exhibitionistic tendencies in masochistic gambling instead of continuing to indulge in the more primitve forms of exhibitionism, he has undoubtedly progressed in the direction of sublimation.[6] Still, we would not call gambling of either type a successful sublimation because of its self-damaging tendencies.

5. There are contradictions between Freud's original formulation on sublimation—that an erotic trend is directly perpetuated after desexualization—and newer formulations which consider sublimitation a defense mechanism. For instance, Jones, in his "Prob-

[5]Cf. Freud: Three Contributions to the Theory of Sex. New York: Nerv. and Ment. Dis. Pub. Co., 1910; also Freud: Leonardo da Vinci: A Psychosexual Study of an Infantile Reminiscence. New York. 1916.
[6]See the "Triad of Gambling" in my paper "On the Psychology of Gambling." Imago, XXII, 1936, No. 4.

lem of Paul Morphy,"[7] speaks of a double layer: "I conceive that (Morphy's) parricidal impulses were 'bound' by an erotic cathexis, actually a homosexual one, and that *this in its turn was sublimated.*" To complicate matters, the newer English theories (Klein, Sharpe), pointing to sublimation as one of the means toward an external symbolic restitution of the "devoured" mother because of feeling of guilt, were never correlated with the original conceptions on sublimation.

6. The inability to produce workable sublimations has always been considered neurotic and the ability to achieve such sublimations after successful psychoanalytic treatment has been taken for granted. There has been no explanation of the method of achieving this sublimation besides that of reducing the neurotic's concentration on his unconscious neurotic conflict. By the same token, the ability to sublimate has been considered normal in non-neurotic individuals without any explanation of why, and especially how, this is accomplished.

The idyllic way in which the process of sublimation has been described in our earlier literature is surprising and fascinating. For instance, Jones wrote in 1912:

"A child . . . . who had conquered a sadistic love of cruelty may, when he grows up, be a successful butcher or a distinguished surgeon, according to his capacities and opportunities. One in whom exhibitionistic fondness for self-display was pronounced may develop into an actor, an auctioneer, or an orator. There comes to my mind a patient who as a child showed an unusually strong interest in the act of micturition, in the guidance of the flow, in the force of it, and so on. When a little older, he was passionately fond of playing with streams and puddles. He is now a well-known engineer and has constructed a number of canals and bridges."[8]

To this Roheim adds:

"In the light of what we know at present, we can add to this that infantile activity itself (exhibitionism, urethral erotism), which appears to be the basic element in sublimation, is really the triumphant denial of a specific anxiety situation."[9]

'Jones, Ernest: The Problem of Paul Morphy: A Contribution to the Psychoanalysis of Chess. Internat. J. Psychoanalyt. XII, 1981, No. 1. (Also in the Psychoanalyt. Bewegung, III, 1931.)
'Jones, Ernest: The Significance of Sublimating Process for Education and Re-Education. J. Education. Psychol., 1912.
'Roheim, Geza: Sublimation, Loc. cit., p. 848.

The same holds true of Freud's description (1910) of Leonardo da Vinci's sublimation. Leonardo's famous screen memory of a vulture flying to him when he was in the cradle, opening his mouth with its tail, and repeatedly pressing against his lips, is interpreted by Freud as an expression of the memory of the infant with the nipple in its mouth and of the many kisses showered on the child by a loving mother. Freud believes that the Mona Lisa and the Mettertia are sublimated expressions of Leonardo's infantile gratification coming from his loving stepmother and grandmother. Once more we find the idea of the direct transition of a desexualized Id wish into sublimation.

Further study casts doubt on this idyllic and direct mechanism and indicates that the ways of sublimations are more dramatic and tortuous. From analyses of writers I came to the conclusion that the sublimation of writing, for instance, had to be explained on a twofold basis: the ability to write *per se* and the specific problem expressed in a specific work of art. The first, ability to write, could be reduced to an oral conflict; the second, specific work, *not*, as is generally assumed, to an *expression of an original drive, but to the defense against that drive.*

In a report[10] on fifteen cases of writers, I came to the conclusion that every writer suffers from oral regression (confirming Brill's statement), but that he is no longer striving to fulfill the friendly desire of "getting" in the repetition of the child-mother relationship, but is rather full of spiteful desire for oral independence. He identifies himself with the "giving" mother because of aggression toward her, thus eliminating her. He achieves oral pleasure for himself through beautiful words and ideas. In its deepest sense, his writing is a repudiation of the "bad" pre-oedipal mother and the disappointment, allegedly experienced at her hands and masochistically perpetuated, by the establishment of an autarchy. Oral autarchy is the primary basis of writing in general. Secondarily—on the more superficial level—the writer tries to solve his specific problems (anal, urethral, or phallic), to which he has turned as an escape from oral dependency. What he expresses in his writing, however, is not the direct oral masochistic wish but the defense against that wish.

Applying this understanding to other forms of sublimation, it

[10]A Clinical Approach to the Psychoanalysis of Writers. Psychoanalyt. Rev., XXXI, 1944, No. 1.

became clear that all the contradictions in the earlier formulations of sublimation could be traced back to two sources: the fact that what was assumed to be the original drive was later found to be only the palimpsest for a deeper one, and the fact that the importance of aggression as a human drive was constantly overlooked. Take Freud's example, Leonardo. Leonardo's homosexuality expressed his oral regression, cryptically hinted at even at that time by Freud in his paper. In other words, Leonardo had a pre-oedipal *aggressive* conflict with his mother (covering masochistic attachment) which resulted in the defense mechanism of homosexuality.[11] In his madonnas he did not express the direct continuation of the mother's love but rather the defensive denial of her *lack of love*. The sublimation represented not the loving mother, but the defense against the hating and damaging mother to whom he was masochistically attached and whose aggression he tried to nullify because it was a narcissistic injury. He executed his hatred of his mother in his homosexuality—which was very near consciousness—and repaired his mortified narcissism in his madonnas who loved the child. At the same time by thus warding off her hatred and sublimating the secondary defense, he denied his own masochistic attachment toward her.

The following four examples of sublimation lead to the conclusion that a *five-layer structure* is involved in its mechanism. The starting point in sublimation is not an Id wish *per se*, but the result of regression. In other words, it is in itself the result of a conflict. That conflict is presented (layer one), immediately counteracted by a Super Ego reproach (layer two), which necessitates the establishment of a defense mechanism (layer three). The Super Ego objects, however, even to the defense mechanism (layer four), which in turn forces the unconscious Ego to sublimate (layer five), which represents the defense against the defense.

Case One is an architect who specialized in country houses. In the gardens of the estates he always wanted to build great fountains. Had he been able, he would have furnished every client with a reproduction of *Menekin Pis*, which he considered to be the greatest work of art ever produced. This patient came into analysis partly because of premature ejaculation. In his early childhood he was, like the

---

[11]Cf. my paper (in coll. Eidelberg, Ludwig): Breast Complex in the Male. Internat. Ztschr. f. Psychoanalyt., XIX, 1933, No. 4; also my paper: Eight Prerequisites for Psychoanalytic Treatment of Homosexuality. Psychoanalyt. Rev., XXXI, 1944, No. 3.

engineer of Ernest Jones, intensely interested in his own and other
boys' micturition and played constantly with streams and rivers
which he "built" in sand. He was, of course, a bedwetter. In his
country forty-five years ago, fresh water was brought in containers
and as a boy of five he played at being a water peddler. He distinctly remembered carrying a tray of bottles filled with water and
asking everyone if he cared to buy a glass of water. When the play
was forcibly interrupted by his father, who was ashamed of having
anyone suspect that his child was trying to make a few pennies in
this way, the boy cried bitterly. His masturbation fantasies later
centered on the idea that a girl was forced to drink from one of his
bottles, which in this version contained "dirty" water.[12]

His first genital attempts always resulted in premature emission.
At nineteen he was unaware of his inadequacy until a girl broke off
relations with him because of it, whereupon he became suicidal. He
soon gave up sexual relations completely and sometime afterward
began his architectural studies. He was fired with ambition and
quickly made money. He finally married an aggressive "gold digger"
who was able to exploit him in every way by holding over him his
potency disturbance. The unhappiness in his family life made work
his only pleasure.

This patient was the only child of a marriage of convenience.
He hated his mother who was a cold woman, and was irritated by his
weak, boisterous father. Analysis brought out a typical oral substructure underlying his personality and symptoms and, as is typical
in premature ejaculation,[13] the "mechanism of orality" was fully
developed. The patient took revenge for early oral disappointments
in his symptom. He unconsciously identified breast and penis, milk
with urine and sperm. He refused sperm in the same way in which
he was supposedly deprived by his mother of milk; more, he spilled
the milk (sperm) to spite her. This aggression, however, was but a
covering cloak for deeper repressed masochistic attachment. At the
same time he was under the pressure of guilt because of his aggressive refusal, a guilt which he counteracted by "giving," but at a time
when the woman could get no pleasure from it—he mocked giving.

[12]Previously I described a similar pattern observed in another patient with
ejaculatio praecox. In this case the girl had to eat dirty grapes. See my book:
Psychic Impotence in Man. Berne: Verlag Hans Huber, 1937, Chapter on
Ejaculatio Praecox, pp. 115-135.
[13]Ejaculatio Praecox. Psychiat. en neurol., bl. (Amsterdam), 1937.

Concomitantly, he "protected" the woman from his "dirty," that is, orally poisoned and anally contaminated sperm (Abraham).

His neurosis manifested itself in his symptom and in his unhappy marriage. He was able, nevertheless, to build some long-lasting sublimations in his work: one had the impression that he built houses only for the sake of his fountains. However, even that escape was gradually blocked as his neurosis progressed, until he decided to undergo analysis because he had lost interest in his profession. When he was at this stage, a friend ironically remarked, "He is so depressed that he does not even enjoy his fountains any more." That remark struck home and the patient decided that he was really sick. It is interesting to note that until the age of fifty his unremitting impotence failed to force him into analysis but the approaching collapse of his sublimation did.

In his sublimation the patient's basic conflict was between an aggressive refusal: "I will not give because my mother did not give," and his conscience which demanded that he give. The solution was a "magic gesture": "I will show you in my behavior how I wanted to be treated." On the surface, therefore, he gave, but hidden behind his giving was a masochistic accusation of his mother: "See how bad *you* were." That weak repartee of a magic gesture, used to counter the accusation of aggression, could be traced back to infancy. Even as a boy of three he always voiced his curiosity about strangers with a standard question: "How does he make his living? Does he earn enough?" This need for constant reassurance that people were not starving was combined with a commiseration for the poor. Later, in the stage of the negative oedipus complex, he was the feminine recipient but was quickly driven out of that relationship by castration anxiety. So he combined remnants of his penis-pride and the denial of his alleged castration, by going back to his own substitute, the breast-penis. This was an act of desperate spiteful defiance both to preserve his Ego and to avoid "aphanisis" (Jones). Therefore his sublimation was also a dramatic and guilt-laden attempt to deny his masochistically perceived oral and phallic castration.

To summarize:

First layer: "I want to enjoy my mother's refusal masochistically" (libidinous).

Second layer: first Super Ego reproach: "You have no right to enjoy it."

Third layer: aggressive defense against the masochistic wish:
"I don't want to enjoy it; on the contrary, I am
refusing in revenge, as did my mother" (aggressive).

Fourth layer: second Super Ego reproach: "You have no
right to be aggressive either."

Fifth layer: aggression is repressed under the pressure of
guilt, the alibi of being a "good boy" produced
by doing something approved and asexual (foun-
tain building), and as compromise, the "magic
gesture" is established: "I do not refuse; I
give." Nevertheless, aggression is hidden in the
magic gesture.

Only the fifth layer represents the sublimation.

Case Two. A patient of twenty-five, a mechanical engineer,
entered analysis because of work inhibition, impotence, and masochistic character abnormalities. After a year of analysis he was able
to achieve erection but during the whole of the next year he suffered
from "psychogenic oral aspermia."[14] Strangely enough, he masturbated with fully conscious early pre-oedipal aggressive fantasies
pertaining to his mother's breast. When asked about his beating fantasies, he declared at first that he had none. He added, however,
that perhaps he ought to mention certain episodes from his school
days in which he, as head prefect, had protested several times against
boys being beaten by their school fellows. It was then that he had
had the "tragic experience" of detecting active beating fantasies more
than once in himself. At the very beginning of his analysis it was
clear that he identified himself mainly with the boys who were
beaten, although he did not know this consciously. After some time
and with great reluctance, he gave an account of the chronologic
development of his masturbation fantasies. When he was three or
four years old his sadistic fantasies were exclusively concerned with
his mother's breast. He generally pictured her with her breasts
fastened by cords to a sort of pulley which hung from the ceiling.
The patient pulled the cord, stretching the breasts until his mother
was dragged upward in great pain and the breasts finally torn off.
Or his mother's breasts were fastened to her feet by means of cords
tied from the back while her head was also fastened to her feet by

---

[14]The case is described in my paper: Further Observations on the Clinical
Picture of "Psychogenic Oral Aspermia," Case B. Internat. J. Psychoanalysis.
London, XVIII, 1937, Parts 2-3.

cords tied from the front. The breasts were pulled backward, the head down, and when both were pulled at once she was torn in two. Or his mother was chased naked in the street, her breasts expanded by means of a cord held by the patient which pulled her arms backward. In this combination of sadistic and scopophilic fantasies the patient played the active role of tormenter in an ever-diminishing degree. Other women made their appearance, then men who became increasingly important—the penis soon took the place of the breast. He could recognize the penis of his father in these fantasies because his father was the only circumcised man whose penis he had seen. (His father was a baptized Jew, but his children had not been ritually circumcised; in his country only Jews were circumcised.)   Men were now tortured instead of women. The "cord, tearing and hanging fantasies," as the patient called them, were replaced by "crushing fantasies." Naked men and women were thoroughly scrambled in a box and then squeezed together. Here for the first time we have a clear shift into masochism: the patient, hitherto the active agent, now climbed into the box and suffered all that he had perpetrated against others. At puberty the fantasies of schoolboys being beaten were in the forefront, but typically masochistic notions, such as that of having a woman sitting on him as he lay supine so that he had to breathe her "evil odor," were also present. He had the fantasy of drinking urine several times. He elaborated the story of robbers who, falling upon peasants, forced them to drink manure drainage to make them tell where their money was hidden.

In these fantasies the patient made the most desperate effort to place his sadism in the forefront as a defense against his masochistic wishes, the recognition of which he obviously tried to avoid. In my essay on Stendhal I showed that that writer was fully conscious of his positive oedipus complex *because* the complex served as a defense against his feminine identification stemming from the negative oedipus complex. The same mechanism held true in this case. He also finally made a regression to the negative oedipus complex and— precisely in order to keep the accompanying powerful masochistic wishes under repression—retained his sadistic interest in his mother's breast in consciousness. By means of this sadism he avoided both his masochistic attachment toward his father ("I am a sadist"), and indeed any attachment toward his father whatsoever ("I am interested only in my mother"). It may seem strange that a deeper oral

layer can be used as defense against a more superficial phallic layer
but the whole problem is less mysterious if we take into account
the fact that phallic passivity is but the continuation of an oral one.
The patient made a desperate effort to flee orality, which, as his
aspermia proved, did not entirely succeed.

This case further corroborates my previously stated[15] affirmative
answer to the question as to whether a preliminary sadistic phase
does exist in masculine beating fantasies, a question left open in
Freud's famous paper on beating fantasies.[16] The masculine beating
fantasy in the male seems to develop by the following stages: 1.
sadistic aggression toward the breasts of the mother in the pre-
oedipal period; 2. turning of the aggression, because of guilt, toward
the boy's own buttocks, which are identified with the breasts of
the mother; "transcription" of executive power from mother to
father; 3. renewed transcription from father to mother as a defense
against unconscious femininity.

Our question is: exactly what did the engineer and constructor
sublimate and to what degree was he successful in his attempt to
sublimate by means of his construction of machines?

First layer: "I want to be masochistically mistreated by my
                 mother (libidinous).
Second layer: first Super Ego reproach: "You have no right
                 to be masochistic."
Third layer: "I don't want to be masochistic, anyhow; I am
                 aggressive toward my mother" (aggressive).
Fourth layer: second Super Ego reproach: "You have no
                 right to be aggressive either."
Fifth layer: "I want to obey and to be a good boy. I shall
                 change in conformity with my father's wishes.
                 I shall construct machines, thus doing something
                 which my father does (his father was a tech-
                 nical theoretician). In addition, I shall be prac-
                 tical (his father had always complained that he
                 was impractical) and construct *real* machines."
                 In this attempt at sublimation irony, hypocrisy,
                 and spiteful derision of his father are visible.

Once more, only the *fifth* layer is sublimatory.

[15]Preliminary Phases of the Masculine Beating Fantasy. Psychoanalyt. Quart.
VII, 1938, No. 4.
[16]Freud: A Child is Being Beaten. (1919) Coll. Papers, 11.

This sublimation was only partially successful. He wanted to be an inventor of machines, but succeeded only in being an imitator of inventions. He had inventive ideas, but could not pursue them. However, he was very gifted in duplicating and understanding the machines of others and in that respect could solve the most complicated problems. In other words, he could not bear the responsibility of inventing machines because that would remind him of his first invention, the pulley. Thus, we see that he could only partially circumvent his Super Ego.

Case Three. A scientific worker awaited the publication of his papers in various scientific journals with impatience and excitement.[17] Whether his papers would appear, whether he would be praised or criticized, seemed to be matters of utmost importance in his life. Everything else, work, love, hobbies, were subordinated to that "publication compulsion." But when the papers were published, he soon lost all of his former interest and began to wonder when his next paper would "at last" be published, and to complain bitterly about alleged neglect. He also reacted paradoxically to being quoted. When quoted with criticism or even passed over, his aggression, always ready to break out, revelled in orgies of hatred. He was a typical example of the "mechanism of orality" mentioned before. Neurotics of this type constantly force people whom they identify with the phallic mother, into the role of refuser, so that they may be aggressive—seemingly in self-defense while repressing their own provocation—and masochistically enjoy the situation of being unloved.[18] They are, to quote a witty patient, "always pulling a 'Nobody loves me.'"

The cause of the patient's mania for publication was found in his voyeurism. Since that voyeurism was directed toward his mother, it was strongly counteracted by a Super Ego reproach. To void that objection he furnished an unconscious defense mechanism: "I am not a voyeur, I exhibit." Publishing scientific papers was therefore an exquisite defense. His sublimation had the following structure:

First layer: "I want to be a voyeur" (libidinous).

[17]We are concerned here with the counterpart of the patient I described in Chapter IV of my paper, "To Reject Somebody—To Accept Somebody." Imago, XXIII, 300 f. 1937.
[18]See the description of that mechanism in: Psychic Impotence in the Male. Chap. on Orality. Loc. cit.

Second layer: first Super Ego reproach: "You have no right to peep at your mother."

Third layer: "I am not a voyeur; I am an exhibitionist. I don't need my mother; I am showing my own body (penis) and am autarchic and aggressive in transgressing educational rules."

Fourth layer: second Super Ego reproach: "You have no right to be aggressive by using exhibitionism."

Fifth layer: "I am not aggressive and I am not exhibitionistic. I want to be obedient and a good boy. I shall publish papers[19] and work for science and help others. Didn't my father tell me to be socially minded?" (irony against his father).

The *fifth* layer leads as usual to sublimation and also permits mockery of the Super Ego.

Case Four. A patient suffering from obsessional neurosis, a student of languages, had occupied himself for some time with the project of a school of agricultural fertilizers.[20] Although he knew nothing of this specialty, he attempted with some astuteness to interest various agricultural authorities. The assumption was justified, however, that his interest in manure represented an attempt at a sublimation of anal wishes. A detailed analysis revealed the following structure:

First layer: "I want to be anally and passively overwhelmed by the penis of my sadistic father" (libidinous).

Second layer: first Super Ego reproach: "You have no right to enjoy passivity."

---

[19]One might object that layers one and five are basically identical because the patient originally wanted to be a voyeur (layer one) and finally achieved his wish indirectly in layer five, since before he could publish he had to observe his scientific material. The fallacy is based on the confusion of two forms of voyeurism: the original one was of the oral-devouring type, the final one a purified "friendly" and observing one. Another objection could be made: why is there no connection established with castration anxiety? That objection overlooks the fact that the "breast complex" in the male starts with "oral castration" in the period of weaning. (See my paper in collaboration with Eidelberg: Breast Complex in the Male. Loc. cit.) The exhibitionistic penis pride is a defense against it, penis and breast being identified. The autarchy is established and the mortified narcissism restored. The patient was very sensitive to typographical errors—he used exhibitionism as a defense against castration. That castration was, however, not phallic but oral in structure.

[20]The case is described in my paper, "Two Forms of Aggression in Obsessional Neurosis." Psychoanalyt. Rev., XXIX, 1942, pp. 194-195.

Third layer: "I don't need my father, don't care for him, and
               don't want to be overwhelmed anally. I have an
               anal penis myself. I am autarchic and want to
               play with my faeces-penis" (aggressive).
Fourth layer: second Super Ego reproach: "You have no right
               to be aggressive toward your father."
Fifth layer: "I want to obey; I want to be a good boy. I
               shall do with all my wishes something you shall
               approve. I shall change them in conformity with
               your commands into something permitted. I
               shall teach productivily the use of manure.
               Didn't you tell me that teaching was produc-
               tive?" (spiteful derision and hypocrisy directed
               at the Super Ego).

The role of aggression remains one of the main unsolved problems in sublimation. It is clear that the old formulation which entirely ignores the role of aggression became untenable after the
introduction of Freud's eros-thanatos theory.

The only analyst who before my paper took into consideration
seriously the role of aggression in sublimation was Karl Menninger,
in his book "Love Against Hate."[21] Menninger believes that aggression alone is the raw material of sublimation: ". . . . This is the
schematized natural history of the victory of the life instinct (love)
over the death instinct (hate). All aggressive energy except that
small quantity necessary for self-defense against real dangers is
turned into useful channels and employed in the services of living
and loving. Aggression, destructive energy, is thus effectively de-
natured, and by a shift in object and modality it becomes construc-
tive. This latter process constitutes sublimation as I view it." The
progress in this approach is in the stressing of the role of aggression, doubt remains in viewing of libidinous energy as "love" without specifications and not stressing of pregenitality. Moreover, the
pre-genital, libidinous material for sublimation is partly disregarded.

What we see clinically is always only a mixture of libido and
destrudo (Weiss) or, to use Eidelberg's terminology, the products
either of "sexual instinct fusion" or "aggressive instinct fusion."
Therefore, something must happen to the admixture of destrudo in
the process of sublimation. In my opinion, destrudo plays a decisive
part. It is precisely that aggression—the spiteful defiance against the

[21]Harcourt, Brace & Co., N. Y., 1942.

Super Ego—which makes sublimation possible at all. Sublimation always contains Id elements even if we assume, as is done here, that what is sublimated is not the Id wish itself but the secondary, not primary, defense against the original conflict (fifth layer). The aggression which wrests Id ground in a disguised form, despite the fierce opposition of the antilibidinous Super Ego, must be considerable. I conceive of sublimation as a desperate and defiant attempt to insist on childlike megalomania. As recently acknowledged by Roheim,[22] this "autarchic fiction"[23] is the basis of magic.

Another approach to the same problem of the use of aggression in sublimation is visible if one takes into account the fact that the execution of even the simplest libidinous wish in childhood is closely connected with aggression. For instance, if a boy plays with his penis he not only satisfies his libidinous wishes but also transgresses an educational rule not to touch his penis. He is therefore also aggressive. We simply must learn to think in terms of libido-destrudo.

In the case of the chess player, Morphy, Jones reversed his earlier standpoint of the direct and idyllic transition of a repressed drive in sublimation. He seems to have been on the right track in this reversal, although some modification of his approach is justifiable. Jones believes that a primary aggressive tendency in Morphy was counteracted by a passive-homosexual one, which in turn was sublimated in chess. I believe that a primary passive tendency stemming from the oral level—the mechanism of orality—was counteracted by an aggressive defense. That defense was not accepted by the Super Ego with the result that a new, secondary defense was furnished: "I am not aggressive, I only play"—chess. One is compelled to assume that unknown oral-passive mechanisms played an important role in Morphy's case, mechanisms indicated by his paranoid ideas of being poisoned.

Let us not forget that psychic development does not start with the oedipus complex. No one has stressed this point more strongly than our English colleagues. What is often visible as anal passivity is but a repetition of oral passivity on an oedipal level. By assuming

[22] Cf. Roheim's paper, "The Meaning of Magic," read before the New York Psychoanalytic Society, March 1943, and his contribution to my paper, "Thirty Years after Ferenczi's 'Stages in the Development of the Sense of Reality.'" The Psychoanalyt. Rev. 1945.
[23] Jekels, Ludwig, and Bergler, Edmund: "Transference and Love." Imago, XX, 1934, No. 1.

the above sequence of events, we solve the contradiction in the case of Morphy. Roheim states:[24]

"It is clear that sublimation is a defense mechanism, but it is questionable whether, like other defense mechanisms, its aim is primarily that of a defense against Id impulses. Dr. Jones is of this opinion: 'By discharging Id energy along a deflected path, and particularly by transforming a sexualized aggressiveness, it protects against the dangers to the Ego which we know to proceed from excessive accumulation of that energy.' Yet what happens in the case of Paul Morphy? When chess as a sublimation fails him, he succumbs to paranoia, i.e., he is left defenseless against the persecution of the projected Super Ego."

The contradiction resolves itself when we assume the five-layer structure. The moment the fifth layer—sublimation—collapses, the aggression of the Super Ego turns against the Ego and masochism overwhelms the personality.

Roheim is correct, with slight exaggeration and terminologic inaccuracy, in stating that the mood in sublimation is manic and that in neurosis, depressive. What he means is that sublimation gives a queer kind of pleasure and satisfaction. It would be more correct to speak of the elated mood of persons with successful sublimations. However, the problem arises as to where elation comes from. Is it the satisfied libidinous wish, as Roheim assumes, or is it the aggressive pleasure of outwitting the Super Ego with a successful blind? I believe that both elements are present. The original wish is enjoyed only in the defense against the defense, but the preponderance of pleasure comes from outwitting the Super Ego.

A part of the outwitting of the Super Ego is found in the return of the repressed in every sublimation but only in a very indirect and roundabout way via the defense. Of course, those who believe in the direct and idyllic transformation of an Id wish in sublimation could argue that childhood sublimations are more primitive and less complicated in structure than those of adults in whom the Super Ego forces the Ego to form new defense mechanisms. That may be so. What I maintain is that the sublimation of adults is the outcome of the above-sketched five-layer structure.

The degree to which hypocrisy and irony directed against the Super Ego are involved in sublimation was illustrated by a schizoid

[24]Roheim, Geza: "Sublimation." Loc. cit., p. 350.

patient who angrily refused, as an adolescent girl, to play the piano when ordered to by her mother. Her explanation of this refusal, which occurred twenty years before she entered analysis, was the following: "At that time I had read in analytic case histories that playing the piano had, in a specific case, the unconscious meaning of masturbation. Since my mother forbade masturbation and approved of playing the piano, I believed her to be a hypocrite. I didn't want to be a hypocrite." Most neurotic persons do not go so far but still use hypocrisy as a weapon against the Super Ego.[25]

Typically an originally libidinous conflict is warded off by aggressive means, always making use of the opposite mixture of instincts in the defense. Why the starting point in sublimation always seems to be a libidinous conflict remains mysterious. A possible answer is that the aggressive tendencies are expended more easily than the libidinous, especially the pregenital ones. To the extent to which pregenital libidinous wishes can be subordinated under the primacy of genitality, all goes well. But even in the most favorable circumstances there are remnants of pregenital wishes, and those are the material for sublimation. Pregenital wishes therefore predominate in sublimation. However, a great deal of aggression is used in constantly warding off the Super Ego even under "normal" conditions.[26]

At this point the question arises as to the quality of sublimations after successful analysis. When one considers the sublimation of the patients described above, one might be led to believe that all sublimations are no more than defense mechanisms. This *is* in both neurotic and "normal" persons to the extent to which they serve the purpose of directing aggression against the Super Ego and the underlying Id-Super Ego conflicts. Likewise, in both the neurotic and the "normal," successful sublimation is brought about by that portion of the Ego which is healthy and is dedicated to a productive use of aggression. There, however, the similarity between sublimation in the neurotic and the "normal" ends. When we look further we see that in the neurotic, pregenital drives (and conflicts) predominate and that it is against the Super Ego reproach for these drives that the defense mechanism is instituted. In such a situation there is very

[25] Bergler, Edmund: "Hypocrisy, Its Implications in Neurosis and Criminal Psychopathology." J. Crim. Psychopath., IV, 1943, No. 4.
[26] See Jekels, Ludwig, and Bergler, Edmund: "Instinct Dualism in Dreams." The Psychoanalyt. Quart., IX, 3, 1940.

little aggressive energy left for productive use in the outer world. The Ego, only a small part of which is healthy, is so belabored by the Super Ego and the pressure of the pregenital and phallic conflicts that any sublimation it is able to establish is almost wholly concerned with inner defense, and its relation to reality is at best tenuous.

Compare this situation with that of a "normal" or analyzed person. During analysis the pregenital conflicts give way to a great extent to genital wishes, the aggression of the Super Ego toward the Ego is reduced, and the expanded, strengthened areas of healthy Ego are able to use more of both libido and aggression for productive, reality purposes. Sublimation in a well person certainly stems from a defense against the Super Ego and the remnants of underlying pregenital conflicts, but it is then concerned with affecting the real world from which the healthy Ego derives its satisfactions.

Only to play the *advocatus diaboli*, I would like to mention that one of the pregenital drives, voyeurism, seems to play some unclear but nevertheless especially important role in sublimation. Sublimation presupposes imagining the success of the desexualized energies in its end-result. Furthermore, exhibitionism in the form of showing off is involved in every sublimation, an exhibitionism which is, as usual, a defense against voyeurism.[27] How and why the role of voyeurism should be so great in sublimation remains to be clarified.

The starting point of sublimation is, by the way, not at all a pure and simple Id wish. Quite the contrary: it is the *result* of a conflict already crystallized between Id and Super Ego, executed by the unconscious Ego. For instance, the starting point in Case One was the mechanism of orality. That mechanism, with its triad ("I provoke a situation in which the pre-oedipal mother is unjust; I don't recognize my provocation and am aggressive in self-defense; I enjoy masochistically the situation of being unloved"), is not the beginning but the result of the oral conflict.

The starting point in Case Two was identical.

The starting point in Case Three was a voyeuristic conflict, which is in itself an ocular modification of the oral "getting" desire (Simmel).

The starting point in Case Four was the anal wish of being over-

---

[27]See my paper, "A New Approach to the Therapy of Erythrophobia." The Psychoanalyt. Quart., XIII, 1944, No. 1.

whelmed by the father, in itself only the continuation of oral passivity on the anal level.

Thus in every case the starting point in sublimation is the frozen conflict between Id and Super Ego.

What happens in cases in which a sublimation collapses? To what level does the person regress? The primary defense (third layer) and the secondary defense (fifth layer) crumble, and the person finds himself once more at the point where the whole process leading to sublimation began (first layer). There he is confronted with the task of furnishing a new defense which is his neurotic symptom.[28] Since his Super Ego aggression against himself is no longer sufficiently counteracted, the results are weak neurotic substitutes for sublimation.

On the other hand, persons with unstable sublimations are frequently strong enough to fight on the primary defense line of sublimation (third layer). Every time that the patient described in Case Three received a journal in which one of his papers appeared he experienced palpitation and excitement. After understanding his defense exhibition through publications, he argued that exhibition must be the decisive point since he was seemingly afraid of exhibitionism and not of voyeurism and because he never felt excited or afraid during his scientific observations (voyeurism). He was wrong: he underestimated the power of the unconscious Ego in sublimation. That part of the personality is so strong in successful sublimation that it forces the Super Ego to fight on the Ego's chosen battlefield. And the chosen battlefield of the Ego is, of course, the defense mechanism and not the original conflict. In other words, if the Super Ego attacks, the first line of defense is the third layer and not the first layer. So we see that sublimation is really a wall behind which the fight against the Super Ego succeeds. Only in cases of complete breakdown of sublimation does the Ego retreat to the first layer.

Looking with the analytic microscope at the process of sublimation in slow motion, we find that in every sublimation a five-layer structure is discernible. The first layer represents the result of a conflict and is itself not a primary Id wish. The second layer represents a Super Ego reproach directed against the original conflict. The third layer represents a defense against the original conflict. The fourth

---

[28] In the case of Morphy we find regression to oral-anal passivity, warded off secondarily with paranoid projections.

layer is again a Super Ego reproach directed against the defense. The fifth layer is a compromise. *Only that compromise—the fifth layer—is sublimated.* Expressed differently, what is sublimated is neither the Id wish nor the defense against the Id wish, but the *defense against the defense against a conflict originating historically in an Id wish.* Sublimation is therefore not the child but the modified grandchild of the original conflict.

The driving power behind sublimation is the tenacity of the original conflict and its modifications. The energy to achieve the aim, however, stems from the aggression of the individual and his intense narcissism and childlike megalomania.

Sublimation contains elements of spiteful defiance, irony, and hypocrisy directed against the Super Ego. The person producing the sublimation unconsciously derives the greatest pleasure from outsmarting the Super Ego. Basically, childish megalomania is triumphant in every successful sublimation.

B. Rationalization

Inner guilt is constantly masked and rationalized, since its cause and indeed its existence are unknown to the typical human being. Rationalization denotes, psychiatrically, a rather naive attempt to explain with "logical" means an unconscious process, visible only in its results. It is a means of explaining away an unpleasant and incomprehensible fact in a way which least damages one's self-esteem.[29] A few examples:

A patient thirty-five years of age, who came into treatment because of agoraphobia, was asked about his sex life. "Everything is all right there," was his reassuring answer. "Could you give a few details?" was my next question. After some time it became clear that the man had not had intercourse with his wife for the last ten years. His explanation was that, since he had been unemployed for a long time and his wife was earning their living, he just had not had the heart to make her submit to the exertion of intercourse. It was undoubtedly more unpleasant for the patient to admit to himself his potency disturbance than his "good heart."

Another patient, a girl suffering from street fear, was asked why

[29]Every unconscious mechanism is covered by a surface layer of rationalization. One can describe these mechanisms by starting either at the bottom, by uncovering the unconscious reasons, or at the top, from the covering cloak of specific rationalizations.

she avoided the street. She immediately produced statistics of traffic accidents in New York. Pressed to explain why other people were not similarly frightened, she replied, "They're just not careful enough." Once more we see unconscious exhibitionism covered up with a rationalization. One might object that the patient could not find out herself the real reasons for her inhibition. True enough, but she could have said: "I just don't know." The intellectual modesty which allows one to accept silly rationalizations is the amazing thing, the ignorance concerning unconscious reasons a truism.

A third patient, sent into analysis because of severe hypochondria, indignantly protested against his diagnosis. "I just worry about my health," was the man's stereotyped answer. Asked how great were his worries, he admitted that they forced him to consult a series of specialists regularly. "We call people who worry about their health, although no organic changes are visible to the specialist, hypochondriacs," I explained to him. The intelligent patient still insisted that he was not a hypochondriac.

On the other hand, it is incorrect to assume that rationalization *per se* is a neurotic mechanism. In the same way as the sun shines on the just and the unjust, the consoling rationalization is at the disposal of normal and neurotic people. It simply denotes ignorance of unconscious factors, and there is no difference between normal and neurotic people in their naiveté concerning unconscious driving forces. When a surgeon tells us that his interest in surgery is based on humanitarian ideas, he is right from the conscious, but wrong from the unconscious, viewpoint. His interest has unconscious reasons. When the historian asserts that his interest in the Middle Ages is "objective," he is ignorant of the unconscious wishes and defenses pushing him into that specific sublimation. The same holds true for every self-chosen profession or interest, hobby, or predilection.

As was seen in the examples, rationalization is not a conscious swindle. It is an *unconscious mechanism of self-deception.* Human beings who don't use rationalizations do not exist. The amount of self-deception of which even intelligent and correct people are capable is amazing: The battle with their conscience makes queer excuses acceptable to them.

It may seem strange to enumerate rationalization under the heading of "normal" antidotes against guilt since we have to destroy these rationalizations in psychoanalytic therapy. One has to distinguish between harmless and neurotic rationalizations. As long as the rationalization makes life easier in a not-too-neurotic individual, there is no objection to it. It is a different tale when rationalization is used to defend the whole structure of a neurosis in a neurotic person.

Two other neurotic mechanisms closely connected to rationalizations of unconscious guilt should be mentioned: pessimism and impatience.

Pessimism is a neurotic mechanism anticipating defeat or bad outcome in every situation. This anticipatory negation of success serves different purposes. First, it represents a face-saving device for childlike megalomania. The pessimist deals, as every other person does, with uncertainties if confronted with situations, the solution of which is necessarily in the future. Whether a specific endeavor will prove a success or a failure in the future cannot be decided at the moment with certainty. Still, whether or not the prospects are reasonably propitious, the neurotic pessimist automatically predicts failure. What he is most afraid of is *not* having anticipated possible failure, which would hurt his childlike megalomania.

Second, the pessimist gets rid of a great deal of inner self-punishment and guilt in anticipating the unhappy outcome. After having used his narcissistic face-saving device, he indulges in anticipation of defeat. He behaves from the start as if the blow had already fallen—and he enjoys it *unconsciously* in a masochistic way.

Third, there are connections between neurotic pessimism and superstition. The superstitious neurotic projects his own aggression outwardly, as Freud proved, is crushed by it when it boomerangs, and at the same time uses preventive magic. A patient of mine suffered, among other things, from an obsession that a concern for whom he worked in previous years would sue him for damages. Amusingly enough, the concern was obviously afraid of the same thing in reverse, and proposed a settlement which would void any unpaid debts or claims—for *both* parts. The contract was sealed on December 31, and the patient called me up to communicate the good news. "I congratulate you that the *New Year starts* so well for you," was my reply. The patient was horrified: "Don't say that, please! If you must congratulate me, say at least that you congratulate me that the *old year ended* so well for me." At the next appointment I asked the man for an explanation: "Well, I always imagine that somewhere in the universe there's a bookkeeping system in which favorable and unfavorable events must be balanced in everyone's account. Since you said that the solution of my conflict starts the New Year so well for me, it means that I shall have to pay an equal amount with unhappiness in the New Year. If, however, we put down my success on the account sheet of the old year, I don't start the New Year with a negative indebtedness. . . ."

Impatience is another neurotic mechanism which acts like a sponge in absorbing unconscious guilt. The impatient person who cannot stand delay believes that his haste is explainable in the desire to reach the goal. Clinical experience proves the opposite. The problem needs some elaboration.[30]

1. *Essentially different attitude is enforced waiting: the practically healthy person strives after the current aim, the neurotic person after the current defense mechanism.*

During the analysis of an obsessional neurotic patient, the cause of his strange haste for intercourse was discussed. On a certain day he had made an appointment with a new girl friend for 5 p.m. and with his usual girl friend for 9 p.m. The patient's explanation was as follows: "I do not know whether the new one will submit to coitus immediately; for safety I have also invited my 'old' girl friend. Provided that the affair runs smoothly with the new one, I shall go to the movies with my 'old' girl friend." I asked the patient what explanation he would give for this double insurance, and pointed out the improbability that it was really only his sexual desire which pressed him so; for he had had regular intercourse, the last time for instance only two days before. Further I reminded him that I had often shown him to be inwardly uninterested in women, and that he often only used them to displace his aggression, and that the strikingly frequently practised intercourse was also often misused as a defense mechanism: "I am not feminine and passive, on the contrary I am hyperpotent with women."

In all probability it was this alibi which again imperatively demanded the coitus. His not being able to wait was therefore neurotic.

[30]First published under the title: "On the Psychoanalysis of the Ability to Wait and of Impatience." Psychoanalyt. Rev., 26:1, 1939. The original publication is more extensive.

After some hesitation the patient admitted this, and inquired ironically if the healthy man is really such an artist in being able to wait.
Was there literature on this ability in the healthy man? I replied
that we know as yet but little about the psychology of the average-
normal man. As far as I knew no special study on the psychology
of being-able-to-wait in the healthy man existed. Experience alone
showed that exaggerated impatience, an instant need to achieve an
aim, roused the suspicion of neurotic behavior, and accordingly, as
in the case of the patient, represented a defense mechanism. The
patient revenged himself by making the ironically reproving statement: "So you are not able to say wherein the difference lies between
the ability to wait of the neurotic and of the healthy man." I replied
that I was not bound to shake a theory out of my sleeve, I was not
so impatient as he was and could perfectly well wait until this riddle
had found its solution, perhaps after several years. As a matter
of fact the patient was not really interested in the explanation at
all, but merely wished to direct a piece of aggression toward me.
Had it been different, then, on the basis of my former remarks, he
could have formulated the required theory himself: *The healthy
man strives only for an aim, the neurotic, under the disguise of an
aim, for a defense mechanism.* Applied to the patient here discussed: The healthy man would never think of playing off one
woman against another as a double insurance; he could wait; for
he *merely* desired the coitus; the patient on the other hand desired
official documentation that he had had intercourse, i.e., that he was
a man, which he could then present to the Super Ego to unburden
his feeling of guilt reproaching him with inner passivity.

The patient accepted this statement too and—preparatory to with-
drawal of forces— struck one more blow: "If being able to wait is
really such an important sign of health, then I am one hundred per
cent healthy, although you say that I am suffering from a moderately
severe obsessional neurosis. For I am able to wait, am opposed to
all precipitation. But did you not only recently point out that my
indecision lasting for years in the affair of K. (the patient wavered
between marrying or leaving a certain woman) was the result of my
neurotic ambivalence?" Therefore, concluded the patient triumphantly, inability to make decisions—*which appears from without as
ability to wait*—is both neurotic and healthy. He would not at first
admit the validity of my argument that mere description revealed
nothing of the genesis and that inability to make decisions caused

by an ambivalent conflict, had nothing to do with the ability of the healthy man to wait. In order to prove him wrong I quoted the following example: A woman patient with a most serious obsessional neurosis[31] which had lasted for half a century, could enter the restaurant where she was accustomed to eat her meals only after going through a series of complicated compulsory actions. It often happened that at 5 p.m. she had not yet had her breakfast. "Do you mean to say," I asked the skeptical patient, "that this patient was healthy because she could wait until 5 o'clock for her breakfast?"

We compromised on the basis that it is necessary to analyze the motives of being-able-to-wait in each individual case just the same as those of impatience.

I think that the formula "the healthy strive after the current aim, the neurotic after the current defense mechanism under the disguise of the aim" gives a general explanation of the phenomenon of the ability to wait as well as of inability for waiting in healthy and neurotic people. Neurotic impatience does not refer so much to the real aim as to the defense mechanism supplied by the unconscious Ego. The healthy person can wait also because his aims are interchangeable. The neurotic finds such difficulty in waiting because his Super Ego chronically presents the bill of the feelings of guilt and the unconscious Ego is compelled to defend itself by the alibi of the defense mechanism. It is evidently easier to change aims than to alter painfully constructed defense mechanisms, as tendencies of the Ego are obviously more plastic than the tendencies to punish proceeding from the Super Ego.

Our formula of the psychology of the ability to wait needs still some completions as well as limitations. For instance the obsessional neurotic just quoted reminded me in a sophistical manner of the tinge of obsessional neurosis in this phenomenon which shams a waiting capacity but on more close analysis turns out to be a *neurotic pseudo-ability to wait*. Other examples of this morbid pseudo-ability to wait are f.i., masochists who at heart do not wish success or types "taking their time" for years because the aggression so expressed represents an unconscious dike against passive-anal wishes to be overwhelmed which are still more repressed: the student who in spite of the despair of his family does not appear for years before

[31]Cf. "Observations on an Obsessional Neurosis in Ultimis." Internat. Ztschr. f. Psychoanalyt. 1936. N. 2.

the board of examiners belongs here as well as the parasite who, at his family's expense "takes his time" for years before following a profession, etc.

2. *In the practically healthy also a long enforced wait gives rise to a severe situation of conflict.*

It would be an error to pretend that even the so-called average healthy person—surely no ideal figure—is not exposed to conflicts in the situation of a too long enforced waiting. The contrary proves to be right: the reaction to the situation of enforced waiting is always the touchstone for relative normality. The advantage of the not too neurotic man consists in the fact that he—as shown—seeks rather the aim than merely the defense mechanism. Aims, however, are interchangeable.

Let us review a few typical reactions to be found in the "not too neurotic," viz., average people in the danger situation of an enforced waiting of years.

(A) Holding fast to the aim or displacing of the interest upon another aim, both without pathologic reactions: This is the most favorable, therefore rarest attempt at solution. It rarely succeeds without internal struggle whereby often appear the transitory phases to be described.

(B) Internal denial: Another type denies the original aim if too strong obstacles are in the way: This denial is at first only external—a kind of outward simulation or mimicry—and is achieved after more or less violent outbursts of emotion. This dissimulation can with time become an *internal* denial. The change from external to internal denial requires a rather long time, and represents a more or less abortive defense mechanism passing through quite a series of intermediary phases. A typical one may be emphasized: the person in question believes he has already given up his aim until a specific situation of temptation shows him the strength of his original desire.

(C) Bitterness and contempt for mankind: A phase of bitterness is not spared anyone who must wait too long for an aim striven after. The question is only how strong this bitterness is. There are all transitions between the quiet bitter intimated accusation, and hate and contempt of mankind accompanied mostly by devaluation of all success. The question is how far the bitterness goes, as the single attempt at solution remains unproductive and whether it impels forward productively. Again and again one may observe that enforced waiting, viz., the not immediate possibility of attaining a present aim draws upon unconscious infantile conflicts.

Frequently the inner bitterness ("I am not loved") leads through the too long enforced wait to incapability of enjoying success when attained at last. There are for example some remarks of H. Heine from his "mattress tomb" depreciating the success of the French version of his works by a "too late."

To this group belongs also the disillusioned poet, because not acknowledged, who is writing only for the desk drawer.[32]

(D) Depreciation of the aim: With every period of waiting lasting for a number of years the depreciation of the aim is as much connected as its idealization. The paradox of this statement disappears if we consider that here we are dealing with the "two ends of the same stick" (Dostoevski): for striving after an aim we must overrate it in order to mobilize the necessary amounts of libido and aggression. To be able to bear that the aim is not attained immediately we are obliged to depreciate it again. So it is only neurotic exaggeration of a normal defense mechanism if the two final phases appear overstressed. In extreme cases the aim is sweepingly annihilated, obscene vociferations are prevalent; the defense against not being loved is aggression.

(E) Reveling in fantasies of revenge: One of the normal ways of handling the waiting time is the fancied enjoyment of attaining the aim. The exacerbation of this attitude leads to the revenge fantasy being placed foremost instead of the fancy of reaching the aim striven after. It is again meeting the situation of not being loved by way of aggression. But these revenge fantasies are completely unproductive having no impelling force whatever—the impotent fancying becomes a neurotic end in itself.

(F) Doubt of the rightness of one's own ideas: This refers to neurotic people setting up a new doctrine, idea or tendency in art, literature, science or a technical branch, and growing to doubt their own ideas because of the lack of approval by the outer world. The rejection by the outer world—a matter of course with each new idea,

---

[32]Another variation on the part of these disillusioned people is silence. They have a presumptuous disdainful kind of silence clearly expressing their aggressive contempt. It is mostly oral defiance, more rarely an anal mechanism. Cf. my paper. "On the Resistance Situation: the Patient is Silent." Psychoanalyt. Rev. 1937.

the incubation time for new ideas is to be reckoned in generations—
is unconsciously also interpreted as an infantile punishment for aggression against the reigning authority; out of fear the neurotic tries
to escape into the situation of "I am a good boy again." A proof
for the psychic substructure of the doubt of the rightness of his own
ideas by the propagandist is the fact that the man who is internally
strengthened by his narcissism attaches only a very conditional value
to the approbation of the outer world. (Nevertheless he can enter
public life moved by exhibitionism united to aggression.) However,
I do not believe that even the most healthy can pass through a
waiting-time of years without a conflict.

(G) Consolation in the idea of being in advance of one's generation: In the case of people of this type there are points of contact
with neurotics who make use of bitterness and contempt of mankind
as typical attempts at solution. It comes to a compensatory increase
in narcissism, which however—as always in secondary narcissism—
gives the impression of being a sham and covers fresh wounds.
("He laughs at scars who never felt a wound." *Shakespeare.*) It
seems to be that the temporary renunciation of real success—concretely expressed in reaching the actual aim — hardly succeeds
even in the most favorable case and always needs some rationalizations for the placing of the feelings of guilt referring to aggression,
for handling the situation of not being loved, etc.

(H) Suggested "artificial paranoia": I am thinking of the fate
of the gynecologist Semmelweiss who, conscious of having made a
decisive discovery in the realm of antisepsis, had to endure being
rejected, laughed at and persecuted by the whole European medical
world. In Semmelweiss occurred the development of megalomania
and the use of fantastic counter-measures. Semmelweiss tried to
exclude the doctors, he addressed proclamations directly to the
mothers and fathers demanding that they refuse to admit to the
woman in labor anyone who had not disinfected his hands. No
wonder the defense reaction of the doctors increased more and more,
which strengthened the megalomania and led to a mania of persecution. On the other hand one must ask if the means employed by
Semmelweiss belong among the average man's weapons, further if
there exists "artificial paranoia" without unconscious homosexuality,
a question probably to be answered in the negative. The correct
formulation would be that certain unconsciously homosexually pre-

disposed types choose the issue of a mild paranoia as an attempt at solution if forced to wait for approval. It is interesting that the facts serving as a basis for the monomania did not represent a fantasm but, as it were, a reality: the idea of Semmelweiss on antisepsis was well founded and made a way for itself, though only after his death.

(I) Hinted at social self-degradation: The impelling motive is unconscious revenge against the infantile imago is projected on the denying outer world. The forms of self-degradation can be very different ones. In the genesis it is always the same mechanism that plays a part: the external refusal is perceived as a wilful denial on the part of the infantile persons which leads to revenge against these objects according to the motto: "It serves my father right that *my* fingers are frostbitten, why didn't *he* buy me gloves?"—Naturally only the "mild," hinted-at forms belong in this category.

(J) Resignation: Without complete shifting of the interest to another aim, resignation always goes a step too far when giving up the actually purposed aim. This "going a step too far" has again the meaning of an unconscious accusation against the infantile image which one again induces to prohibit too much so as to carry it *ad absurdum*.

(K) Tearful fantasies of rehabilitation: A variety of attempts at solution tending more to psychic masochisms lies in a chronically picturing to one's self the sentimental situation that the wicked world will one day do justice to the wrongfully misunderstood person,[33] and will acknowledge him "with tears in their eyes" as a genius. In many cases these fantasies alternate with bloody ideas of revenge.

This short review of some typical kinds of reaction which in no case pretends to be complete shows at all events that even the average healthy person does not very easily overcome the conflict situation of long enforced waiting.[34]

On the borderline between rationalization and collapse of a rationalization is a process which one may call "half-admission" of

[33]Here belong also the well-known attempts to pass over enforced waiting with jokes. A well-known gynecologist in an anti-Semitic country alleged the following reasons why he had not been appointed chief of the clinic: "First they said I was too young, later on I was too old, in between times I was—a Jew."

[34]A special form—waiting for one's own death—has not been treated here. Reference may be found in my work: "A Clinical Contribution to the Psychogenesis of Humor," Psychoanalyt. Rev., New York, 1937, N. 1.

guilt. It consists of acceptance of guilt for a lesser "crime" to disguise the real source of the guilt. This mechanism is built upon the ironic principle: "I couldn't have killed the girl in Manhattan of which I'm accused because at the time I was stealing a watch in Brooklyn." Many confessions in literary form are extracted that way. The poet H. Heine knew this one hundred years ago. In his "Memoirs," written in 1850 on his deathbed, he stated in reference to Rousseau:

> "For instance, I am convinced that Jean Jacques did not steal the ribbon which caused a chambermaid to be unjustly accused and dismissed, costing her her reputation and her position. . . . . Probably there was another offense of which he was guilty, but it was not theft. . . . . Nor did he send his children to the foundling hospital, but only the children of Mademoiselle Therese Levasseur. Thirty years ago one of the greatest psychologists pointed out to me a passage in the 'Confessions,' from which it seems certain that Rousseau could not have been the father of those children. The conceited old growler preferred to let himself be thought a barbarous father rather than bear suspicion that he was altogether incapable of fatherhood . . . ."

The following is a clinical example of this process of "half-admission": A patient had the peculiar habit of confessing little "crimes" in society. These were his constant topics of conversation. He was a master in imagining and describing situations which made him appear in a "bad light." He walked, so to speak, always on the narrow borderline of the not punishable but not quite correct. He would start in general by quoting different criminal cases of the day. He would then remark on the danger of life and the ease with which one could arouse unjustified suspicion. From that philosophical introduction he would proceed to reminiscences of his own, incidents in which he "nearly" came into conflict with the law—*ad infinitum.* He followed his usual procedure also in analysis. A little exasperated, I asked him: "What are you hiding behind these constant confessions? When did you have, not an imaginary, but a real conflict with the law?" His reaction was immediate and surprised: "How did you know?" After some time he confessed that he had been under arrest for a few hours many years before, although "of course" he was completely innocent.

It is clear that rationalizations are but intrapsychic crutches which collapse as time goes on. In psychoanalysis the first thing we do is to unmask these superficial covering-cloaks. The majority of people live—for better or for worse—with their changing rationalizations. In general, one can agree with Ch. N. Bovee's observation: "Many an honest man practices *upon himself* an amount of deceit sufficient, if practiced upon another, and in a little different way, to send him to the state prison."

C. *"Pathos"*

The constant battle which every human being must fight with his conscience is responsible for a type of reaction which is classified as "pathos." The Greek word has no adequate English equivalent,[35] and denotes scientifically the lofty expression *in speech* of a passionate emotion and has *no* connection with the usual connotation of pity. But inasmuch as emotion and its expression in words overlap with one another, the word pathos signifying the state of suffering, of being carried away by emotion, is used to describe any vehement affect underlying this mode of expression, and in particular a mood of solemnity and exaltation. Pathos is not unknown, either, in music, architecture, painting and plastic art. The idea of it is readily associated with the notion of something inflated, vague, shallow and rather spurious; the type of person with little command of expression mostly regards the pathetic individual as half a lunatic, half a comedian.

The psychology of pathos has nothing to do with conscious misuse of that reaction by swindlers and speculators hoping for a response of the lachrymal glands of their listeners. Excluded are also cases in which a fraudulent "dictator" offers his "indignation" to his dupes for the purpose of exciting them to criminal actions of the pogrom type. Also outside the scope of a scientific discussion, fall cases in which a person, cornered and proven guilty of a specific misdeed, uses pathos convincing the victim—that the victim did him an "injustice."

The psychology of pathos starts, where pathos has no rational reason at all. The classic situation of this type is an *unjust* accusa-

---

[35] I submitted in 1934, in collaboration with Dr. A. Winterstein, a paper, "Psychology of Pathos," to the Internat. J. Psycho Analysis, London. The paper was published there (Vol. XVI, 4, Oct., 1935) with the following remark: "The German word 'pathos' has been translated into its English equivalents, but it is not necessary to read beyond the first line of the present paper to discover that the German sense of the word is very different from the English. . . . No adequate English renderings appear to exist."

tion, which can be easily refuted and the matter closed. Clinical observation proves that the intrapsychic reaction is quite different. Whether it is visible on the surface or not, the victim reacts in his thoughts with pathos and indignation. The question is: Why does everybody react that way?

At first, lack of experience with human malice has to be excluded. If an immature boy, confronted with the fact that real people react differently than nursery rhymes let him expect, uses "pathos," nobody wonders about his indignation. If, however, people after passing their twentieth birthday, react similarly, one has reasons to suspect deeper motivations. We expect that the mature person adapted himself to the aggression of his fellowmen, and learned to protect himself. With or without being familiar with Goethe's dictum:

> No use to complain
> Of the baseness of one's fellows.
> It has might behind it
> Whatever folks maintain.

—the not too neurotic average person learned his lesson, provided gratis by experience. Nobody asks him to approve, or to associate with "impossible" people. Analytic experience proves that the pathos of indignation has intrapsychic reasons. The child's education was not only objective. The child was forbidden certain actions with four methods: persuasion, threat of loss of love, punishment, and —a moral factor, too. Just remember, how often you were told: "You should be ashamed of yourself." The result is that the language of reproach, later taken up by the severe inner conscience, continues the "pathos-form" of reproaches. The "pathetic reaction" preserves remnants of that early experience. A great deal of inner reproaches is presented to the frightened Ego in a pathetic form.

If the Ego is not completely submerged in masochistic submission, it finds an amazing way out: it turns the tables. It accuses now the malefactor *outside,* of the same crimes, the inner conscience accuses the Ego *inside.* It amounts to an *endopsychic reversal of roles by means of projection.*

Chapter IX

PARADIGMS OF NEUROTIC ANTIDOTES AGAINST GUILT: THE TRIAD—CYNICISM, HYPOCRISY, SELF-DERISION

There are literally hundreds of unconscious specific techniques neurotics use to fight their losing battle of conscience. Of course, the chief *general* technique is imbedded in the neurotic symptom of living out unconscious fantasies and defenses against it at the price of suffering. But *characterologically* the list of their techniques is incalculable, and not all are yet known. I shall isolate the triad: cynicism, hypocrisy, self-derision, not because it is the only technique of that type but because it is a fairly typical one.

A. Cynicism

What is a cynic? To use Oscar Wilde's definition, it is a person who "knows the price of everything and the value of nothing." A cynic is characterized by Henry Ward Beecher as follows: "The cynic is one who never sees a good quality in a man, and never fails to see a bad one. He is the human owl, vigilant in darkness, and blind to light, mousing for vermin and never seeing noble game. The cynic puts all human actions into two classes: openly bad and seemingly bad." Which means that the cynic has a cold-blooded attitude toward human values, suspecting behind every decent or even harmless action some low or dirty motive.

Psychologically the problem is complicated because the cynic covers up his neurotic attitude with so-called "facts" which he allegedly observes; completely oblivious to the unconscious reasons behind his own attitude.

The only psychoanalytic attempt to investigate that problem is contained in my paper "Psychology of the Cynic"[1] written in 1932. In this work sixty-four different forms of cynicism are enumerated. Here is a summary of the "mechanism of cynicism." The cynic is faced inwardly with a guilt problem concerning his exaggerated ambivalence—love and hate for the same person at the same time.

The cynic is subjected to the constant pressure of his ambivalence and—grotesque as it may sound—to the equally constant

[1]Psychoanal. Bewegung, V, 1933.

150

pressure of his punishing Super Ego, whose prohibitions relate to this very ambivalence, so that the unconscious compulsion to confess becomes the mainspring of action. The Ego of the cynic frees itself from this conflict by "turning the tables," by showing to the rest of the world (the despised "other fellows") that this forbidden ambivalence is to be found in them too. Implicit in all cynicism is the challenge to the listener: "Confess that in your heart you think exactly the same as the cynic who rouses your indignation." Here, the "other fellows" are conceived as a part of one's own Super Ego. At the same time, this demonstration of the ambivalence in others is a means of forestalling the attack that is expected as a punishment from the external world, the latter being perceived by the individual as part of his own Super Ego. It is indeed a peculiar war on two fronts which the individual carries on against his Super Ego, which appears in a double shape: as the internal unconscious conscience and as the external world. The cynic's onslaught appears to be aimed at this external-world aspect of the Super Ego; but in reality he is defending himself against his severe internal Super Ego, which is beyond the reach of his consciousness and is only perceived as a sense of guilt. The "rabidity" of the cynic does not proceed simply from aggression; it is equally the expression of his desperate struggle to ward off his "inner foe," the endopsychic Super Ego, and he sees to it that the contest is carried out on "foreign soil." The cynic treats the external world with the same severity as his Super Ego treats his Ego; and at the same time he is attacking his own Super Ego in the external world. The formula is something like: "He hits out at others, but it is his conscience he aims at."

The cynic always attacks authority or opinions accepted by the majority. Intrapsychically he still fights his neurotic battle with authorities in childhood: his parents. He captivates and appeases his inner conscience with the expectation of punishment or of at least rebuff, on which he cashes in from the environment. In general opinion, cynicism has something disreputable about it; the world which is ridiculed and allegedly unmasked takes revenge by not receiving the cynic completely. The habitual cynic suffers in his cynicism a good deal of self-punishment for his unconscious confession.

The cynic is thus a "debunker" of acknowledged values and opinions, not because he so chooses but because he is *forced* by an intrapsychic conflict to be thus. He is basically a passive person torn between two intrapsychic powers. He wards off the attack of his Super Ego by means of pseudo-aggression, and cashes in on his punishment by being rejected by the environment, which laughs at his jokes and rebuffs him at the same time.

Man, the "tireless seeker after pleasure" (Freud quotes this phrase from an unknown author), has understood, however, how to extract a certain amount of compensatory pleasure out of even as painful a process as that of solving an internal conflict of ambivalence and self-punishment. The cynic has done this in the following ways:

1. By means of the resolution from time to time of his internal ambivalence conflict, the cynic is temporarily free from guilt. In this a self-punishing and masochistic attitude plays a part.
2. The indignation, bewilderment and rage of those allegedly "unmasked" gives the habitual cynic pleasure—in living out compensatory aggression in fractional doses.
3. Voyeurism and exhibitionistic tendencies assert themselves and are experienced unconsciously as pleasure, especially in masochistic combination—the cynic utters his blasphemies publicly.
4. Narcissistic pleasure is enjoyed. As a general rule the cynic is somewhat admired and feared because of his sharp tongue. This gives him also the mirage of being "aggressive," whereas in reality he is the opposite.
5. Insofar as cynicism is expressed in the form of wit, the pleasure derived from wit, described by Freud, is to be included.[2]
6. The cynic gratifies in cynicism a number of infantile strivings—the "enfant terrible" motif, infantile megalomania, etc.

As a representative example I would like to quote the remark of one of the most famous cynics—Napoleon's secretary of state, Talleyrand.[3] Talleyrand, in negotiating a treaty with a foreign diplomat asked the latter, after their introduction: "Did you bring money with you?" The puritanic diplomat was taken aback and indignant. "You see," explained Talleyrand cynically, "in this country political affairs are difficult; one must have a great deal of money."

What is the technique of this cynicism? The honest and prudish diplomat was put on the spot by the French statesman, whose embarrassment Talleyrand enjoyed (attack against authority in child-

[2] See Part III of this chapter.
[3] See my book on psychoanalytic biographies.

hood). At the same time the foreign diplomat was asked to consider whether he himself was above pecuniary considerations. He was made to understand that the cynic just expressed what was hidden and not admitted by the partner. At the same time, Talleyrand's admission ridiculed his own superiors (the "Directoire"), once more a pseudo-aggression toward the same authority he himself allegedly represented (ambivalence). Masochistic exhibitionism was visible, too: His reputation could not be improved by this technique. Last but not least, manifestation of infantile megalomania ("I can afford such behavior") coupled with expected punishment—exposure of venality through indiscretion—were discernible.

Superfluous to state, the "great" cynic Talleyrand was one of the most unhappy people ever encountered. Cynicism was just his mask in the neurotic fight with his inner conscience.

B. Hypocrisy

Goethe once remarked ironically that the greatest difficulty in a problem lay exactly where one did not search for it. That observation holds true especially for all "obvious" human reactions. Layman and scientist alike have first to overcome an inner resistance when confronted with a hidden problem which seems to them no problem at all. "What is there to explain?" is their first reaction. The skeptic of this attitude is immediately accused of complicating matters unnecessarily or of drawing far-fetched conclusions if he points out that "there is more to it than meets the eye."

Let us forget therefore for a short time our prejudice about the self-evident and obvious and ask ourselves whether we know all about so common a psychic reaction as, for instance, hypocrisy.[4] Our first impulse is to pass in review certain of our acquaintances and choose a few outstanding examples of hypocrites who angered or amused us, depending on whether we were victims or onlookers. Looking more closely we will soon discover that what made us so sure that we knew all about a hypocrite was simply the fact that we confused description with underlying reasons for hypocrisy. True, we can describe precisely the hypocrite's behavior—his perversion of the truth, his smiling pseudo-submissiveness, his tendency to "hit below the belt" when giving distorted information to our personal enemies,

[4]First draft published in Internat. Ztschr. f. Psychoanal. 1935 and in the present form, in J. Crim. Psychopath. 1943.

his malicious cowardice, his ingratitude, his feeling of superiority in succeeding in fooling us with his pseudo-flattery and pseudo-approval. But *why* does he react that way? What are the *unconscious* reasons for his behavior? What differentiates him from the man who tells "white" lies because he is forced to and against his will, while the hypocrite uses deceit voluntarily, even in uncalled-for situations, and with noticeable pleasure?

The naive observer would be even more dumbfounded if he were to know that the unconscious reasons leading to hypocrisy are an important incentive in neurotic *and* criminal actions. We do well, therefore, to "eat humble pie" and to approach the problem without prejudice.

Let us start with three clinical examples of neurotic hypocrisy:

Case I. Eighteen years ago in the Vienna Psychoanalytic Clinic I made the following experiment: I was interested in finding out to what degree of human "stupidity" psychoanalysis was still effective. Since in private practice we deal with persons who are more or less educated, with some degree of intelligence, I wanted to find out whether people with a low I. Q. could still be influenced analytically. With the help of one of my superiors in the Clinic, I selected among 2,000 patients on our waiting list a man who appeared mentally the most primitive, one who made his living by means of what even his wife called his "low intelligence." The man was a peddler of soaps, and his customers bought his wares out of pity. On the advice of a physician he wanted to be treated, without fee, because of erective impotence, threatening to commit suicide if his condition could not be changed. I felt that even he could be helped provided the analyst took the trouble of explaining, as far as the intellectual part went, the complicated phenomena of an hysteric impotence in a simple, childlike language. I was sure that in the affective, therefore unconscious, level, there would be not the slightest difference between him and intelligent patients. The patient entered analysis, behaved very submissively, but, as expected, started very soon to repeat in the transference-situation his oedipal aggression toward his father, which was for him defense-mechanism against his deeper repressed passivity. By no means could he be brought to admit his inner aggression and resulting feeling of guilt. After a few months his sexual interest toward his wife improved, and after the typical ebb and flow of success and failure performed normal intercourse one morning for the first time in his life. He did this at exactly 7:30 a. m. At 9 a. m. he had his analytic appointment and was over-enthusiastic about the success, wanted to kiss my hands, and cried from happiness, especially since he was treated without charge. At exactly 2 p. m. of the same day he appeared without previous announcement in the office of my immediate superior in the Clinic, a colleague with whom he had spoken in my presence before being definitely sent to me. There he complained about me. *He did not mention his successful intercourse,* but simply stated that he was wasting his time with me since no improvement was visible. My colleague behaved correctly and told him that if he had resistances he should fight them out with me. The patient implored him not to mention his complaint to me. My colleague, of course, refused to do this; on the contrary, asked him specifically to analyse the whole affair with me on the following day. The next day the patient came for his appointment and started with the question: "Have you seen Dr. X already?" My colleague had not informed me of the incident, considering it simply a typical "acting out" not worth mentioning, but the word "already" was suspicious to me, and I asked the patient why I should have seen him. "Only because you know him well." I insisted on some explanation, and word by word had to be extracted from him until his action of the day before could be reconstructed. I asked him: "Why did you complain on the very same day that you had intercourse successfully for the first time in your life and why did you not mention the fact to my colleague?" At that the patient *smiled hypocritically* and informed me that he had some doubts of a "general" nature. "Is intercourse really so important?" was the tune he repeated. I reminded him that he had threatened to commit suicide if he could not achieve intercourse. At once the patient changed his approach, cried, and accused himself of hypocrisy and ingratitude, and begged for some humiliating work in expiation. After that incident the analysis progressed normally. He was cured and discharged a few months later, and I was repeatedly invited by him to the ritual circumcisions of his sons, who were produced regularly for a number of years.

What was the reason for his queer behavior? That he repeated in the transference his hatred of his father was clear. That he repeated that hatred in self-damaging conditions was also apparent, since his lies could have been detected through a single telephone

2

2

call. That he masochistically did not want to be cured was visible, too, since he assumed that I would dismiss him after his insolent act; that we do not react in such a manner in analysis he did not know. All of these facts are unimportant with regard to our problem; the explanation of hypocrisy. I believe that we could observe in this case in *statu nascendi* the re-enactment of the genesis of the hypocritical reaction. The patient repeated in the transference the father-son relation. His father was a severe disciplinarian; he preached authority, especially the orthodox Jewish one. The patient acquired toward him the attitude of deep submission with a defense counter-reaction, pseudo-aggression. Both he repeated with me, despite the fact that I behaved very differently from his father. He simply projected the old pattern upon me in the transference-repetition. Where his father was authoritative I was friendly, explaining, trying to make him cooperate without coercion. For a long time the discrepancy in his behavior was explained to him without effect. His attitude was that of submissive non-acceptance of interpretations. He was so submissive that he did not even dare to come out with his aggression; only once he accused me of trying to force my interpretations upon him. In other words he projected upon me the aggressive father who had really forced him to accept his opinions without contradiction. In his objection the patient repeated the feeling of being passively overwhelmed (negative, inverted oedipus complex in feminine identification) and the defense-reaction of pseudo-aggression. I explained to him that his conscious belief or disbelief was unimportant for us in analysis. However, since he projected the father-repetition upon me, he did not accept that. We see in this case the following prerequisites for the "mechanism of hypocrisy": a very weak and frightened Ego confronted with an authoritarian educator who enforces acceptance of his dictum without contradiction. The first reaction in some cases seems to be a false submissiveness ("pseudo-submissiveness"). That pretense of submission is one of the indispensable features of hypocrisy.[5]

[5]Hypocrisy can be observed as a transitory phase in every analysis before an interpretation is inwardly accepted. Since in analysis a change in the Super Ego takes place, it is understandable that the patient uses the old mechanisms of warding off educational authorities. This interpretation fits well with an unpublished remark of Ferenczi to the effect that hypocrisy seems to be a typical transitory phase of childhood. That remark was made to Anna Freud, who quoted it in the discussion of my paper. "The Psychology of Plagiarism," in the Vienna Psychoanal. So., June, 1932. Details are published in that paper, Psychoanal. Bewegung, 1932.

After his complaint to my colleague, I was of course interested to see if hypocrisy was a new acquisition of my patient. Of course it was not; it was only the resuscitation of an old mechanism. His "stupidity," widely publicized in his environment, gave him—only unconsciously, to be sure—a queer feeling of superiority: All of these people were convinced that he was stupid, whereas he was cleverly capitalizing upon their pity. What happened in analysis in this case was the change from an unconscious to a conscious hypocrisy as a transitory phase. The reason was: Once more the patient's Ego was confronted with an inescapable superiority of a person who, in his opinion, wanted to force his opinions upon him as his father had once really done. Naively the patient assumed that if he did not *consciously* believe my interpretatons, he simply could not be cured, and persisted in that misconception despite all my protests. On the other hand, the old situation of pseudo-aggression toward his overpowering father was brought to the fore; that was his *modus vivendi*. His first successful attempt to have intercourse was interpreted by him, not as lessening of his neurosis, but as inner danger. Since he had lost his symptom, he felt that he was overwhelmed by me, via interpretation, as he had been overpowered by his father. Therefore he was forced, exactly on the day of his success, to be aggressive toward me in defense, by complaining to my colleague. Since he wanted partly to be punished and partly to be passively overwhelmed, he chose this transparent way of complaining with an easily discernible lie.

All of that explains his actions on that, for him, fateful day but not his hypocrisy. He was confronted with the fact that he really believed my interpretation; this was his way of explaining his success in coitus. But he could not accept anything in common with his father, since that meant, in his unconscious vocabulary, being overwhelmed once more sexually by him. So he chose once more the outlet of ironic pseudo-acceptance in hypocrisy, giving him the following advantages: He proved to his unconscious conscience (Super Ego) that he made fun of his father without depriving himself of the advantage of accepting the interpretation, that is the loss of his symptom of impotence. That procedure, moreover, gave him the alibi that he was not passively submissive but was aggressive toward his father. That man really "ate his cake" and had it too.

We see, therefore, that the patient's hypocrisy was basically associated with his *inner fight between his unconscious Ego and his Super Ego.* Secondarily he *projected* that conflict upon me. *The actual victim of hypocrisy is comparable to the innocent bystander who is killed during a fight between two rival gangster bands.*

Case II. The second clinical example is of a patient from a completely different milieu. He was the son of an old aristocratic, devoutly Catholic, Austrian family. His father was a high dignitary in the court of the emperor and a convinced monarchist. His son, unconsciously to be aggressive toward him and also to prove to himself that he was not passive-submissive but aggressive, had chosen to join the Nazi party. In the last months before the father's death the two had violent scenes; one "Weltanschauung" fought the other without the slightest understanding that they were both fighting, not political and religious, but intra-psychic situations. What made the son especially furious was the fact that his father ridiculed the Nazi party as a "hopeless" one which could never come to power. Since these conflicts took place in the early twenties, at a time when the Nazis in Austria were more of a joke than a real threat, the old man's viewpoint was understandable. A few years later the patient continued his analysis with me, his first attempt with a colleague of mine having been given up after some time. Very soon his anti-semitic tendencies projected upon his previous analyst and myself were used as resistance. I asked him how he could reconcile his Nazi principles with his voluntary acceptance of treatment by Jewish physicians. The patient smiled half-ironically, half-hypocritically and answered: "Well, our main argument against Jews consists of the fact that they are *the* destructive element. Since, in analysis, you have only the laudable purpose of destroying my neurosis, which is independent of my being a Nazi, and the destructive tendency is used for a good purpose, there is no objection to it from the racial viewpoint."

That elegant piece of double talk, worthy of a Goebbels' disciple, had a complicated superstructure. All educational rules were given to the patient directly or indirectly by his tyrannical father, who introduced military discipline into his household. As in the case previously discussed, not only were the educational rules given tyrannically but every attempt at opposition was crushed at the start. What the parents asked for in both cases was *lip service, not inner conviction,* since both believed in education by force. The result was pseudo-acceptance and retaliation by the mortified narcissism in the form of hypocrisy toward the tyrant. That pseudo-acceptance thus became a weapon of the Ego against the stern and sadistic parent.

The following episode shows to what extent the father placed his emphasis on lip service only. The man found out that his wife was unfaithful to him and achieved annulment of their marriage. The two children—the patient was seven at that time—were asked by a servant to see their father in his room. He was seated at a table, before him was his army pistol, having just returned from army maneuvers, in which he took part as a reserve officer. He informed the children that their mother, who was absent allegedly to visit friends in the country, would not return home. They were to forget her completely. He was asking now for "absolute loyalty." Should they not show the allegiance to the degree he expected, he would kill himself with the pistol, which he demonstrated. Needless to say the children promised everything, despite the fact that they could neither understand nor forgive being deprived of their mother, whom they loved.

The patient's conflict in making use of Jewish physicians did not start with my ironic question, but was only culminated by it, since it resuscitated an old pattern of behavior. Of course, for a long time he had feelings of guilt from the "party viewpoint," fearing that he would be evicted from the Nazi organization were the leader to find out his "unpardonable" crime. A masochistic element was involved, especially in his toying with the idea that he could be found out by his party or that I could be indiscreet. On the other hand, the Nazi fanaticism was in his specific case only a superimposed feature, since he had constantly to ward off old "aristocratic remnants" in his personality. Consciously he despised himself for that; in reality he caught himself constantly thinking "in the old way." Austrian aristocrats, as, for instance, his father, were in general not anti-semitic in the Nazi sense. They considered themselves superior to most people—the old emperor, Franz Joseph, for instance, never gave his hand to a non-aristocrat—had a mild irony toward everyone, but did not hate the Jews; indeed, they felt themselves so exalted that they often scoffed at anti-semitism as something "plebian." Amusingly enough, the patient's choice of Jewish physicians was therefore in conformity with his father's ideas, even a

proof of inner submission toward his father, who, were he alive at the
time of his analysis, would not have objected to his choice of physician specifically.⁶ Of course, his choice of a Jewish physician was
a great sin against his newly-acquired Nazi conscience. Since he used
his being a Nazi unconsciously only as a defense mechanism against
his father, he repeated in it, too, the old pseudo-aggression toward
his father. The result was that it was inwardly a pleasure for him
to be aggressive also toward his super-imposed Super Ego. He was
simply incapable of "accepting" a set of principles in a form other
than that of lip service. His sophistic interpretation of Jews as a
"destructive" element used for the good purpose of "destroying"
his neurosis was paradigmatic for that attitude. Here he unconsciously made fun of the Nazi principles, simply repeating the old
irony and defense mechanisms originally directed against his father;
once more, lip service instead of inner acceptance.

Case III. A schizoid student of protestant theology entered
analysis because of—to quote him—"personality difficulties, especially shyness, blushing, and occasional fits of violence toward
my family." He was a scholar, and one of the first in the theological
seminary. A few days after the start of his analysis, the director
of his religious academy called upon me to ask my help in "getting
rid of that impossible and dangerous man for the Church." He explained that he and his colleagues were exasperated at having to
let that pupil pass with high honors because of his scholastic achievements in the theory of theology when they felt reluctant that "such
a hypocrite" should be a preacher and represent the Church one
day. Said the man, "We cannot prove it, but we feel that he is a
hypocrite." I replied that an analyst is hardly the person to solve
such a conflict of church dignitaries such as he and his associates,
and suggested that he speak to the young man himself. "That is
hopeless," answered the professor. "We have explained to him time
and again that his personality does not fit into preaching, but he is
convinced that it does. He never objects directly but is very stub-

---

⁶The patient's choice of Jewish physicians had other unconscious determining factors as well, especially in connection with his castration complex. He
unconsciously identified Jews with castration. On the one hand, he consoled
himself with the fact that others, who were in his opinion "really" castrated,
were even worse off than he. On the other hand, his neurotic fear of Jews was
based on the idea that they would castrate him in revenge for their own
castration; in other words, masochistic elements were involved.

born." We compromised on the basis, that, should analysis be successful, the patient would probably accept the reality factors involved. It was conceivable that he would either change or choose some less compromising theologic work, for instance, that of bibliothecary in a foundation. The latter alternative was, by the way, the way in which the patient solved that part of his conflict, despite the fact that external reasons made continuation of analysis impossible after a few months.

In his conscious attitude the patient was extremely subservient and submissive. He raised objections in an extremely polite, never direct manner. At first glance his religious beliefs gave the impression of sincerity. However, it became clear very soon that he used his calling for neurotic reasons. He received deep satisfaction from the fact that his father did not approve of his decision to become a pastor. He remembered even how he had made his decision to become a pastor at the age of six. One Sunday, during a vacation in the Alps, his father, a very neurotic individual who was a severe and unjust disciplinarian, settled his son's weekly "spanking" account. The man enforced upon his son some complicated and queer point-system, whereby every offense was rated during the week. On Sunday the spanking was executed, the amount of strokes depending upon the points which the father arbitrarily had marked against his son. On this day the man beat the boy mercilessly, without explaining what offense had made him so angry on that specific occasion. He interrupted the punishment only to go to church with the family. There the boy was greatly impressed with the fact that his father, who a few minutes before was so autocratic and cruel, listened with devotion to the pastor. At that moment his decision was made; he wanted to become a minister himself. He could give me no more information; he remembered the facts but could not connect them. On a more conscious level the reason for his decision was to escape his father's tyranny by becoming an authority which stood even above him. What the patient did not even suspect was his deep masochistic desire to be mistreated by his father. In his calling, he wanted, in the more superficial level, to overcome his father by becoming an untouchable authority, respected even by him. In the deeper level, he wanted to use his calling to be mistreated; he felt clearly that he was not wanted by his superiors, and in addition was tortured continually by an obsessional thought which he concealed in analysis for weeks, that one day in delivering his sermon he would use blasphemous language. Expressed differently, he wanted through his choice of profession to cling to his defense mechanism of aggression toward his father in order to fight his inner wish to be overpowered. His superiors were on the right track in questioning his motives. What they did not understand was that his hypocrisy was an unconscious one and not, as they believed, a conscious one.

The patient was confronted with the fact that he misused religion for neurotic reasons and that his inner convictions were not acknowledged by his superiors. Of course, the accusation of conscious hypocrisy was unjustified and he fought it. During analysis the following incident occurred: All of the pupils of the seminary had to deliver "test" sermons in small churches. The young man did so and seemingly succeeded. However, he used such ambiguous language and quoted religious authorities in such a way that some protest came a few days after his test. A few of the members of the congregation wrote to the church, asking whether the quotations were correct. As it happened, they were, but the youth had used them in an objectionable manner, mentioning, for instance, the theological dispute during the arianic heresy as to whether God was "homoousios" or "homoiousios" and elaborating at length over the small difference of an "i," "which was responsible for the death of many persons." Without knowing it consciously, the man was making fun of religion, neurotically projecting upon it his conflicts with his father and his defense mechanisms against him. He could not be convinced that he used unconscious hypocrisy, but accepted the post of a bibliothecary because during his sermon he had been so tortured by blasphemous ideas, which he refused to let me analyze.

Our assumptions culminate thus far in the following formulations: Hypocrisy is a mechanism which acts in the *un*conscious Ego. It expresses the result of an inner conflict and has originally no connection with the outer world victims of the hypocrite. The existence of the pattern of hypocrisy proves that a constant intrapsychic conflict between Ego and inner conscience (Super Ego) does exist. Both the Ego and the Super Ego of the hypocrite are characterized by specific features. The Ego of the hypocrite is weak and on the other hand elastic and cunning, unable to renounce its high-pitched narcissism. The Super Ego of the hypocrite was originally built according to patterns of educators who tyrannically insisted on acceptance of their rules, aggressively enforcing them without regard to whether the acceptance were real or only by lip service. In typical circumstances such as that—weak Ego, aggressive Super Ego— the result is submission of the Ego. In the case of the hypocrite exactly the opposite occurs: The Ego tricks the conscience on the basis of *pseudo-submission.* It accepts, in other words, all demands of the conscience only as a formality, accompanied by constant mockery of the "stupid" introjected educator who takes pseudo-acceptance as a real one and lip service as real conviction. From that *outsmarting of the Super Ego* the Ego derives a great deal of hidden narcissistic pleasure.

In the case of the hypocrite the unusual fact is that under the disguise of a victory of the Super Ego a mockery of the Super Ego takes place. The Super Ego is made fun of in its own house, so to speak, thereby reversing the typical role of Ego and Super Ego. In this case the victory of the Super Ego is only a Pyrrhic victory.

That domestic struggle between the different provinces of the personality is secondarily projected upon innocent victims, since the process leading to hypocrisy has the tendency to be generalized and made external. The outerworld victim of the hypocrite is now aggressively dealt with, whereas in reality the inner Super Ego is being fought. The fight is simply projected upon persons in the outer world.

The distinction between "conscious" and "unconscious" hypocrisy is therefore of little avail, since in conscious hypocrisy only the action against the object of the projection is conscious, not that against the original enemy, the Super Ego; the action against the latter is always repressed.

The problem of projection is of decisive importance in the understanding of the "mechanism of hypocrisy." The aggression is diverted and re-directed *four times,* to be exact. First, it is directed toward the real educator (mother-father). Second, after the educator has been internalized and the inner conscience (Super Ego) built up, it is directed toward the Super Ego. Third, it is projected upon people in the outside world who are directly identified unconsciously with the introjected educators. Fourth, the aggression is generalized and projected upon Tom, Dick and Harry. In that fourth step there is also an additional hidden, unconscious irony discernible: "What kind of shabby Super Ego is it that can be materialized upon every idiot in the world!"

The reason for the use of projection in hypocrisy is not specific for hypocrisy itself. Projection has always the same inner purpose —to diminish inner tension by creation of the fiction that our repressed wishes are not inside but outside, belong, not to us, but to other persons, a fiction which also gives us a better opportunity to fight these forbidden wishes. For example, Freud has described a jealous man of a specific type who wants unconsciously to get rid of his wife and "feels" that *she* is unfaithful to him. This "feeling" gives *him* the advantage of lessened inner tension created by the unconscious, repressed wish (aggression toward her), which is counterbalanced by a Super Ego reproach. By projecting his wish upon his wife, he diminishes his feeling of guilt and even creates an alibi for himself, since he fights constantly against his own inner wish, which is, however, externalized.

The whole problem hinges on the pivotal point of the strength of the inner conscience. The problem of the development and working of the Super Ego is still controversial in psychoanalytic literature. A few facts are clear and more or less accepted. The core of the Super Ego consists of the introjected educational authority (father-mother and their successive representatives), as shown by Freud. What is introjected, however, is not the *real* mother and father but the mother and father *as the child sees them*, a fact stressed especially by English analysts. The child sees them through the spectacles of his own projection. When, therefore, the child projects a great deal of his own aggression on his parents, he later introjects them as cruel and malicious, even though in reality they were mild and benevolent.[7] That tragi-comedy of education explains its relative unimportance in the subsequent neurosis of the child. That does not mean that a neurotic education could not produce artificially a neurotic product; of course it could. It implies, however, that even the most intelligent education cannot always prevent the development of neurosis.

We have furthermore to distinguish between an "assimilated" and a "non-assimilated" Super Ego. Normally the inner conscience

[7]The whole problem is complicated by the introduction of Freud's Eros—Thanatos theory. See my paper "Transference and Love," in collaboration with Jekels, Imago, 1934, and my contribution to the "Symposium on the Theory of Therapeutic Results," Int. Psychoan. Convention in Marienbad, 1936, published in Internat. J. Psycho Analysis, London, 1937.

becomes a part of our own personality; it is more or less assimilated. In the case of certain neurotics—as, for instance, hypocrites— exactly the opposite happens. The introjected Super Ego is treated constantly by the Ego as an inner enemy, is fought and made fun of. As long as he lives the hypocrite repeats his fight against the educator, who has been first introjected and then projected. The disguise of mistaken identity is therefore perfect. There is a *constant tendency to show up the projected Super Ego as mean, base, and aggressive.* Thus, the queer phenomenon of the hypocrite's "good conscience" is explainable. First, since the hypocrite always has a feeling comparable to that of a patriotic Frenchman toward the Nazi invaders of his homeland, he has the conviction of always being right and justified in his actions. Second, he seems so undisturbed in his possession of a "good conscience" since *he expects unconsciously to be punished.* He is a perpetual collector of ill will. Third, he is so proud to have proven that he is not passive but aggressive that his successful defense mechanism gives him the feeling of being right, since his inner passivity is the greatest crime of which he accuses himself.

That constant tendency to fight the inner enemy, the Super Ego, in its outerworld projection explains furthermore why the hypocrite gives the impression of being extremely "aggressive." Unconsciously he is not; indeed, he is just the opposite. His continual fight against the victims of his projections shows only—on a different battlefield— how helpless he is without his perpetual device, the "mechanism of hypocrisy." The old saying, "The lady doth protest too much," is applicable here. The hypocrite is *inwardly a very passive person* who fights desperately to disguise his passivity.

The term "typology" must be taken with a grain of salt as far as hypocrites are concerned. There is, as my clinical experience has taught me, only *one* type of hypocrite with *one* mechanism as *vis a tergo.* But the technique of provocation varies. With that fact in mind, we may describe some of these techniques.

Another warning is necessary. Examples taken from history, *belles lettres,* and casual experience always give the impression at first glance that the hypocrite is very "aggressive." That impression is, as has been explained, erroneous; it takes the defense mechanism at face value, confusing the defense with the drive behind it. History and literature record, furthermore, only the "successful" examples, without mentioning the self-provoked punishment that ensues. That eclectic tendency reminds one of the technique of superstitious persons. They record the chance "successes" of their superstitious guesses and repress the failures.

Since none of the figures in literary and historic examples can be analyzed (they are products of imagination or dead, and cannot even protest), we can only assume by comparing them to clinically accessible people that the same mechanism applies for them too. True, it cannot be proven in a specific case. We can either dismiss these examples as meaningless or make use of them, realizing these limitations, for one purpose only: to learn a few tricks of their *external* technique. I propose to do the latter.

Having been interested in the problem of hypocrisy for a long time, I collected a great variety of types, fifty-one to be exact. I do not believe that there is any reason to mention all of these; on the contrary, a small selection is sufficient.

Hypocrisy in the form of a reciprocal compliment as trap. As a first example I shall use one of the classical hypocrites of history, Fouché. Fouché, the traitor on a grand scale of the nineteenth century, was police chief under Napoleon, but "served" *and* betrayed all French governments from the beginning of the French Revolution until the restoration of the Bourbons. Here is an instance of his technique: After Napoleon's second abdication in 1815 the French Chamber of Deputies elected a provisional government consisting of five men. Carnot received the highest number of votes, 324; Fouché received only 293. Carnot was clearly chosen to preside over that government. At the first meeting of the Council Carnot automatically took the president's seat. Fouché, however, proposed, as if mentioning an obvious procedure, that the Council should *constitute* itself. "What do you mean by that?" asked Carnot in surprise. "Well," answered Fouché innocently, "to elect a secretary and president." And with hypocritical self-denial he added, "Of course, I give my vote to *you* as president of the Council." Carnot did not see the trap and answered politely: "And I give *you* my vote." But two of the five members being "in" with Fouché, he received three votes and Carnot two, and before Carnot understood what had happened to him, Fouché was sitting in the president's chair.

By chance we know some details about Fouché which show us the nature of his neurosis. Typical is an episode of his life in which he provoked Napoleon to such a degree that he was dismissed as cabinet member. But after his dismissal Fouché refused to deliver to Napoleon the latter's confidential notes, thus infuriating and frightening the emperor. Fouché fled through half of Europe, attempted to escape to America, became seasick on the ship he had hired (he was the son of sailors!), returned, and capitulated. History books describe that episode as a "nervous breakdown," whereas it represents a typical example of acted castration fear under a pseudo-aggressive facade.[8] Other signs of that fear may be found in Fouché's spying on his superiors; as long as he did not know all of the details of the private lives of others, he felt insecure.[9] The power he acquired in that manner had, in addition to external advantages, the internal one of pacifying his fear of the little boy who is a Peeping Tom. Thus, we find, for instance, that Napoleon's first wife and his permanent secretary were Fouché's well-paid spies.

Hypocrisy in the disguise of help. Dr. Lecher, the well-known physicist, once asked a nineteen year old female medical student during an oral examination to describe the medical fever thermometer. She described it correctly, but added that there were marks also for temperature below zero. The professor nodded approvingly, as if to encourage her, and asked innocently: "What purpose do the marks below zero serve?" "To measure the temperature of dead bodies," was the prompt answer.

Hypocrisy in obeying. Napoleon treated his secretary of state, Talleyrand, contemptuously, never being able to forget that his cabinet member was of aristocratic descent while he himself was a parvenu. Once, so reports F. Blei in his biography of Talleyrand, the emperor asked his cabinet member for a glass of lemonade at a party in Warsaw. Talleyrand obeyed, but placed a napkin under his arm to imitate a waiter and served "his" emperor the lemonade. Talleyrand's despising attitude[10] was so noticeable that Countess

[8] I have had no actual experience in analysing diplomats. I can therefore only guess that diplomats of the old school, who excel in hypocrisy and even make hypocrisy their life business, have a psychic structure similar to that of hypocrites in general. The few details known about their private lives seem to confirm this assumption.

[9] Details of his life can be gathered in Stefan Zweig's "Fouché" and my attempt to interpret that book in "Biography makes concessions to psychoanalysis: one step forward—two steps backward," Psychoanal. Bewegung, 1933.

[10] The intrapsychic reasons which made it possible for Talleyrand to assume this attitude are discussed in my book, "Talleyrand—Napoleon—Stendhal—Grabbe," Psych. Verlag, 1935.

Potocka, who was present on that occasion, mentioned the incident specifically as characteristic of the relations between the two men.

Hypocrisy using the technique of "jokes of overbidding." The technique of a "joke of overbidding" reduces a statement to absurdity by hypocritically accepting it and offering further, exaggerated "proof" of it. For instance: Two newcomers in New York exchange impressions on the amazing tempo of American life. "Yesterday," says the first, "I saw how they build these skyscrapers. In a few hours they finished one hundred stories." "Well," answered the second, "that is nothing. A man committed suicide in that building, and during the fall from the hundredth floor, he saw on the second floor a man reading a newspaper account of his suicide."

Scientific hypocrisy. In totalitarian countries science is treated in the same fashion as every free opinion in general; it cannot be expressed, or, even worse, must be adapted to the specific use of the specific dictator. One has to think only of the "scientists" who supplied the Nazis with their "scientific" racial theories. One might say, varying the word of the Russian satirist, Saltykov: *"That* brand of 'science' is the adaptation to every dirty trick."

Hypocrisy in the disguise of optimistic belief in human nature. An old story reports of a "wonder" rabbi who visited a small Chassidic community. The believers decided to honor the famous man by giving him a barrel of wine. The elders prescribed that every member of the community should provide two pints of the finest wine *in natura.* The bottles received were placed into the big barrel, which was eventually filled—with water. Every believer trusted his neighbors to deliver *real* wine, not believing that they would be so cheap as to cheat the holy man.

"Altruistic" hypocrisy. I asked a patient who entered analysis because of agoraphobia whether he had any complaints regarding his sex life. "Not at all," answered the man convincingly. Asked to elaborate on his statement, he divulged that he had not touched his wife for many years. "My wife earns our living since I cannot leave the house because of my street fear. When she comes home I simply don't have the heart to make her undergo the strain of intercourse since the poor darling is so tired . . . ."

There are connections between "rationalizations" and hypocrisy. Undoubtedly it was more agreeable for the patient to believe in his goodness of heart than to acknowledge the bitter fact of his impotence.

Hypocrisy in the disguise of faked naiveté. Casanova mentions in his memoirs that someone objected to his assuming the title of "Chevalier de Seingault." Without hesitation the famous cheater replied that the twenty-four letters of the alphabet were free and that he had chosen with good taste, since his were not better nor worse than others.

Hypocrisy on the death bed. In this category belong promises of being mentioned in the will, the falseness of which can be proven after death of the bestower, threats of non-existing memoirs, etc. A good example is the following: In the memoirs of Alexander Dumas (vol. V, p. 305) there is to be found a description of the last hours of the former chief of the French Directoire, Paul Barras. Barras was chief of the French government after the execution of Robespierre until Napoleon's coup d'état in 1799. During that time he carried on a compromising correspondence with the Bourbons. After Napoleon's abdication in 1815 the dynasty of the Bourbons was re-established, and the king and his advisors, and later the king's brother, wanted to obtain the correspondence, in vain. On his deathbed Barras was justifiably worried that after his death his papers would be confiscated. To prevent this, he deposited the letters in question with friends. To fool the king, he purchased thirty or forty very pompous briefcases and dwelt upon the idea that these should be opened in a session of the king's most confidential advisors. "Do you know what they shall find there?" Barras asked his friend Cabarus. "The bills of my laundry woman for the last thirty-five years . . . . and they will have to decipher a great deal, since I have had since the ninth day of Thermidor (Robespierre's execution) a great deal of dirty linen to wash . . . ." "And Barras," adds Dumas, "laughed so heartily about his pun that he succumbed to a new attack. In the evening he was dead, as he had predicted."

Hypocrisy with the alibi of loyalty. Barras mentions in his memoirs that Robespierre was feared to such a degree that a member of the French Revolutionary Convention, being by chance watched by the dictator at a moment in which he meditatively supported his head on his hand immediately withdrew his hand, giving an excuse, "He could believe otherwise, I think about something."

In a new Russian satiric novel, "Fischbein Conducts War," a Soviet clerk, previously a bourgeois merchant, is described early in 1919 as not knowing where to turn, since it is not clear whether the Bolshevists will hold Moscow or the counter-revolutionists will be capable of occupying the metropolis. One evening Fischbein comes home and shows his wife an official document strongly warning him to abstain from "counter-revolutionary propaganda in the office." His wife is desperate, since such a warning is usually the first step to the firing squad of the Tscheka. Fischbein, however, laughs hypocritically; he himself has swindled the document in order to have an alibi should the white army enter Moscow.

In another new Russian satire, Katajev's "Defraudants," the main character comes to a small Soviet village. There he finds that many places and streets are named for a local hero, Djeduschin. The only remarkable feature about this is that the nameplates also have a strip of cardboard attached changing the name, for instance, from "Square of the Comrade Djeduschin" to "Square of ex-Comrade Djeduschin." The visitor asks for an explanation. He learns that Djeduschin was a local boy who had made good. Unfortunately, he later had stolen money, belonging to the Soviet, so that he was placed in jail. Since, however, the change of all of the plates would involve too much expense, the Soviet decided simply to put the word "previous" before his title and leave all as it was . . . .

Hypocrisy using seemingly "objective" facts as excuse. A typical example of this is the business of criminal lawyers of a certain type who are expected to be shrewd rather than in love with the truth. The best satire on this type of lawyer is found in W. Rode's "The A.B.C. for Defendants." One story in this, obviously invented for ironic purposes, is of a well-to-do man in a European capital who is surprised with his "girl friend" and a seven year old child in a morally objectionable situation. A famous lawyer takes the case and brings forward the following defense: It is simply ridiculous to assume that his clients were doing something immoral with the child. True, they were caught when the child was fully undressed. But the reason is simple. Both defendants are admirers of the science of eugenics and both are superstitious. The financier's friend, whom he wants to marry, of course, is pregnant, and they were making use of the superstitious tradition that the sight of a healthy body might help to produce a similar one.

Hypocrisy after the shock-experience of loss of confidence. A patient, an hysteric woman, remembered a symptom which started in her fifth year and persisted for many years afterward. She was puritanically educated, and her question regarding the sex relations of

dogs which she had observed was sharply answered by the objection
that she simply imagined things. A few months later she observed by
chance an act of sexual intercourse between a maid and her husband.
She repressed this experience but developed the symptom of answer-
ing always the opposite of what was obviously expected. Confronted
with facts, she would laugh obstinately and reply that her meaning
was not the one interpreted. She entered analysis because of frigidity
of the hysteric type[11] and showed in addition many symptoms and
signs of a psychopathic personality. She was a pathologic liar, and
reacted to disagreeable facts which contradicted her lies with the
ironic excuse, "All truth is uncertain."

Hypocrisy justified by a "set of inner principles." The classical
example of this form of hypocrisy is found in Moliére's "Tartuffe."
"There are ways," Tartuffe proclaims, "of enlarging one's own conscience" and "He who sins in secrecy does not sin at all." It is obvious
that we deal here with rationalizations which obscure the hidden conflict. Tartuffe's device is reminiscent of the "mechanism of the cynic"
described by me elsewhere.[12]

I wonder why, until now, no satiric writer has brought together
the three most outstanding literary examples of hypocrites: Moliére's
Tartuffe in the play of that name, Shakespeare's Gloucester in "Richard III," and Dostoevski's Foma Fomitsch in "The Farm Stepantschi-
kovo." These three gentlemen could give some good advice—on
rationalizations of their hidden, unconscious conflicts.

Looking over our secondary or auxiliary material concerning
the typology of hypocrites, we find that all of the examples give at
first glance the impression of—jokes. That proves, first, that there
is some similarity between the results of the "mechanism of hypocrisy" and wit. Both contain aggression toward someone else, but
that in wit[13] seems more original, while that in hypocrisy represents

[11]See Hitchmann and Bergler, "Frigidity in Women," Nerv. Ment. Dis.
Monograph Series No. 60, New York. 1936.
[12]"The Psychology of the Cynic," Psychoanal. Bewegung, 1933.
[13]Literature Freud, "Wit and Its Relation to the Unconscious" (translated by
A. A. Brill), "The Basic Writings of S. Freud," Modern Library, N. Y., 1938;
Freud, "Humor," Imago, 1928; Brill, "Freud's Theory of Wit," J. Abnorm. and
Social Psychol., 1911; Brill, "The Mechanisms of Wit and Humor in Normal and
Psychopathologic States," Psychiat. Quart. 1940; Hitschmann, "The Psychology
of the Jewish Joke," Psychoanal. Bewegung, 1930; Reik, "Nechdenliche Heiterkeit," Internat. Psychoanal. Verl., 1933, and "Lust und Leid im Witz," Psycho-
anal. Verl., 1929; Dooley, L., "A Note on Humor," Psychoanalyt. Rev., 1934;
Bergler, "A Clinical Contribution to the Psychogenesis of Humor," Psychoanalyt. Rev., 1937.

only a defense mechanism. The objection that something that looks like a joke cannot be used for scientific purposes, since science is "serious," boils down to a misunderstanding of the psychology of wit. Every manifestation of wit contains a deep and complicated unconscious mechanism; only the facade is brilliant, as Freud has conclusively shown in his book on wit. Let us also not forget what the humorist, W. Raabe, once said: "Laughter is one of the most serious things in this world."

C. Self-Derision[14]

In discussing this problem we meet with a terminologic difficulty. The English term "humor" comprises both "wit" and "irony directed against one's self." The latter is called in other languages— humor. To avoid this misunderstanding, let us differentiate between wit and self-derision.

The problem of *wit* was solved in an admirable fashion by Freud in 1905, in his book, "The Wit and Its Relation to the Unconscious." Freud proved that we are laughing when another person expresses *our own* repressed tendencies; since the other person takes the responsibility our own psychic energy holding down the repressed material becomes, for a few seconds, superfluous. That freed "counter-cathexis" is transformed into laughter.

Freud finds that "what is fine about self-derision is the triumph of narcissism, the Ego's victorious assertion of its own invulnerability. It refuses to be hurt by the arrows of reality or to be compelled to suffer. It insists that it is impervious to wounds dealt by the outside world, in fact, that these are merely occasions for affording it pleasure. This last trait is a fundamental characteristic of humor."[15] In this connection, Freud characterizes the relationship between the Ego and the Super Ego of the humorist as follows: The humorist displaces large quantities of cathexis from his Ego to his Super Ego, resulting in a hypercathexis of the latter. The Super Ego, otherwise the "stern master," allows the Ego a slight but intense gain in pleasure in accordance with the motto: "Look here! This is all that this seemingly dangerous world amounts to. Child's play, the very thing to jest about!" The Super Ego, in humor, "speaks kindly words of comfort to the intimidated Ego," and tries to "comfort

[14]First published in Psychoanalyt. Rev., 1937.
[15]"Humor," Gesammelte Schriften, XI, 404.

the Ego, and protect it from suffering." The dynamic conception of the displacement of large quantities of cathexis from the Ego to the Super Ego is a completion of the psychoeconomic aspect of humor described by Freud in 1905, which consists in a saving in expenditure of effect. There are many types of humor, in accordance with the nature of the effect which is saved in humor: sympathy, pain, pathos, fright, horror, disgust, etc.

Anna Freud has stated the fact that a humorous mood may develop in children after they have overcome the fear of punishment. The lecture given by Anna Freud at the Oxford convention has not been published. Her own report[16] says: "The very same elements which in other cases may be demonstrated in the structure of the infantile animal phobia have been used, in the two cases reported, in the construction of an animal fantasy which compensates the fear of the father, and converts it into the opposite. The same mechanism may also be found in dreams, children's stories, and fairy tales."

Alfred von Winterstein[17] has called attention to the strange fact that the Super Ego, "otherwise a stern master," is ascribed by Freud in humor a kindly, comforting attitude toward the Ego. Winterstein attempts to make this easier of comprehension in that he assumes a pronounced mother-section of the Super Ego in the humorist. The characteristic aggression peculiar to the father-section of the Super Ego appears here only as a devaluating view of the matter at hand, not taking it seriously. Winterstein is of the opinion that humor has its origin in Abraham's first oral (sucking) stage. The question as to why the Ego desires to save expenditure of effect is answered by Winterstein as follows: "On account of fear of the consequences of the instinctual demands of the Id, for behind the spared expenditure of effect stand the instinctual drives. These are in part of a sadistic nature (for example, anger, contempt, indignation), in part, masochistic (sympathy, pathos, pain, fright, disgust). In both cases, the external danger to the threatened narcissistic masculinity (humor is a masculine characteristic) in the same. The humorist, however, does not repress the painful conceptual content attached to the effect, but, according to Freud, he is able to deprive the intended release of pain of its energy, because of his peculiar constitution, and to

---

[16] "An Example of Children's Animal-phobia," Internat. Ztschr. f. Psychoanal. 1929, p. 518.
[17] In his article, "Observations on the Problem of Humor," Psychoanalyt. Bewegung, 1932.

displace this energy, to the Super Ego. Here we have an act of defense."

Theodor Reik[18] defines humor as an "act of mercy of the Super Ego," which statement he then limits, however, as follows: We "know too little as yet about the nature of the Super Ego." Reik calls attention to a special case of humor, in which narcissism is not threatened from without, as in Freud's example of the grim humorist at the gallows, but by dangers from within, by guilt. He gives as a typical example the words of a patient with an obsessional neurosis: "How I have tortured myself! And all because I have killed a few people. When you think of the World War, that is nothing at all!"

Franz Alexander[19] draws a parallel between the "Spartan attitude" and humor: "Except that in humor the Super Ego's reflective, kindly characteristics are manifested, whereas in the Spartan attitude, the disciplinary nature of the Super Ego appears. Although the two procedures demonstrate a similar principle formally and as to topic and dynamic, their mental content is as opposite as the poles. The Spartan mentality gives an impression of extreme dryness and lack of humor, its content is the direct opposite of humor. Moreover, it originates from an opposite situation. Whereas, in humor, one finds a way to comfort one's self in a disgreeable situation. By means of humor, the individual pretends a superiority in the situation which is really not present, whereas the Spartan-Puritan attitude exhibits a superiority completely unnecessary in the situation. The tourist who climbs up a mountain, panting and heavy-laden, alongside the funicular, behaves as though he were in a wilderness. Both situations are paradoxical, and unsuited to the situation. In the one case, the seriousness of the situation is underestimated; in the other, the situation is taken more seriously than necessary. Humor (self-derision) allows the individual to stand in the shadow of the gallows and laugh, whereas here, alarm is raised to no purpose. In humor (self-derision), the life principle triumphs in spite of the desperate situation; it will not be downed, and overcompensates the external danger, whereas in the Spartan reaction, the individual is deceived by a danger which is not present at all.

[18]"Humor and Mercy," in the collection, "Nachdenkliche Heiterkeit," page 115, International. Psychoanalyt., Verlag, 1933.
[19]"Need of Punishment and Death Tendencies," Internat. Ztschr. f. Psychoanal., 1929, page 237.

Here, the death principle puts in an appearance, although merely in playful form."

Anny Angel[20] finds a relationship between optimism and humor. "Whereas in humor, the Super Ego is only able to assume a mild, comforting attitude for a few seconds at a time, and thus abandon itself to a happy illusion, with genuine optimism, the Super Ego appears to be able to preserve this comforting attitude toward the Ego constantly."

Lucile Dooley is the first to attempt to prove the principle set forth by Freud by means of clinical material.[21] She describes a patient who produced the following fantasy during the third year of treatment, when the reliving of the suffering and disappointments of the oedipal phase, and of her masculine desires, in the transference had reached particular intensity: "There is a tiny girl. It depends on how she is treated whether she lives and grows up or whether the life is crushed out of her. She is in my stomach, but sometimes she gets out and runs all over the place. I feel like laughing because she is so tiny. I laugh and am amused when I'm most depressed." Dooley believes that the patient is describing her immature Ego and its escape from pain. She considers the fact of great importance that these "proto-humorous" fantasies developed only when the patient was dealing with the experiences of the oedipal phase, from which the Super Ego originally developed. "This is of great importance because only the Super Ego is capable of detachment from the real situation, and of giving the Ego the assurance that external dangers cannot harm it." "Irony," according to Dooley, "is the forerunner of humor, has an admixture of sadism, and is mediated by the more primitive and sadistic Super Ego." The difference between wit and humor (self-derision) also lies in the open sadism of wit. Humor (self-derision) is never sadistic, it serves to fend off suffering. Dooley's patient had masochistic fantasies, of being an ant and a fly, further, desires to be devoured and destroyed by the father. From the masochism of her patient, she deduces that there is a special relationship between humor (self-derision) and masochism, which may correspond to that between wit and sadism. In Dooley's article, a theory of Wälder's which he communicated to her orally, is cited. In accordance with this, humor (self-derision) can develop only when

[20]A Few Remarks on Optimism, Internat. Ztschr. f. Psychoanalyt., 1934, page 199.
[21]"A Note on Humor," Psychoanalyt. Rev., 1934, No. 1.

the conflicts of childhood have not been too severe, and the Super Ego developed is not too strict.

Ernst Kris[22] devoted a few remarks to humor (self-derision) which have to do with its peculiar position: "It alone of all the phenomena of the kingdom of the comic also borders on the uplifting. Not only because it does not stand on the ground of the ambivalent— it is post-ambivalent, and the contribution of the Super Ego to the comic—but above all because humor (self-derision), complete in one person, does not need a partner for increased enjoyment. That it is the property of the mental household of the individual may be the reason for its approach to the uplifting. It appears to be the form of the comic which the individual develops latest in the course of his life, is considered a sign of spiritual maturity, and is less bounded by the narrow limits of a particular society and time than other forms of the comic. In this, it is nearer the uplifting." Kris attempts to define the special position of humor more exactly by calling attention to two lines of thought: "The saying of the criminal on the way to the gallows, 'This is a good beginning for the week'—one of Freud's fundamental examples—may *also* be considered as irony directed against himself. One is tempted to believe that humor (self-derision) also may have the character of tipping, especially when the irony of grim humor (self-derision) dominates the effect. Another difference between humor and other related effects is that humor (self-derision) has no special technique, no special forms of speech. This seems to accord well with the fact that it is seldom met with alone,[23] usually in alloy, as a contribution to or shading of some other comic effect."

The attitude which Freud assumes the Super Ego to take in humor (self-derision)—mercy instead of punishment—brings in its train a series of problems which the psychoanalytic authors quoted

---

[22]"On the Psychology of the Caricature," Imago, 1934, page 465.

[23]This assertion is not absolutely true as a generalization, as humor (self-derision) frequently appears without admixture. May I call the following example to mind: In J. Popper Lynkeus' "Philosophie des Strafrechts," there is a section where the author speaks of the cruelty of Chinese justice, and its ineffectiveness in arousing fear: "There are criminals who endure the greatest torture not only with equanimity, but even with humor (self-derision). And a case is described, for example, where a criminal who was to be hanged was carried into the prison yard in a basket by four guards. He was carried because his arms and legs had been hacked off. And in this situation he called laughingly to the populace present: 'I never thought that a poor devil like me would be carried by four lackeys.'" (page 55)

above have so far avoided in part. They have either shrugged their shoulders and admitted our slight knowledge of this institution ("We know too little as yet of the nature of the Super Ego—hardly more than of the nature of God himself—to recognize when and why each an act of mercy comes about." Reik), or they have undertaken an explanation which cannot be verified clinically, such as Winterstein's hypothetic assumption of the more pronounced mother-identification in the Super Ego of the humorist. Freud himself, in his article on humor (self-derision), speaks these modest words:

"If it is really the Super Ego which, in humor (self-derision), speaks such kindly words of comfort to the intimidated Ego, *this teaches us that we still have very much to learn about the nature of that institution.*"[*]

In his "New Introductory Lectures on Psychoanalysis," which appeared after publication of the article on humor (self-derision), we find the following:

"The Super Ego seems to have made a *one-sided selection* and to have chosen only the *harshness and severity* of the parents, their preventive and punitive functions, while their loving care is not taken up and continued by it."

The lofty conception of Freud's work on humor (self-derision) has caused all the later workers in the field of humor to stare fascinated at one point: at the conciliatory and comforting in the production of the humorous effect. Thus, several other partial problems of humor, *which have not received consideration so far*, are neglected. In my opinion, in humor (self-derision), the process is as follows:

Act 1. The Super Ego of the humorist has brought about *aggressively*, or helped to bring about, a desperate situation for the Ego (for example, toleration of neurotic wishes at the price of punishment, whose executor is the outer world).

Act 2. The masochistic Ego turns to the Super Ego in a sort of prayer for help and love, begging at least to be loved by the Super Ego after punishment, and at the price of it.

Act 3. The answer of the Super Ego is to scorn the Ego and undertake *aggression* against it, under the mask of comfort.

[*]The italicizing in this and the other citations is mine.

Act 4. Driven to desperation, the disappointed Ego now undertakes
aggressions itself, against the Super Ego (more exactly,
against the Ego-Ideal section of the Super Ego[25]), relapses
into primary narcissism, deceives itself as to the reality for
a few seconds in a kind of negative hallucination, and enjoys itself in a sort of intoxication.

Let us start with the apparent but insufficiently considered fact
that *humor (self-derision) always presupposes an unhappy situation,
humiliating to the Ego.* The so-called grim humor of the criminal
who was led to the gallows on Monday, and who called out, "Well,
this is a good beginning for the week," presupposes that he was
condemned to death. We are therefore rather taken aback when we
hear of the "kindness" of the Super Ego of the humorist, the same
Super Ego which brought the Ego into this situation of conflict.[26]

In "Transference and Love," Jekels and I attempted to separate
the insufficiently differentiated portions of the Super Ego more
clearly, making use of the Eros-Thanatos theory. We came to the
result, that both portions of the same, *Ego Ideal* ("Thou shalt") and
Daimonion ("Thou shalt not") are various as to instinctual psychology and genesis.

One of the defense techniques of the threatened Ego consists in
aggression against the Ego Ideal, which has become irksome. As
manifestations of this technique of attack, we have named the following: mania, wit, comedy (Jekels), hypocrisy (myself).

Humor (self-derision) is also to be counted among the methods
of attack of the Ego against the Ego Ideal. Its purpose is to wrest
the instrument from the Daimonion with which it tortures the Ego,
and to bind the indifferent energy of the Ego Ideal to itself. This
more or less unsuccessful attempt on the part of humor (self-derision) is made in a very exceptional manner:

This exceptional manner consists of the four acts referred to pre-

---

[25] This last portion as to the threefold direction of the aggression in humor
(self-derision) appears in my article in collaboration with Jekels, "Transference
and Love," Imago, 1934, No. 1

[26] The objection may be made that the Super Ego is not responsible in all
cases for the unfortunate situation of the Ego, for example, in organic disease.
This tempting looking objection is of no consequence, as experience teaches us
that the Ego unconsciously considers every misfortune as punishment from the
Super Ego. This is shown by the question of almost all individuals in misfortune as to what the misdeed is for which they are being punished, a question
which indicates that the Ego is always ready to accept reproach.

viously, from which results the *tragi-comic effect of humor (self-derision)*.

The question as to the *origin of the instinctual energy of the aggression of the Ego against the Ego Ideal* (4th act) may be answered as follows: The Ego courts the Super Ego in vain, in spite of hypercathexis of the Ego Ideal. On the contrary, the Daimonion succeeds in getting possession of the indifferent energy of the Ego Ideal, and it becomes aggressive against the Ego, as the latter seeks for love— as described above. This, however, frees a certain amount of instinctual energy in the humiliated Ego, which the Ego uses in tame, masochistic aggression against the Ego Ideal. This is illustrated by the following two clinical examples:

Example I: A frigid woman patient with nymphomanic tendencies, who lived out prostitute fantasies as posthumous revenge against the father.[27] She was completely disinterested doing coitus, and she had not the slightest genital gland secretion, a fact which disturbed her particularly in the advanced stages of the analysis. During this temporary stage, the patient had a peculiar double relationship to the sperm of the man: on the one hand, she was offended if the man did not ejaculate vaginally, as she interpreted the ejaculation unconsciously as castration of the man. On the other hand, she had an unconquerable fear of impregnation. This fear was many faceted and had to a great extent a very deep oral foundation: Sperm, among other things, was identified with the milk from the breast of the mother (=penis), and the conception of being poisoned or injured was built up out of her own projected aggression. In the transference, the patient repeated in this phase the relationship to the fancied wicked, withholding, phallic mother. The patient, for example, once expressed the idea that I grudged her the glandular secretion, wanted to spoil all her sexual pleasure, etc., although she knew herself that the physician desired to cure her frigidity by means of analysis. Then the following mishap occurred: Her lover withdrew too late, during intended coitus interruptus, and ejaculated vaginally, against his will. The patient reacted in bed with an outburst of anger and desperation, reproached the man with having "besmirched her honor," and began to weep hysterically. This was interrupted only by the constantly repeated phrase, "Oh, I hope nothing happens."

---

[27]The case is described in, "Frigidity in Women," Nerv. Ment. Dis. Publ. Comp., 1936.

This hysterical crying spell, which became more and more violent, was suddenly succeeded by a laughing spasm, as the following thought occurred to her: "Well, anyway, *I* have had an ejaculation." In spite of the fact that the patient knew intellectually that she was identifying herself with the man in this ("*I* have had an ejaculation"), and was playing a joke on her malady in other layers, in a certain sense, she got around the forbidding mother and "got something" in spite of being forbidden—she had a short but intense feeling of well-being. As her lover, delighted that the patient was no longer in such despair, began to minimize the danger of possible pregnancy, the patient had another outburst of anger—more to "save her face" than anything else—and suddenly declared again that the man had "besmirched her honor" and that a woman like her had no honor, anyway. As her lover protested violently, the quarrel raged on for a time, and was terminated by a spasm of laughing from the patient, who suddenly recalled a saying of Lichtenberg's: "It is a fine kind of honor women have, that lies only half an inch from the rectum."

In the analysis, first a purely descriptive differentiation was demonstrated between the intense feeling of well-being after the occurrence *of the humorous idea* ("*Well, I had an ejaculation, anyway*") and in the form of the quotation from Lichtenberg. This latter was found to be cynicism, and showed all the stigmata of the "mechanism of cynicism" as I have described them.

Let us inquire, first of all, whether the thought, "Well, anyway, I had an ejaculation," really bears the external signs of humor (self-derision). The thought is humorous for the following reasons: the external situation dangerous to the Ego is present (danger of pregnancy, along with extreme neurotic fear of the same), and also the narcissistic attempt of the Ego not to be downed by this real danger, as is proved by the short intensive feeling of well-being after the thought quoted above occurred to her. Thirdly, this thought is directed only to the patient herself, it has no need of a listener.

Let us attempt to trace through the *four acts of tragi-comedy of humor (self-derision)* as enumerated above as characteristic of the humorous effect:

Act 1. The Super Ego allowed the patient to be so "incautious" as to allow the man coitus interruptus, although she usually insisted on the use of preventive measures. In other words, the Super Ego allowed a neurotic action (oral, anal, and phallic desires in the retention of the man's ejaculation), on condition of the expected punishment, pregnancy, or the fear of the same.

Act 2. The masochistic Ego turns to the Super Ego again, in spite of this unfortunate affair, with the prayer, "Oh, I hope nothing happens." This pious wish addressed to the Super Ego obviously corresponds to the formula, "Love me, spare me, and comfort me."

Act 3. But in spite of this prayer, the patient cannot quiet down for a long time, because—this portion is of course not conscious—she is given an aggressive answer by the Super Ego, something as follows: "But you wanted it yourself."

Act 4. Forsaken by the Super Ego, and the object of aggression, the Ego, hard pressed, resorts to aggression itself, turns the tables, and ridicules the Super Ego, in that it outwits the wicked, forbidding mother, and declared defiantly that it has gotten its wish to "receive something" in spite of being forbidden. Negative hallucination of the danger solves the problem of the latter for a few seconds, and *this aggression of the Ego against the Super Ego manifests itself in an intense feeling of pleasure.*

It is unnecessary to state that the entire process, described here as though under the microscope, takes place *unconsciously*. Only the initial feeling of despair and the terminal feeling of consolation are conscious. A connecting phrase, "Oh, I hope nothing happens," also remains conscious but without making the sense of the process clear.

Example II. An effeminate, unconsciously passive male patient, in analysis on account of impotence, had a slight flat foot. The patient declared that he had "violent pains," although the orthopedic findings were in extreme contrast to the subjective complaints. There was well grounded suspicion—and the patient's dreams proved it very definitely—that a displacement from the penis to the foot had taken place. But the patient had little understanding for this psychic hyperevaluation of his foot complaints, although he repeated the following ironic refrain again and again: "I will have my feet cut off." In the transference, he repeated the aggressive and likewise passive relationship to the father in accordance with the formula: I will forego the penis as punishment for my desire for the mother, and my aggression against the father, but, father, you must love me as you loved my mother. The dissatisfaction which arose from this unconsciously desired situation, in the analysis, appeared as strong aggression against the analyst. In this situation, he began to discuss his foot complaints once again, in a whiny tone, and suddenly, after a short silence (this short silence is typical of the *forum internum* to which the humorist appeals), he said in a gay tone, "I will have my feet cut off, and then have my old nurse push me through the streets in a carriage, and say, like Caesar, 'The whole world lies at my feet.' "[28] All the requirements for humor are here present: a distressing inner situation, narcissistic unconcern in rising above this, production of humor (self-derision) for himself as an audience. The conflictuous situation, here, is not the harmless foot complaint, but the great disappointment arising from repeated attempts to win the love of the father (the analyst) in the analysis. Not even the sacrifice of the fancied renunciation of the penis was great enough to make the father love the child.

Let us attempt to reconstruct the four stages of the humorous effect in this example also:

Act 1. The Super Ego of the patient compelled the renunciation of the penis at the time by means of unconscious feelings of guilt, and forced it into the feminine position. Here, again, it is in large part the direct cause of the patient's misfortune, by allowing the passive repressed desires, unsuited to reality, to emerge, under the condition of the illness (punishment).

Act 2. The masochistic Ego of the patient now turns for love to the Super Ego, and brings attention to its sacrifice of masculinity.

Act 3. As answer, the Ego does not get love, but new aggressions and reproaches, in that the Super Ego holds up his passive desires to the patient, and the Ego Ideal of masculinity as the model, in reproach.[29]

[28] I was very much interested in whether the patient was acquainted with a similar saying of H. Heine's, whether his remark was original or a plagiarism. I was able to determine with considerable certainty that he had never heard the following quotation from A. Stodtmann's "Heine's Leben und Werke": "In the morning, Heine (who was a cripple) usually had a bath, when his condition allowed. His nurse, a strong mulatto woman, lifted him from his 'mattress grave'—and carried him in her arms like a child to the bathtub. 'Just see the way I am carried around on people's shoulders in Paris!' he called with grim humor (self-derision) to a friend who saw him carried back in the same manner from the arm-chair to the bed." Quoted from H. H. Houben, "Gespraehe mit Heine," page 838. See also my book, "The Misunderstanding about H. Heine." (In preparation)

[29] In my work on Stendhal (in the book of essays cited above), I described a similar conflict of the poet's as follows: "Stendhal once said that he was con-

Act 4. The Ego itself fends off this aggression by a counter-aggression against the "ungrateful" Super Ego,[30] and relapses regressively to a still lower level, apparently that of mother love, but in reality that of primary narcissism (for the patient is the tiny child as well as the nurse, as in Dooley's

---

sumed with scorn for the outer world. He might have added: with scorn and psychic masochism. For everything serves Stendhal as an excuse to enjoy the aggression directed against himself lustfully: getting on in the world, love, and poetry. All of his heroes are decided seekers for masochistic pleasure. More precisely, psychic masochists and seekers for punishment, who cannot allow themselves forbidden pleasure otherwise than under the condition of punishment. Stendhal's Fabrice del Dongo ('Certosa Parmesienne') only becomes a happy man in prison, facing death. Julien Sorel ('Rouge et Noir'), according to a phrase of M. de Frilair, commits 'a sort of suicide' during his defense ('I killed with intention,' the accused man says) and he does everything to cause himself to be sent to the guillotine (provokes the jurymen in the extreme, for example). In the face of death, he is calm, and he says humorously that it is queer that the verb 'to guillotine' cannot be conjugated through all the tenses. The masochistic enjoyment of fear is found all through 'Certosa." Fabrice speaks when in the greatest danger of 'a pleasant fear,' and in the face of death, 'heavenly joy filled the depths his heart, a strange fact that he did not stop to analyze.' In many cases, Stendhal's heroes only taste love just before they go to the gallows. Love itself becomes the greatest and most pleasant of all self-tortures for Stendhal, and in 'De l'amour,' he coins the principle, 'Love is a costly blossom, but one must have the courage to pluck it on the brink of the abyss.' And Stendhal says of 'Amiele': 'Even in the midst of wildest passion, her glowing fantasy reaches out for the still more immeasurable, and above all, for danger, for passion without danger is not passion to her.' Stendhal is, of course, not at all clearly conscious of this masochistic self-torture, and enjoyment of self-torture. On the contrary, his conscious ego-ideal is that of the reckless, open and merry deceiver of women. It is copied after his uncle, Romain Gagnon, a provincial Don Juan. Consciously, Stendhal appears only to suffer from his timidity, shyness, fearfulness, and disturbance of potence, where women are concerned. As a matter of fact, Stendhal suffers from stasis of his passive feminine desires, of which he is unconscious, whereby his suffering appears to be increased by the discrepancy between the 'masculine' and the 'feminine' Ego Ideal. For the Daimonion, the result is the same: self-destruction and self-torture. This neurotic process takes place in the Ego, and the Ego—the greatest triumph of Eros—enjoys the punishment of the Daimonion masochistically. The unconscious character of his Ego Ideal is that of the castrated, feminine Stendhal: Lucien Leuwen, for example, in Stendhal's novel of the same name, begins his wooing of Mme. de Chasteller by falling from his horse twice. But these desires can neither become conscious nor be realized, inasmuch as they are incest-bound (mother, father). And thus the picture changes, the Daimonion continues holding up the model of the Ego Ideal, whereby the Daimonion gains advantages for purposes of torture from the difference between the 'old' masculine and the 'new' feminine Ego Ideal. The entire procedure is a peerless grotesque: under pressure from the Daimonion, self-castration is carried out, and the feminine Ego Ideal erected. But secondarily, the Ego is made to suffer guilt by the Daimonion's holding up the masculine Ego Ideal and comparing it with the feminine Ego Ideal."

[30]It is interesting that the declaration that there is also an aggression of the Ego against the Super Ego present in humor (self-derision) appears so strange. Ernst Kris, for example, has only allowed the truth of this aggression of the Ego as a "tip phenomenon," citing the remark in "Transference and Love": "One is tempted to believe that the achievements of humor can also have tip

example), and thus rids itself of the commands and tortures of the Super Ego, hallucinates all tragedy away for seconds at a time, and has the narcissistic pleasure of the Caesar-like mania besides, which, *eo ipso*, is an aggression against the oppressive Super Ego.

May I clear away a possible objection: I can imagine that some reader may declare that all that has been said so far has nothing to do with humor (self-derision), but is only true for *"irony directed against one's self."* The difference between the latter and humor (self-derision) may be characterized something as follows: The nature of irony directed against one's self is *preventive,* that is, the individual makes fun of himself in order to forestall ridicule coming from the outer world. The *audience* of the ironic individual is always *outside.* With the humorist, it is different: the *audience* is the *forum internum* alone, *his own narcissism;* he has no need of an audience. The individual making use of irony does not achieve the mechanism described in this chapter; he merely intends to do so, in part. But one cannot say, as Kris does, that irony is "unsuccessful" humor (self-derision). There is *another* form of solution of the conflict here. I also believe that we can *admire* the humorist, *just because of his narcissism*: instead of allowing himself to be crushed by real misfortune, he rises smiling, above it. The conditions are similar to those which Freud, for example, describes for the narcissist in general: ". . . the charm of the child is due in large part to its narcissism, its self-sufficiency, an unapproachableness, just as the charm of certain animals which appear to pay no attention to us, such as the cat and large predatory animals. Even the great criminal and the humorist command our attention in poetical reproduction through the narcissistic consistency with which they are able to keep everything at a distance from themselves which would reduce their

---

character, for example, if the irony of grim humor (self-derision) dominates the effect. In this sense—and in this sense only—am I able to understand a remarks of Jekels and Bergler, in accordance with which humor (self-derision) serves the technique of attack of the Ego Ideal." ("Zur Psychologic der Kari-katur," Imago, 1934, page 465.)

Under "tip character" of comic phenomena, Kris understands the fact that when the comic effect is unsuccessful, there is a reversal of the effect: instead of pleasure, the opposite results. Kris is therefore of the opinion that the sup-posed aggression of the Ego against the Super Ego, here, can only take place when the humorous effect is unsuccessful, and for this reason fails to develop. On the contrary, I believe that the aggression of the Ego against the Ego Ideal is an integral component of the successful humorous effect.

Egos. It is as though *we envied them the preservation of a happy psychic condition, an invulnerable libido position, which we ourselves have long since relinquished.*[31]

I purposely avoid giving more examples from analyses of patients, as I am familiar with the objection that the analyst has the advantage of his opponent in an argument when he speaks about a case which he alone knows. I therefore choose an example from a joke book, to prove the point in question, that the Ego is aggressive against the Ego Ideal in humor:

"Motke, the thief, was sitting out time again for thievery. On this occasion, it was two years. When he came home, he found an addition to the family: a child of four months. It was very ill, when Motke returned home, and died a few days later. After the funeral, Motke and his wife sat 'schiwe,' as is the custom among orthodox Jews (as a sign of mourning for the dead, the nearest relatives sit for eight days on the floor or on low stools). A visitor came to give his condolences. Motke acknowledged this token of sympathy with a deep sigh: 'My friend, I've sat (out time) often enough in my life, but never when I was as innocent as I am now.' "[32]

Leaving aside the play on words in the double meaning of the word "sit," there is another typical humorous expression here. The unhappy situation, humiliating to the Ego, is present, and also the attempt of the Ego not to be crushed by this reality. *But the third element is a severe reproach to the Ego Ideal* (and secondarily to the object on which this Ego Ideal is projected, the wife). This *bitter and at the same time woeful reproach* might be reproduced something as follows: "Instead of loving me, while I was in an unhappy position, in prison, my wife betrayed me." The wickedness and unkindness of the Ego Ideal in this justifiable reproach is all the more pronounced because the pitiable situation is brought out as making the new misfortune worse: "Not enough that I was imprisoned, I was betrayed by my wife as well." The humorist Motke thus piles up a double reproach to the introjected authority of the parents, petrified in the Ego Ideal.

---

[31] "On the Introduction of Narcissism,"Gesammelte Schriften, vol. VI, page 172.
[32] Joke 103, "Innocent" from "Jewish Jokes," published by Lowit, Vienna, 1928. Freud says in his book on wit that we ask no patent of nobility of the joke; we are satisfied if it is good.

Here we see that the humorist is a *psychic masochist*,[33] an individual who bewails his misfortune and enjoys it unconsciously at the same time. It is as though he allows himself his aggression against the Ego Ideal only under the condition of taking punishment upon himself, which he uses secondarily as a reproach *against* the Ego Ideal. *This is the reason why individuals with free aggression at their command which can be directed at objects are never humorous.*

The objection might be made: but what else is there for an individual to do, even if he has free aggression at his command, in a desperate situation—such as under the gallows—besides be humorous? This question will be discussed with the aid of a literary example.

I quote the following from a novel, "Apis and Este," by Bruno Brehm:

Captain Apis, Major Vulovic, and Rade Malobabic were to be shot as leaders of the Serbian terroristic organization, 'The Black Hand,' on June 25, 1917, by command of the prince-regent in Saloniki. The judge, Lieutenant Colonel Dabic, who read the long sentence, asked for a drink of water:

"The gendarme comes back with a jug of water. Lieutenant Colonel Dabic drinks, and as he puts down the jug, Major Vulovic calls out to him, 'Do please give me a drink, too, as we share the same name; Apis, here, has heated me all up with his hopes (for the victory of Serbia).' Lieutenant Protic hands Vulovic the jug. 'Let's hope you haven't got syphilis,' said he, looking at Lieutenant Colonel Dabic.

" 'It wouldn't do you much more harm, anyway,' replied Dabic with a loud laugh, 'It's a little late for you to be worried about your health' " (page 548).

Here we have a combination between wit and humor. Insofar as there is an aggression directed against the judge of the military

---

[33] I agree completely with Lucile Dooley that humor (self-derision) is connected with psychic masochism, and I consider this statement, at which we arrive by very different paths, as of especial importance. Dooley's contribution, aside from Reik's emphasis of the equal values of the inner and the outer dangers to the Ego of the humorist, is, in my opinion, the most valuable in the special field of humor (self-derision) since the appearance of Freud's article. It agrees well with the relationship between masochism and humor (self-derision) that, according to Eidelberg ("Contribution to the Study of Masochism," Internat. Ztschr. f. Psychoanalyse, 1934), masochists are possessors of a secret megalomania. See the meaning of narcissism for the genesis of humor (self-derision) brought out in this chapter.

court, that is, against a real person, in the words of the major, the saying is to be considered as wit; insofar as it is aggression against the Ego Ideal of the person speaking, it is to be considered humor (self-derision). This mixed case is chosen purposely in order to bring out the difference between wit and humor.

Let us analyze the humorous effect more closely, assuming that the humorous major felt humoristic pleasure. The effect on the environment is clear: it consists in a saving of expenditure of sympathy.

The saying of the condemned man is humorous because it complies with the three requirements mentioned above: First, desperate external situations: the major is to be shot in a few minutes, and he knows it. Second, he rises above the situation humiliating to the Ego, in a sublime, narcissistic manner, and gains pleasure from it. The condemned man acts as though he had time for syphilis to develop, or as though the disease might have some consequence for him, although he will be dead in a few minutes. Third, aggression and woeful reproach directed against the Ego Ideal.

If we go into this mechanism more in detail, we find, above all, numerous aggressions of the Ego against the Super Ego: the Ego of the major brought him into conflict with the official powers. The Ego is therefore under pressure of the tendency of the Id to aggression, *with the consent of the Super Ego*, the originator of the whole miserable situation. Inasmuch as the authority, that is, a representative of the Super Ego, is the recipient of the aggression, this aggression is also directed against the Super Ego. (All terrorists are at least neurotic characters.) The Ego of the major is also in aggression against this authority in making fun of its instruments: a fine authority that is represented by a syphilitic (this aggression is in part wit). The decisive aggression, in my opinion, characteristic for humor, is a direct intrapsychic reproach addressed to the Ego Ideal: instead of comforting me, you have me shot.

In this example, the function of the Daimonion—the thanatic section of the Super Ego—can be studied especially well. For the Super Ego in question holds up the poor Ego to ridicule, and is aggressive against it, in an especially cruel manner: after the Daimonion has made use of the Ego Ideal for its own purposes of torture, and has attained its end, the destruction of the individual (the major is to be shot), it gives the poor Ego still another kick *by showing it the insignificance of the instrument of torture of the Ego Ideal.* It is as though the Daimonion wanted to say to the Ego: "See here, this is what I have used to scare you with all your life: a child's plaything." The phrase coined by Freud for the comforting Super Ego: "See here, this is the world, that looks so dangerous. Child's play, the very thing to jest about!" in my opinion, may be used *in this special case* in the sense of mockery. The Ego is destroyed, and added to that, *irony* is directed against it *by the Daimonion,* by *showing the insignificance of the means used for terrorization.* Both acts are carried out by means of the same instrument—by the chronic demonstration of the discrepancy between the Ego and the Ego Ideal. It is as though a criminal had forced a person to sign a very important paper by pointing a revolver at him, and afterwards had showed the terrified individual that the revolver really contained, not cartridges, but—cigarettes. *The Ego is therefore not only the object of comfort, but also of mockery*: the Ego, driven to desperation by this punishment and by the senselessness of its ideals (Ego-ideals, through following or not following which it brought about the punishment), rebels completely against the persons of authority absorbed within itself, and brings about the infantile situation present *before* the absorption of the persons of authority into the Ego: *boundless primary narcissism dominates for a few seconds, with all the consequences of denial of reality.* This primary narcissism, which, unworried as a baby, acts as though there were no outer world, explains the negative hallucination of reality, lasting for seconds, which is always manifested in humor (self-derision).

The "heroic" procedure in the Ego of the humorist is in reality not so grandiose: it lasts only a few *seconds* or minutes, and is always handicapped by the *fear of the Ego* which has not been overcome. The major in our example might, for instance, have gotten the commanding officer to come near him under some pretense or other, such as in order to tell him something of importance (betrayal of accomplice), might have given him a blow, spat upon him, insulted him, in short, carried out some aggressive *act.* But the humorist does *not* do this; his aggression against authority is very tame. He uses indirect and not very transparent ridicule of its representatives by degrading them to luetics. And even in this rebellion against the Ego Ideal there lies an attempt of the individual to free himself of guilt; the intrapsychic process of defense is carried further by concealed ridicule of authority: "I am punished as a criminal, but you who punish me are no better, yourselves." Heine's verse in ridicule of a farewell letter of a lover:

> "Twelve pages, close and fine,
> A little manuscript.
> One does not write so many a line,
> When one must bid farewell. . . ."

might be used *mutatis mutandis* for the humorist: A rebel who is always looking in the direction of the authority that he is supposed to have overcome is *no* rebel at all. That is, the narcissism of the humorist intends rebellion, but this is soon quelled, which is not surprising, considering the psychic masochisms of the Ego of the humorist. The fact that the Ego of the humorist still turns to the Ego Ideal for love and help, in *spite of* the lost situation, points in the same direction.[84]

The tortured Ego then appeals to its only friend, the original narcissism of the Ego. A weak, much misused Eros portion of the same, but still the only standby.

---

[84] I am not at all of the opinion that the Super Ego of the humorist is very mild. Also I doubt the spoken statement of Wälder, quoted by Dooley, according to which humor (self-derision) can develop only when the conflicts of childhood were not too severe, and the Super Ego developed was not too strict. This view of Wälder's is very much like that of Winterstein; both are struggling with the same difficulty: how is it possible that the otherwise cruel Super Ego suddenly becomes kind? Nor do I believe that the strictness of the Super Ego alone is responsible for the development of humor (self-derision). Megalomania, and the psychic masochism of the Ego, above all, play a part here. Humor (self-derision) is one of the most complicated psychic acts, and presupposes a very exceptional attitude of the Ego. But I doubt that humor (self-derision) is "postambivalent," as Kris assumes.

CHAPTER X

IDENTIFICATION AND INNER GUILT

In studying character formations of neurotic persons and those who are not too neurotic (sometimes euphemistically called "normal"), we are constantly confronted with cross sections of unconscious identifications.[1] These identifications refer partly to different people in the child's environment; and every analyst is familiar with the patient's resentment and indignation on having pointed out to him the source of his identifications. Obviously, only the choice and the "mixture" of these identifications are original in the psychic make-up of each human being.

What determines this choice? If we are to believe our patients, their identifications mirror simply their specific environment. Analysis has proven time and again that such an assumption is a mirage. First of all, it does not account for the exercise of choice among possible objects of identification. For instance, a boy confronted in childhood with a severe, aggressive father and a kind, weak mother may grow up to be a sissy of the feminine, hysteric type. How are we to explain his identification with his weak mother instead of with his aggressive father? Obviously we must take into consideration the castration complex, which forced the child into his feminine position. Furthermore, we can prove in such a case that a short but futile attempt to identify with the father preceded the feminine identification but was shattered by the oedipal castration fear, as pointed out forty-five years ago by Freud.

Second, the identifications are not at all photographic pictures of real persons. They all go through narcissistic modifications, and thus take on to a large degree the characteristics of the person performing the identification, a fact stressed first by Edoardo Weiss.

Third, the fate of an identification is further complicated by the defense mechanisms which the individual sets up against it. For instance, the man mentioned before with the hysteric feminine-passive identification builds up an inner defense against his passive wishes and shows all the signs of a cramped "he man" attitude on the surface. He treats women contemptuously, and, despite his weak

---

[1] First published under the title: "The Leading and the Misleading Basic Identifications" in Psychoanalyt. Rev., 1945.

potency, is aggressive toward them, in order to ward off his inner feminine identification. He usually marries an aggressive shrew finally, is mistreated by her, and despite all his conscious protests, stays with her.

Fourth, since the child does not see reality as it is, but only through the spectacles of his own projections, as has been stressed especially by English analysts, the original identification may be a caricature from the start. For instance, the child often projects his own aggression onto his educator and later introjects this "severe" educator in identification; reality and environment can hardly be blamed for the distorted image of them petrified in the identification.

Fifth, the inner reasons for identification are manifold, as Freud has proven. A person may identify with someone unconsciously because of fear, because of love, because of guilt feeling, because of loss of the object, because of identical "etiologic claims," etc.

In studying the identifications of our patients, we are confronted by the following facts:

a) When we have discovered a specific identification, we must not be content simply to state the fact of the identification; we must also find out the *unconscious reason* for it.

b) In doing so, we find with regularity that the identification *was preceded by an inner conflict*. This can be proven easily in connection with the best-studied type of identification—that of the boy with his father in the end resolution of his oedipal conflict, establishing the last stages of the Super Ego (inner conscience). Freud pointed out that castration fear shatters the oedipal wishes; the boy introjects the stern father into his Super Ego and *avoids thus the danger of overwhelming drives* corresponding to libidinous wishes toward the mother and aggressive wishes toward the father. In a process of simplification, the reasons for this identification have often been forgotten by Freud's followers. This accounts for the rather ironical fact that when Nunberg[2] pointed out in 1932 that this type of identification was a *defense*[3], his observation was hailed as something new. Anna Freud could correctly call the defense element

---

[2]"General Theory of Neuroses," Huber, Berne, page 199.
[3]Nunberg also claimed that part of this identification was not defense; he called this other part the "positive" side of identification, and believed that it was evident, for instance, in love as described by Freud. I personally doubt this direct and simple identification in love, and believe that the contents, especially of tender love, are more complicated. See my paper in collaboration with Jekels, "Transference and Love," Imago, 1934, No. 1.

in the formation of the Super Ego "well known"[4]; it was a correct statement, as far as analytic knowledge based on Freud's discoveries goes, but an exaggeration as far as the typical simplifications of this knowledge were concerned.

c) Every identification presupposes an *"inner readiness"* for it. It is therefore erroneous to conclude that certain actions are the result of certain identifications. Quite the contrary; genetically the ground is fertile for such an identification, and *therefore* the identification is accomplished. Often the person used for the identification serves simply *as a tool* to solve the inner conflict.

To put it paradoxically, we cannot simply claim that one person identifies with another. What goes on is far more complicated: A person tries unconsciously to solve an *inner infantile conflict*. His "solution" is under the *pressure of inner reproaches* stemming from his unconscious conscience (Super Ego). To counteract these reproaches and still cling to his specific conflict-solution, the person chooses persons in the outer world *as evidence that other people also do the "forbidden" thing.* He then identifies with such a person, and establishes a *"leading identification."* But even this alibi does not satisfy his inner conscience, and the pressure of guilt feelings continues. As a *secondary alibi* and inner denial of the original conflict-solution, his unconscious Ego establishes new identifications. These might be called "misleading identifications" rather than "inner defense mechanisms" in order to distinguish them clearly from the first type of alibi, also a pre-stage of "inner defense mechanisms."

d) Having once determined that a specific identification has taken place, we have to discover whether it is a "leading" or a "misleading" identification. The latter is the defensive palimpsest for the former. In other words, by "leading" identification we understand the *petrified solution of contradictory basic drives of the unconscious personality, crystallized as the result of early infantile conflicts. Secondarily, images are sought in reality for the representation of* the results of these conflicts; these are introjected. We see that the solution of conflict *precedes* the identification. The sequence of events is exactly opposite to what naive assumption would hold "probable." Needless to say, the basic conflict solution is *unchangeable* in later life, except through psychoanalysis. By "misleading" identification we understand *the series of defense mechanisms against*

---

[4]"The Ego and the Defense Mechanisms" Psychoanal. Verlag, 1936, page 129.

the original petrified conflict-solution, also executed via various un-
conscious identifications, but exchangeable often in life.

The following table lists schematically the differences between
the two types of identification:

Types of identification:	"Leading"	"Misleading"
Time of Establishment	2 - 4 years of age	Exchangeable throughout life
Psychic level:	Established by unconscious Ego as attempt at compromise between Id and Super Ego	Established by unconscious Ego under pressure of Super Ego exclusively
Status:	Unchangeable	Exchangeable as defense mechanism wears out
Genesis:	End result of infantile conflict	Defense mechanism against end result of infantile conflict
Sequence of events:	1. Solution of infantile conflict	1. Establishment of identification as end result of infantile conflict
	2. Adoption of identification as alibi	2. Adoption of exchangeable identifications to cover up first line of defense

If we ask ourselves what is different in this approach, we find
that it is the revival and partial reformulation of the following facts:

1. An inner drive, whatever its contents, can never come to the
psychic surface in its pure state. It is always modified by a covering
defense mechanism. This excludes the old theory of "Triebdurchbruch,"[5] that is, volcanic eruption of deepest unconscious drives in
direct form.

2. Identification *per se* are not the reasons for human actions.
Quite the contrary, they are adopted to serve the purpose of already-
established neurotic or "normal" solutions of an inner conflict.

3. The terms "leading" identification and "misleading" identification are rather antiquated terminology, since they represent a
compromise with the old form of thinking in our science, which
assumed, on the basis of simplification, that identifications in them-

[5] The last pillar of the "Triebdurchbruch"-theory collapsed when Eidelberg
and I proved that even in the perversion homosexuality such a volcanic eruption
does not take place. See "The Breast Complex in the Male," Internat. Ztschr. f.
Psychoanal., 1933. See also my paper, "Eight Prerequisites for the Psychoanalytic Treatment of Homosexuality," Psychoanalyt. Rev., Vol. 31, No. 3, July,
1944.

selves did explain something. There is no objection to this compromise in terminology, provided one bears in mind the actual genesis of identifications.

4. The problem often discussed in our literature, of whether or not new decisive identifications can take place in *adulthood*, the most outspoken proponent of this theory being P. Schilder, who stated: ". . . during the whole life identifications take place which basically never end,"[6] is based on a slight misunderstanding. We are obviously discussing at cross purposes if we deny obvious facts and stick to misunderstanding of theory. The truth is that the *psychic* elasticity of the human being is exhausted after the age of five—as absurd as this may sound. On the other hand, it is also true that Schilder's observation is clinically correct. How can we reconcile both facts? Very simply, by differentiating between leading and misleading identifications. What Schilder described pertains only to the secondary defense mechanism, that is, the *misleading* identifications. The basic *leading* identifications, once established, become petrified and are unchangeable during the lifetime (except by psychoanalysis). But the inner defense mechanisms against them are time bound; time wears them out. Therefore *new types of defense and inner alibi must be furnished,* and they are via new identifications. These identifications are the *new* defenses used to cover the basic, old, leading identifications. To put it precisely: Only the secondary defense mechanisms change after the age of five.

5. The search for the "disjecta membra" of different identifications often occupies too great a place in clinical analysis. Not that finding out whom the patient "copies" unconsciously is not a legitimate part of analysis; but the decisive factor in understanding the psychic mosaic is *the reason leading to the specific partial identification and the differentiation between wish and defense.* The moment greater attention is placed on the hunt for the original image, we find that the patient cooperates too willingly once he understands what it is all about. In some kind of masochistic self-denunciation, he will even bring forward minute details proving whom he plagiarizes unconsciously in tone, posture, opinions, behavior, prejudices, etc. On the other hand, the moment the emphasis is placed on the genetic reasons for this identification, he offers very little cooperation, indeed, a distinct reluctance, in following this

[6]"Psychiatry on Psychoanalytic Basis," Internat. Psychoanalyt. Verlag, 1925, page 5.

path. I once analyzed a patient who had previously spent one year being analyzed by a beginner. The other analyst had tried to solve the puzzle of the patient's complex personality by hunting down mechanically every trait copied from someone else; he made a mistake typical to beginners. He did not even discuss the dynamically effective reasons for the patient's choice of such identifications. The patient, once he understood the difference in procedure in his second analysis, remarked ironically: "I see now; the psyche is more than a collection of plagiarisms and missing persons' bureau."

6. The greatest danger in therapy is the possibility of confusing the original drive with the covering defense mechanism.[7] This confusion is responsible for numerous failures in therapy, since it does not break down the neurotic symptom but, on the contrary, bolsters the unconscious defense mechanism. In a typical process of displacement, such a therapist does not see his own shortcomings but accuses the patient of hopeless resistance.

SPECIFIC FEATURES IN IDENTIFICATION

1. *Meagerness of our knowledge of the genetic reasons for different types of identification.* There is no denying the fact that we have little knowledge of the possible reasons for unconscious identifications. The very few established facts we do have were described by Freud, and little has been added to them.

To what degree uncertainties are the order of the day regarding the theories of identification can be seen from the following conception. We know from Freud's and K. Abraham's studies on identification that it is *psychologically* akin to devouring. From this clinical fact R. Waelder has drawn the conclusion that the tendency to solve inner conflicts preferably through identifications "is especially developed in oral characters."[8] This deduction is not borne out by clinical facts.

If we pass from theoretic speculations, often proved faulty, to practical empirical facts, we find ourselves on firm ground as far as the following types of identification, described by Freud, are concerned.

[7] For a typical example, see my paper, "A New Approach to the Therapy of Erythrophobia," read at the XVth Internat. Psychoanal. Convention, Paris, 1938. Published in Psychoanalyt. Quart., Vol. XIII, No. 1, 1944.

[8] R. Waelder, "The Principle of the Multiple Function," Internat. Ztschr. f. Psychoanal. XVI, 1930. page 295.

(a) *Identification as the result of solution of an object-relationship.* Freud proved that one of the ways in which the Id gives up sexual objects is by establishing these objects in the unconscious Ego. This mechanism of total introjection is observable in depressive psychotics, and the special technique for accomplishing this process is as yet unknown. Freud states that this type of identification corresponds to a regression to the oral phase, and surmises: "Identification is perhaps in general the condition under which the Id gives up its objects."[9]

(b) *Identification on the basis of "identical etiological claims."* In contrast to the mechanism just mentioned, this is a partial identification, observable in hysterics. Freud gives the example of a girl in a boarding school, who receives a letter from a clandestine lover which arouses her jealousy and causes her to react with an hysterical attack. Some of her girl friends take over this attack through "psychic infection." These girls would like to have a clandestine love affair, too, and accept also, because of their unconscious feeling of guilt, the unhappiness connected with such an affair.[10]

(c) *Identification because of "borrowed guilt feelings."* Freud describes "borrowed" guilt as the result of unconscious partial identification with another person, who once was the object of an erotic cathexis. Freud states that such a taking over of inner guilt is often the only difficult discernible remnant of a renounced love-relation.[11]

(d) *Identification is building up the Super Ego.* This type of identification and the misconceptions concerning it have been discussed in previous chapters.

(e) *Identification in a specific type of homosexual perversion.* Male inversion of the type described by Sadger and Freud is based on identification of the boy with the disappointing mother, narcissistically seeking himself in his love objects in a form of negation of the disappointment.[12] This explains why some homosexuals revert to children as love objects, who represent the age in which the process of conflict "solution" took place in their unconscious. It would be erroneous to assume, and never Freud's intention, that this mechanism explains the whole problem of homosexuality. The best proof that Freud did not intend this is the fact that he also described

[9]Freud, Ges. Schr., VI, page 373.
[10]Ibid., VI, pages 305 ff.
[11]Ibid, page 395.
[12]Ibid, page 307.

two other mechanisms allegedly leading to homosexuality. The problem of homosexuality becomes even more complicated if we take into account its pregenital, oral basis, at which Freud hinted.[13]

(f) *Identification through "important common."* Freud pointed out that in some cases an important common can lead to identification; for instance, identification of members of the mass, or of lovers with each other, with the representation of the Ego Ideal, etc.

(g) *Identification through projection of Super Ego.* Freud also stressed that in certain situations one's Super Ego can be projected (transference, relation to the "leader") and thus an identification indirectly accomplished.

If we overlook the analytic contributions to these basic facts stressed by Freud, we find that little has been added. The most important addenda (I have no claim to being complete in this enumeration, which is essentially subjective in evaluation) are the contributions of the English school, Ferenczi's description of the psychologic contents of hypnosis, Reich's ideas on the "precursors of the Super Ego," Ferenczi's "sphincter-morality." The most puzzling contribution is that of Schilder, in his theory about varying changes of "Ideal Ego."

All of the aforementioned facts pertain very likely to but a small fragment of possible identifications. I have come to this conclusion since I myself have been able to observe a few additional types. Since limitations of experience, material for observation, and, to a variable extent, ability to interpret what is observed—disadvantages experienced always by the single individual—preclude completeness, a great deal is yet to be learned on the subject. The following are the additional types which I have observed:

(a) *Identification of the "captatio benevolentiae" type.*[14] This mechanism presupposes the wish to be loved (either original or as a defense against fear) by a specific person and the horrifying observation that this wish cannot be fulfilled, since the object loves only himself. Unconscious identification then takes place with the object, the formula being: "You must love me, since I am as you are, and you love yourself."

[13]For a review of the literature and our present knowledge of the subject, see: "Eight Prerequisites for the Psychoanalytic Treatment of Homosexuality," l.c.
[14]This type was first described in my paper, "Plagiarism," Psychoanal. Bewegung, 1932, pp. 393-420. It is mentioned in that paper as underlying the 16th form of plagiarism described (page 415).

(b) *Identification in dramatization of an inner alibi.* I previously pointed out[15] that certain neurotic symptoms make use of the mechanism of reducing two widely different facts to a common denominator for the purpose of inner defense via identification. The term "tertium comparationis" is used in poetry to denote a comparison of two widely different objects on the basis of one element which they have in common. For instance, Homer's comparison of the Greek soldiers storming Troy to a swarm of bees seems farfetched. The common denominator or *tertium comparationis* is the noise which both make. This device seems to occur in neurosis as well as in poetry. For example: An obsessional patient produced the symptoms of fear of acquiring a tic. Every time he saw a person with a facial tic, especially a tic involving the neck muscles, he was terrified and disturbed lest he himself should acquire the symptom, and often actually produced the symptom via identification. The patient was an actor, and every night faced an audience in a theater. Automatically he would "choose" among the spectators a person with a tic—not too difficult a feat among 1,500 people, and then worry and often produce the tic via identification. He could offer no explanation for his symptom except that, after the annulment of his marriage because of his impotence (twenty years before he started analysis), he became "more conscious of human suffering." The analytic interest was automatically centered on the fact that his preoccupation with tics and his potency disturbance had become apparent at the same time. It was obvious that in the superficial layer the patient identified his penis with the heads of his various "tic models" (as is found typically in, for instance, ereuthophobia), and consoled himself, so to speak, with the facts that his symptom of impotence was not as conspicuous as a tic and that other people suffered, too. Furthermore, his fear was related to masochistic exhibitionism: "Everyone will see that I am impotent" was the unconscious wish which he was warding off. Still, the two explanations did not suffice and did not change his deep-rooted symptom. The next question was: What attracted the patient's attention to a tic, specifically? He explained that it fascinated him because of its *automatic nature*, the inability to control it. Projecting this idea upon the penis, he seemed to be saying unconsciously: "I am not responsible for my erections; I did

---

[15]See my paper, "On a Specific Group of Neurotic Symptoms—Dramatizing the 'Tertium Comparationis' as an Alibi," Internat. J. Psycho-Analysis. London, 1943, Vol. XXIV, Parts 1 and 2, pp. 56-58.

not play with my penis, and the erections came without volition."
Here we seemed to have an impasse. Why should the patient be
afraid of erections and apologize for them when their absence was the
very thing he deplored so much? The answer was that his reaction
was that of the child in him. His potency disturbance was based
on his anal misunderstanding of sex. The idea of anal soiling pre-
dominated for him. The fact that his potency was disturbed, and his
marriage therefore annulled, served to activate his old masturbation
fear. He behaved as if his sexual disaster in marriage were a direct
punishment for masturbation: "You played with your (anally perceived) penis too much; as a result you are impotent." To defend
himself against this Super Ego reproach, he furnished the alibi: "I
did not play with my penis; the erections came of themselves." In
other words, the automatism of an erection and movement of the
penis were used by the patient as an inner excuse. The tic then became for him the symbol of his defense that certain things were
automatic, independent of wilful action. This automatism was the
tertium comparationis between an erect penis and a tic-movement
of the head. He took an example from another field, stressing unconsciously the *tertium comparationis,* to prove his innocence. He
procured the material for his alibi by changing partial and transitory
identifications with indifferent people afflicted with a facial tic.

    (c) *Identification in love.* Commenting on the *psychology of
love,*[16] L. Jekels and I came to the conclusion that tender ("romantic") love presupposes an inner tension because of feeling of guilt.
In this form of love, identifications, projections, and re-introjections
are unconsciously used by the Ego for the solution of the inner conflict with the Super Ego, which reproaches the Ego for not living up
to its self-created Ego Ideal (the idealized conception of one's unconscious self containing megalomania plus introjected parents).
The lover first projects his Ego Ideal on the beloved object. If the
process is the same for both of the lovers, and their love mutual, the
tension between the Ego and Ego Ideal of each is eliminated. Since
lovers see in each other the materialization and embodiment of everything beautiful, clever, and admirable, the discrepancy between Ego
and Ego Ideal is no longer felt. In other words, love achieves the
paradisiac situation of eliminating the weapon of torture of the

---

[16]"Transference and Love," Imago, 1934, No. 1. A summary is contained in
"Thirty Years after Ferenczi's 'Stages in the Development of the Sense of
Reality.'" Psychoanalyt. Rev., Vol. 32, No. 2, 1945.

inner conscience, which consists of the constant holding up before
the frightened Ego of the self-created Ego Ideal, every discrepancy
between the two being felt as depression and feeling of guilt. The
lover then re-introjects (identifies with) the projected object, a procedure which implies that the object is tinged with narcissistic libido.
This conception of love on a narcissistic basis explains the ridiculous
overvaluation of the beloved object; it is one's own self whom one
admires so much. Basically tender love has the purpose of restoring
the narcissistic unity of the personality.

(d) *"Stream of changing, transitory identifications."* In some
hysteric cases in which the inner emptiness experienced because of
not achieving Ego Ideal goals (through clinging to oedipal fantasies)
is a source of depression, a constant stream of "split second" identifications is observable. Often these identifications are expressed
verbally and lead to logorrhoea. As a representative example, I
mentioned the following case in my paper on "Logorrhoea"[17]: A
logorrhoeic patient spoke during her analytic appointment of a friend
who had "performed miracles" during her passage from Le Havre
to Boston, after the outbreak of World War II. It seemed that her
friend had studied nursing as a hobby and had had to use her
knowledge on the ship, when a severe storm had injured many of the
passengers and the number of doctors and nurses was inadequate
for the emergency. The woman had acted as an angel of mercy,
giving first aid, bandaging children, preventing panic. There was
nothing unusual in my patient's description with one exception—
her tone of voice. She started her story in the condescending, partly
indifferent tone of a casual spectator, gradually changed to that of
a proud officer praising his men, then to the modest tone of a person
concealing in public his pleasure in being decorated, and ended on
a note of accusation, as if in identification with her protegée, complaining that the ship company did not reward her with so much as
a small present. In the space of a few minutes my patient changed
her identity intrapsychically at least four times. At first she was the
disinterested spectator, then the congratulatory superior, then the
sheepishly modest yet proud recipient of praise, and finally the
aggressive, complaining hero who considers himself unappreciated.

[17]Psychiat. Quart., Vol. 18, 1944, pp. 26-42. This specific type constitutes
one of many types of logorrhoea. It is mentioned on page 36 of that paper.

In other words, the harmless narrative gave her the opportunity to "be" different persons by means of identification.

The same mechanism can be observed in readers of novels, and is familiar to everyone in that pastime. Some people, in later relating the contents of the novel, indirectly assume the character of the hero or heroine, at least in tone. A special form of this mechanism is found in readers of mystery stories, a form too complicated to be discussed here.[18]

(e) *Identification in substitution.* That different organs can be identified unconsciously is a well-established analytic fact. There is one identification, however, which, coupled with the "unconscious repetition compulsion" leads to the foundation of psychic health in man.[19] By the term "breast complex" is meant the entirety of reactions that arise in the psyche as a consequence of weaning. To make a long deduction short: The male child reacts to weaning with grave psychic disturbances, especially with a mobilization of aggression. His megalomania is hurt by weaning, and he seeks and finds a substitute of the breast or bottle in his own body—he identifies penis and breast. Parallel with the psychic discovery of the penis, the child repeats *actively* what he has experienced *passively*: He identifies milk and urine. Thus, applying Freud's conception of the "unconscious repetition compulsion" to a new field, we come to the conclusion that the identification just described plus the overcoming of the narcissistic mortification by means of active repetition of a passive experience lead to the foundation of normality in man, impossible, as K. Abraham has stressed, without overcoming oral traumatic experiences. Our conception explains also the strange but never sufficiently explained fact that the *parasitic* baby changes eventually into the *giving* man. This is possible only via identification with the "phallic mother" (Freud). Instead of continuing to be the passive recipient of milk, the boy denies the disappointment felt in denial of the breast (bottle) by overvaluating "production" or urine. Hence the overvaluation of urine in early childhood, later shifted to sperm.

The enigmatic and at the same time clinically evident "penis pride" in boys has an oral foundation. Normality in man presupposes the

[18]See "Mystery Fans and the Problem of Potential Murderers." Am. J. Orthopsychiat., Vol. 14, No. 2, 1945.
[19]I am referring to phenomena described by me in collaboration with L. Eidelberg in "The Breast Complex in the Male." Internat. Ztschr. f. Psychoanal., 1933.

unconscious identification of his penis with the mother's breast: He becomes the giving person, identifying the women with himself as child, milk with urine, and, later, sperm.[20] If this transition is not accomplished, oral neuroses result with a constant repetition of the masochistic refrain: "I am unjustly treated."

(f) Identification in performing "magic gestures."[21] The problem of "magic gestures" in psychoanalytic literature is one of confusion. I have tried to clarify the problem elsewhere.[22] The confusion arises from the ambiguous use of the term. H. Liebermann uses it most sensibly in describing a group of neurotics who dramatize in their symptoms "a magic gesture with the purpose of demonstrating to the person against whom they (unconsciously) direct their neurosis how that person should suffer or perish."[23] More often the term "magic gesture" is used in our literature to denote a modification of this meaning, of anonymous origin: "I show you (bad Mother, Father) unconsciously in my behavior how I wanted to be treated— kindly." Elsewhere it is mentioned that a three-layer structure was visible in this type of magic gesture (other types cannot be discussed here). Behind the superficial kindness (first layer) is hidden an aggressive reproach against the educators ("You treated me badly") (second layer). But even this aggression is only pseudo-aggression, a palimpsest to cover a deep masochistic basis (third layer). As far as identification is concerned, the strongest part of this modified magic gesture is that the unconscious identification is not with a real person but with a fictitious one — the parent as the child *allegedly wished him to be.* In layer 1 (display of kindness) we see identification, not with the mother (father) as the child perceived her (him) to be, but with the *corrected* parent.

2. *The problem of active repetition of passive experiences in identification.* Freud's description of the "unconscious repetition compulsion" consists of two facts: First, this repetition is beyond the pleasure principle. Second, passive experiences are actively repeated

---

[20]The most impressive example of a disturbance in this identification is found in psychogenic aspermia (inner refusal to ejaculate). See "Further Contributions to the Clinical Picture of Psychogenic Oral Aspermia," Internat. J. Psycho-Analysis, London, 1937.

[21]The problem was dealt with in Chapter VI.

[22]"The Problem of Magic Gestures," Psychiatric Quart., Vol. 19, No. 2, 1945. See also Chapter I of "Four Types of Neurotic Indecisiveness," Psychoanal. Quart., 1940.

[23]H. Liebermann, "On Monosymptomatic Neuroses," Internat. Ztschr. f. Psychoanal., X, 1924, pp. 213-214.

in order to restore a lesion in narcissism. Freud's classic example is that of the little girl who was forced to open her mouth for a long time in the dentist's chair. On coming home, she repeated the situation with one variation: *She* played the dentist and forced her little sister to be the patient and open her mouth. Thus, her mortified narcissism was restored.

This second factor in the unconscious repetition compulsion has not received enough attention, since many authors have been interested only in the first factor—that repetitions are directed not alone by the pleasure principle, in other words, that painful experience can be repeated. The second factor, active repetition of passive experiences, is of great importance in the study of identifications, as has been proven, for instance, in "The Breast Complex."

3. *Choice of specific "little details" in the process of identification ("identification-torsos").* To illustrate this type of identification, let us make use of three examples:

A patient had a peculiar way of writing the capital letter "S." He made it look like an overdimensional serpent. He took great pleasure in writing this particular letter, and one had the impression that he started his letters with "Dear Sir" rather than with "Dear Mr. ...." simply in order to use his favorite letter often and in a conspicuous place. In analysis one could trace that he had adopted this "S" in imitation of a school director of his high school days, whose name began with "S" and who wrote it in exactly the same way.

Another patient had a particular way of sitting in a chair. He would place his right elbow on his knee with arm erect, as if holding some great weight. His left arm was placed similarly, but raised to a less degree. It was eventually discovered that the patient, a man of Polish extraction, had seen, as a child, a picture of a medieval Polish king in full regalia, holding a scepter in his right hand and the royal insignia in his left. His attitude was simply an exaggeration of the tiring duty of this king during coronation.

A third patient had an aversion to using any gesture at all during his many speeches. Being a politician, he had ample opportunity to be in the midst of excitement, both real and faked, and on those occasions he fought strenuously against his natural inclination to use gestures, even though his political friends advised him to show more "umph." Only in his prepolitical days, as a lawyer, had he made use on several occasions of one gesture—a strange one, consisting of spreading the second and third fingers of his raised right hand, the hole between the fingers pointing to an imaginary enemy. In analysis one could prove that in this gesture he identified with a teacher of mathematics in his childhood who had a somewhat shady reputation, having been accused of fraud and acquitted. This teacher's second finger of the right hand was missing through some accident.

Let us scrutinize these examples. At first glance they do not seem to be unusual, since all three models for identification were authoritative persons— king, teachers—representing continuation of the parental authority. Nor do the symbolic meanings of the serpent-like "S," the long scepter, and the round royal insignia ("The golden apple") cause puzzlement, since they are all representative of masculinity (or denial of femininity). We meet with difficulty, however, in trying to determine just why these little details were chosen, and why borrowed from precisely these people. Even harder to answer are why the third patient demonstrated his castration and why the second patient was not modest enough to stick to imitation of the king's right hand instead of having to imitate the breast symbol, too, in the left hand.

Obviously all three partial identifications were of the "misleading" type, in other words, had the purpose of bolstering the inner defense. The first man fought inwardly his "leading" feminine identification; consequently he had to prove that his penis was as big as his father's or that of this father's substitute. The second was troubled by the same problem, and tried to solve it via a symbolic scepter-penis. Being an oral case, however, he had to deny his loss of the breast; he did this by displaying his autarchy in having both penis and breast. The third patient fought against the inner accusation of masturbation; as a defense he used no gestures in public, proving, so to speak, that he never used his hands for forbidden purposes. On the other hand, his natural tendency to use gestures also meant unconsciously a defense: "You see my hands; they are not at my penis." Obviously the first defense was more convincing to his Super Ego. Moreover, we see that he imitated the *castrated* teacher, which signified: "Since I am castrated, I cannot use my penis sexually anyway; so why the excitement?" Interestingly enough, his defensive gesture—of spreading the two fingers—was used only in connection with his legal examples. He first used it in a crisis in his life, when he was afraid of being accused of embezzling funds of a client although completely innocent. Still, his strong exhibitionistic tendencies (which pushed him into politics) were used for the defense, since the gesture also expressed the thought that the teacher with whom he identified by means of it was innocent, or at least acquitted. At the same time it served as masochistic memento and indirect confession.

It is therefore not enough to say that identification-torsos are picked up here and there. The purpose of defense must be determined in every case.

4. *New facets of the original basic conflict emerging gradually as the years pass by.* As I have stated before, I agree with Schilder that new identifications take place during adult life, but these new identifications are but *new props for old conflicts.* To express it differently, the old basic conflict grows stronger as the years pass by. Every neurosis increases with age. To ward off these pressing conflicts, new identifications are inwardly established to bolster the neurotic equilibrium of the personality. The fact to remember is this: All of these "new" identifications are of the "misleading" type.

Also to be considered, however, is the fact that *new facets* of the basic conflict emerge with time. This may seem strange, but clinical experience indicates its truth. For example: A patient, a stockbroker of forty, entered treatment because of irrational conflicts with his partner. He fought his partner on every issue, even when he was obviously being obstinate "on principle." Analysis proved that he was repeating with his partner a typical oral conflict, provoking himself situations in which he could enjoy the feeling of being unjustly treated. The patient was not too unhappily married. His conflicts with his wife were more of a characterologic sort, his potency not being disturbed. During the height of his conflict with his partner, which, according to him and his wife, had reached "intolerable" proportions in the six months before his coming into analysis, he had developed a liking for a friend, also the friend of his wife, a well-preserved widow of sixty-five. His wife was not jealous but teased him constantly about his "love for the grandmother." The patient did not pay much attention to her, reiterating his innocence on the grounds that it would be ridiculous to make a love affair out of his liking for an old woman's company. During the analysis it became apparent that widow represented for him an old relative, the sister of his grandmother, who in her sixties had sometimes spent her vacation with his family. At that time he had been sexually attracted to his relative, especially to her full bosom and buttocks. Particularly significant for him was the recollection that as a boy of six he had been granted the special favor of following her in medical baths which she took at a nearby sanatorium. He had always arranged to come into the room a little early, in order to see the woman's back as she left the tub. Until the incident with the sixty-five-year-old widow, he had never in later life been attracted by older women. Certain traits in his personality could be traced back to this relative, through, for instance, a certain type of boasting, a certain way of using allusions in a veiled sexual sense, and even a tendency to cultivate deep facial folds. Behind the superficial repetition of the oedipal conflict, there was visible also an amusing identification with his aunt in his Casanova attitudes, which mimicked her "sexy" reputation. The widow whom he met thirty-five years later reminded him consciously of this elderly relative. He was right in saying that sex did not enter into his liking for the widow. It did not partly because it was shifted, partly because he was inwardly compelled to repeat something else with her: He seemingly had never forgiven his aunt for treating him, as he expressed it, as a "sexual nonentity." He sought revenge by reversing the roles with the widow, avoiding seeing her without his wife, thereby indirectly proving to her that he did not need her (since he was sexually satisfied). He also achieved a reversal of the infantile situation by enjoying the elderly widow's admiration for his knowledge of the stock market, whereas as a child he had admired his relative's wisdom. The episode with the widow lasted a few months, until he lost interest. While it went on he adopted strong transitory identifications with her, which he later quickly relinquished.

The question arises as to the significance of this partial identification with the widow. It served repressed oedipal wishes and the need for revengeful active repetition of an early passive experience, etc., but it seemed to fill an even greater need. Which one and why so late in life? Where was the conflict buried earlier? We have to remember that the patient's liking for the image of the elderly relative coincided with the exacerbation of the conflict with his partner. Obviously the patient's neurosis had progressed, and he was repeating a full-fledged pre-opeidal conflict with his partner. The masochistic enjoyment of this mobilized his feeling of guilt; to ward off his inner reproach of passivity, he needed an aggressive defense, and this he found in the aggressive relation to the widow, whom he teased mercilessly. On the other hand, the allusion to the "grandmother" was an alibi, too, since it reminded him of an old injustice allegedly done to him ("sexual nonentity"). By *not* being sexually interested in the widow, he accomplished an aggressive denial of his sexual attachment in early childhood.

"Age does not prevent stupid escapades," says an old adage. Scientifically speaking, it is always possible for a new trait to come to the fore, which has to be expressed and reeled off. In the evaluation of human conduct, we have to remember this: Even old acquaintances surprise us sometimes. Since we cannot be familiar with all of the facets of a specific person, even though we know that personality well, simply because new facets may appear, the "prediction business" in psychology is a poor bet.

5. *The problem of typical psychic patterns.* It is a well-established fact that patterns built up unconsciously in early childhood become general in application for each individual, and are automatically repeated throughout the remainder of life. Take, for example, the attitude toward authority, the "submission pattern," as one patient called it. A patient attended a reception at which he was presented to the highest dignitary of his state. The patient was a political opponent of the dignitary, still he was, to quote him, perceptibly shivering in his boots. "Why?" His answer was, "Authority in itself makes you shiver." A more rational answer would have been that the father-pattern established in infancy sought repetition.[24]

Another example: A French patient voted on principle for a new man at every French election. He always toyed with the idea of voting twice in succession for the same candidate, knowing that in the end he would not. It was difficult for him to conceive that authority must be delegated. Once the authority was established, he inwardly overdid the submission-pattern, and as inner defense against it, overdid the "independence pattern."[25] He was always full of

[24] The patient was consciously furious that he acted in this fashion. He consoled himself with the observation that some of his friends felt the same way about authority.

[25] The fact that a reactive pseudo-independence pattern exists does not exclude the possibility of a real independence in attitude existing toward the elected dignitary. One of the highest achievements of democracy is that it educates its citizens, not in blind submission, but in inner independence. This independence cannot, however, be achieved in too-neurotic individuals.

hatred toward the new office holder, even when he had voted for him. As was to be suspected, he later developed rather fascistic leanings, long before World War II and the emergence of the Pétain-Vichy regime. (He was analyzed in 1934.)

Other patterns are, for instance, the "commiseration-pattern," the "injustice-pattern" (see "mechanism of orality"), the "anger-pattern," etc. It is perhaps not superfluous to mention that patterns identical on the surface can have completely different psychologic meanings in different people. In other words, the outward similarity of two reactions does not inform us automatically that the genetic reasons for them correspond. Individualization is necessary in dealing with behavior patterns; generalizations lead to false conclusions.

There are many such patterns, too many to be described here, which correspond to either leading or misleading identifications. The only pathognomonic point is the automaticity of the reaction. One can state that remnants of these patterns are present in everyone; the relative ability to avoid following them *blindly* gives us the clue to the amount of normality or neurosis present.

Analysis has always been accused of oversimplifying the complicated structure of personality. This objection is only partially justified—as far as the analytic conceptions of forty or fifty years ago are concerned. At that time Freud was just discovering the basic contents of the Id. In their enthusiasm or naiveté, some of his followers mistook the Id for the whole personality. Freud himself was always more cautious. Later these colleagues had to learn from him that the decisive problem of the personality structure was to be found in the unconscious Ego, which elaborates the repressed wishes of the Id under pressure of the inner conscience and creates the inner defense mechanisms. The fact that some analysts oversimplified because of their misunderstanding of analysis does not mean that psychoanalysis as a science has the tendency to oversimplify. Quite the contrary. We have greatest respect for the complexity of the psychic apparatus. This does not mean that we are not able to reduce very contradictory personality traits in a specific case to a common denominator. One could compare the psychic apparatus to a diamond having hundreds of facets. We don't claim to be able to explain everything by focusing our attention on one specific facet at a time. Still, by getting to know more and more of the facets, we approach an understanding of the whole. These facets in the human being are intimately connected with identifications. True, some of the facets are not yet understood. No analyst of scientific standing claims psychic omniscience. We do claim precisely, however, that we have an inkling—to make use of understatement—of what makes the unconscious in its different departments "tick" and "click."

Future generations of analysts will smile condescendingly at our present relative ignorance, but will perhaps kindly give us credit for the fact that we did the most we could with the tools at our disposal. Perhaps they will react with the same smiling respect with which our generation of analysts regards Freud's report of the first dream he analyzed by his methods. This report, published in his "Interpretation of Dreams" in 1899, describes a dream which he had himself in 1895 and called "Dream of Irma's Injection." In the report the creator of analysis defends himself against the inner reproach that he did not fully cure a specific patient, using between others as argument that Irma did not accept his interpretations and therefore could not have been cured. Freud had not yet discovered the tremendous importance of unconscious "resistance," and believed at that time, fifty years ago, that two types of patients existed, those who accepted and those who did not accept the analytic interpretations. He believed that only patients of the first type could be cured. In the light of his later discoveries, this viewpoint lost its validity, but it serves to show us a little how every step in analysis has to be discovered and rediscovered gradually, on the basis of bitter experience. Freud and his pupils had to console themselves: Knowledge of the workings of the different parts of the unconscious personality did not spring like Pallas Athene from Zeus' head—at once beautiful and complete. This is the difference between mythology and science.

The more we know about the unconscious personality, the more humble we become in regarding this miracle. The miracle seems to be composed at first glance of identifications. But these identifications in themselves do not explain anything. They are built up because they bolster the solution of an inner conflict. In other words, the inner conflict and its more or less normal or neurotic solution come first; then come identifications as props. These identifications support the specific solution of the inner-conflict—and are the "leading" identifications. Against the solution with its props new reproaches of the inner conscience are brought forth, with the result that new opposing identifications are established as defense mechanisms—the "misleading identifications." The basic conflict solution established unconsciously in childhood is unchangeable during the remainder of life, whereas the defense mechanisms are exchangeable many times during life. The confusion of the two types of unconscious identification leads to a complete misunderstanding of the human psyche and to tragic therapeutic errors.

So far we know too little about the whole problem of identification, especially about its details. Here is a field for whole generations of scientific investigators to explore.

CHAPTER XI

SUCCESS WITHOUT THE BLESSING OF CONSCIENCE SPELLS DEPRESSION OF A SPECIFIC TYPE

External success in life has two results: acknowledgment from the outer world and an inner feeling of satisfaction. Large checks and the social achievement of being a "substantial citizen" are the manifestations of the former; absence of constant reproaches stemming from the inner conscience is a sign of the latter. I became interested in the problem of patients whose external success was astonishing and even out of proportion to their merit, *without* stemming the "hell within," to use Milton's prophetic phrase for the inner conscience (Super Ego). In comparing experiences in psychoanalyses of six cases, I came to conclusions concerning a special type of neurotic person which I propose to call the "pseudo-humbug" or "pseudo-bluffer" type.[1] Pseudo-humbugs can be distinguished from humbugs (swindlers) in that, while the latter have psychopathic personalities with criminal involvement, the former are "correct" persons who observe the accepted standards at the same time that their Super Egos constantly acuses them of being "fakes." We are concerned here exclusively with the pseudo-type.[2]

It is very likely not by chance that four of these six patients were specialists in advertising. The fifth patient was a journalist, the sixth a dramatic critic. In other words, all six were exhibitionistically constantly in the public eye.

We shall deal first with the advertisers: Advertising, for instance radio advertising, is new and does not have the public backing that older types of business have. The outer world has in general the feeling of ironic spite for the "swindle of selling swindle," coupled with jealous admiration for the ability to amass money that goes with it. In reality, there is *basically* nothing dishonest or even suspicious about advertising. The moment you have mass production and masses, a contact must be made between them, and there advertising in its different forms plays its part. Still, it is interesting

---

[1] First published in the Psychiat. Quart., Supplement, 1946.
[2] I have described the criminal variety in previous papers: "Suppositions About the Mechanism of Criminosis," J. Crim. Psychopath., Vol. 2, 1943. Further, in "Psychopathology of Impostors," J. Crim. Psychopath., Vol. 4, 1944. See also Chapter XV, this book.

that the pseudo-humbug has a certain attraction toward that business, despite the fact that we can find him sporadically also in practically every other profession or field of endeavor. The argument which is often advanced that there is more swindling in advertising than in other fields has reference either to the "crooks" found in every profession or to the unheroic beginnings of every profession. *Every* profession goes through a process of purification until it reaches maturity and social standing. Advertising is no exception.

The pseudo-humbug type of advertiser is difficult to describe phenomenologically since the type appears in two contradictory forms, the one openly cynical, the other pompous. Individuals in the first group are always making fun of human stupidity, sparing neither the manufacturer nor the buyer of his products, the public. Those in the second group constantly stress, in a highbrow manner, that advertising is a science, although one which cannot be formulated. Inwardly, both are full of irony and self-reproach, whatever their covering cloak.

Whether these neurotic individuals are copywriters, commercial artists, designers, or business executives, they have certain characteristics in common and a certain specific genetic background. They are basically frustrated writers or artists. The publicity profession attracts persons with artistic or writing *aspirations,* who, because of their inner inhibitions, cannot succeed in their specific fields. With the condition of "prostitution," as one patient expressed it, and of renouncing their "high ideals," they make money. Secondarily, they even look down on the real artist or writer because of his poverty.

The important point is that these persons are constantly haunted by dissatisfaction. One of the patients in question was once an unsuccessful writer. Another insisted that his wife, who showed at one time some ability to write, should write, so that he could, at least by way of identification, enjoy being an author. A third spoke of a book which he wanted to write and never did. Another had ideas that other writers had to execute. The common denominator of these patients was, however, artistic frustration.

The situation of the fifth and sixth patients, the journalist and the dramatic critic, was different, insofar as both belonged to a more acknowledged profession. Both were frustrated writers, the journalist admitting it, the critic hiding from himself his unproductivity. The journalist was extremely cynical and was proud of having views similar to those of a city editor described in a novel by Kaestner, "Fabian, History of a Moralist" (1932). The city editor in this tale is told that five lines have yet to be filled on the first page, and immediately fabricates the following news item:

> "In Calcutta, street fighting flared up between Mohammedans and Hindus. There were 14 dead and 22 injured, though the police soon had the situation in hand. Peace reigns in Calcutta."

The episode continues:

> " 'But in Calcutta there were no disturbances!' objected Irgarg reluctantly. Then he bowed his head and whispered, out of countenance, 'Fourteen dead.'
> " 'There were no disturbances?' answered Muenzer with indignation. 'Please prove that to me. In Calcutta there are always disturbances. Should we inform our readers that in the Pacific Ocean a sea serpent once more made an appearance? Keep in mind, news items, the untruth of which cannot be proven at all or only after weeks, *are* true!' "

A few pages further we read:

> " 'Don't blame him,' remarked the editor of the economic section of the paper to Fabian. 'He has been a journalist for some twenty years, and believes his own lies already. Above his conscience lie ten soft beds and above them Mr. Muenzer sleeps the sleep of the unjust.'
> " 'You disapprove of the indolence of your colleague,' Fabian asked Mr. Malley. 'What do you do beside that?'
> "The economist smiled, though only with his mouth. 'I lie likewise, but I know it. I know that the system is wrong. A blind person sees that in economics. But I serve the wrong system with devotion. In the framework of the wrong system to which I lend my modest talent, the wrong measures are naturally the right ones and the right ones obviously wrong. I am an admirer of iron consistency, and besides . . . .'
> " 'A cynic,' introjected Muenzer, without looking up."

A few pages beyond this:

> "Muenzer was sitting in the chaise longue and cried suddenly. 'I am a pig,' he was murmuring."

The problem arises as to why these patients, who made more money than they could have made in other fields, were constantly, either directly or indirectly, on the defensive. They gave the impression that they were always apologizing for their "queer" professions.

All of these people were lonely, having drinking companions but no real friends. All of them were either heavy drinkers or had inclinations to be which they fought, a few more, the majority less, successfully.

The basic mood of all of these patients was superficial flamboyance covering latent depression or cynicism, or instability of feeling, or depression without any defensive cover. All of the advertisers could become easily excited about propagandistic "campaigns" for a product, for a few minutes identifying with the commercial product, to sink soon into their stage of depressed indifference or cynical teasing of themselves and others.

What unconscious drives are expressed in that and similar professions, or, more precisely, what is sublimated? Even a superficial observation shows that people of this type have the "vision," in their flamboyant moments, of seeing their product as the center of the universe. Genetically speaking, voyeuristic (scopophiliac) tendencies are mobilized. That "vision" is transformed into exhibitionism—they must show the public their form of propaganda. There is undoubtedly a short *inner identification with the product they advertise* necessary to achieve such a vision. Here seemingly the difficulty starts: The discrepancy between a five-cent product (to take an exaggerated example) and the megalomaniacal superinflated Ego results in the inner ironic reproach: "That's you. You are worth exactly as much as that five cent product, you fake!" The end is that the masochistic Ego is engulfed in self-irony, and the conscience mercilessly flogs the whole personality.

Paradoxically enough, the amount of money made by means of the five-cent product does not mitigate the inner reproach; on the contrary, it increases it. The millions of dollars made through the cheap product are not taken into account except to increase the sense of inner unworthiness. The result is that the person feels like: five cents.

The pseudo-bluffer is therefore always under the pressure of a feeling of guilt, his habitual unconscious refrain being, "You are a fake, a phony, a bluffer." The next question to arise is the reason for this reproach of the inner conscience.

The external reasons given by these six persons (five men and one woman) for entering analytic treatment varied: Two entered because of potency disturbance, two because of personality difficulties, two because of marital difficulties. All of them were *orally regressed* and clearly showed the symptoms and signs of the triad of the "mechanism of orality." This mechanism consists of a constant unconscious provocation in life of the situation of being disappointed, followed by great aggression toward the self-created enemies, seemingly in self-defense, and afterward by self-pity and the unconscious enjoyment of psychic masochism. Of that triad[3] only the pseudo-aggression in the act of "self-defense" based on "righteous indignation" and the feeling: "Nobody loves me," are conscious. The initial provocation and the psychic masochism are repressed and unconscious.

Besides these oral difficulties, all of these patients had the typical conflicts encountered in creative persons in general—writers, artists, etc. I have emphasized elsewhere[4] that all writers are orally regressed, a fact first pointed out by A. A. Brill, but that they are no longer striving to fulfill the friendly desire of "getting" in repetition of the child-mother relationship but are full of spiteful desire for oral independence, identifying with the "giving" mother because of *aggression* toward her, thus eliminating her. They achieve oral pleasure for themselves through "beautiful" words and ideas. In its deepest sense, writing, for the creative writer, is designed to *refute* the "bad" pre-oedipal mother and the masochistically-perpetuated disappointment experienced through her by the establishment of an "autarchy." That oral tendency of autarchy and alleged self-sufficiency is the primary basis of writing in general. Secondarily, on the more superficial level, the specific writer tries to solve his specific inner problems (anal, urethral, phallic, etc.) to which he has turned to escape from orality. What he expresses in his writing, however, is not the direct unconscious wish but the unconscious defense against that wish.

Productive activity in artists is therefore some kind of "self-cure" (Rank). The self-cure is imperiled in the following conditions:

[3] I have described that mechanism repeatedly in all of its ramifications. The compilation is found in my monograph, "Psychic Impotence in Men," Med. Edition. Huber. Berne. 1937.

[4] "A Clinical Approach to the Psychoanalysis of Writers." Lecture delivered before the N. Y. Psychoan. Soc., Jan. 22, 1942. Published in Psychoanalyt. Rev., Vol. 31, No. 1, 1944.

(1) disturbance of oral giving; (2) inability to substitute the mechanism of exhibitionism for that of voyeurism (See below); (3) flight from one's problems through a breakdown of the defense function in the creative work; (4) unproductive masochistic moods. Without going into details, I want to stress the fact that in the case of pseudo-bluffers a specific difficulty in the sphere of scopophilia is of prime importance in causing their lack of ability for real artistic creation. Every artist is basically a voyeur (Peeping Tom). Since his voyeuristic wishes are in connection with his mother's breast, he wards them off by means of the defense: "I am not a Peeping Tom; I exhibit my own body" (in artistic sublimation). To illustrate the use of exhibitionism as a defense against voyeurism: A woman patient attended a circus performance with some friends. As she was watching two women acrobats performing on the trapeze, she grew dizzy, covered her face, and exclaimed, "I can't stand it! Please tell me when *that* is over." Voyeurism in this instance was warded off by means of exhibitionism: The woman exhibited by making a spectacle of herself.[5]

It is difficult to understand why, in the moral code of the infantile conscience, it is a greater crime to look than to display oneself. Perhaps the answer can be found in the fact that voyeurism belongs to the oral phase and exhibitionism to the later phallic phase of psychic development.[6]

In every writer and creative artist, that substitution of exhibitionism for voyeurism *must* occur or productivity is impaired. *In the case of the pseudo-humbug, a specific solution is unconsciously found: The transition occurs, but only on condition that—humbug is displayed.* In other words, a caricature is set in motion.[7]

The result is that real artistic productivity is prevented, but its caricature, for instance advertising, is not. Thus we see why pseudo-humbugs are usually frustrated writers and artists.[8]

---

[5]For details see "A New Approach to the Therapy of Erythrophobia," Psychoanalyt. Quart. XIII; No. 1, 1944.

[6]In the discussion of the lecture on writers delivered before the N. Y. Psychoanalytic Society, Dr. O. Knopf remarked that one reason for the preponderance of exhibitionism was perhaps the fact that the child is pushed more into exhibitionistic channels by education, which permits him to show off with clothes, achievements, gifts, etc.

[7]That in the superficial layer *phallic* castration is displayed, too, is obvious.

[8]One could object that perhaps some of the pseudo-humbugs are simply lacking in creative talent. That is possible; their Super Egos behave, however, as if they were guilty of misuse of their given talents.

The combination of oral-masochistic tendencies and the *specific* solution of the scopophiliac ones gives us the clue to the types of pseudo-bluffs. Men of this type also contribute to the understanding of the tragedy of "not taking one's self seriously." The pseudo-humbugs are habitually under pressure of their inner feeling of guilt that they are humbugs. Seemingly, one of the prerequisites of living in peace with one's conscience is the Super Ego's acceptance of one's work as real and serious. The moment the Super Ego does not accept the work as such, it reproaches the Ego, with disastrous results. One could say that the pseudo-humbug does attempt a self-cure, but achieves only a self-cure in—humiliation.

Interesting are the different devices with which the pseudo-humbug of the advertising variety tries to prove to himself that his constant inner reproaches are unjustified. From what I could observe, I would say that that type of neurotic uses the four following inner defenses:

1. *Paternalistic attitude.* The advertiser behaves as if the product he is handling is created, not by manufacture, but by advertising. *He* "makes" it.

2. *Contempt for the public.* The pseudo-humbug has a deep-rooted contempt for the common man whom he wishes to reach, is full of irony toward him. He reminds one of a bit of advice which a famous critic gave to dramatic writers: The writer must pretend to be as stupid as his audience really is, so that the audience can believe itself to be as smart as the dramatic writer.

3. *Cynicism.* Cynicism is a specific defense mechanism. Years ago I could prove[9] that the "mechanism of cynicism" has the following structure: Constant pressure from ambivalence and equally constant pressure from the punitive Super Ego, which penalizes this very ambivalence, so that the "unconscious compulsion to confess" (Reik) becomes the motive power of behavior. The unconscious Ego of the cynic relieves itself of this conflict resulting from the cross fire of an Id striving and a Super Ego prohibition by means of repartee couched in the same form as the original thrust of the assailant. It attempts to prove that *other people possess the same ambivalence.* These "other people" are conceived as part of the sub-

---

[9] "Psychology of Cynicism." Psychoan. Bewegung, 1933; "Obscene Words," Psychoanalyt. Quart., 1936; Chap. 1 of "Talleyrand—Napoleon—Stendhal—Grabbe," Psychoanal. Verlag, 1935. See Chap. IX.

ject's own projected Super Ego. The cynic's attack is apparently directed toward this external world moiety of the Super Ego; in reality, the cynic is defending himself against his stringent internal Super Ego, unconscious, and perceptible to him only in the form of a sense of guilt. The rabid behavior of the cynic does not spring from his aggression; it is the expression of a desperate defensive warfare against his "internal enemy," the intrapsychic Super Ego, and it permits the battle to be transferred to "foreign territory." The cynic treats the external world with the same aggressiveness with which his own Super Ego treats his Ego. At the same time, the cynic attacks his Super Ego in and via the external world, somewhat according to the formula: "I strike others but am aiming at myself." Basically, every cynic asks the outer world (here, projected Super Ego) to admit that it is no better than he.

4. *Pessimistic outlook and doubts concerning stability of "talent" and "productivity."* All pseudo-bluffers are inwardly full of pessimism, arising partly from their undigested orality, consciously rationalized with doubts as to the continuance of their specific productivity in the form of "ideas." Very typical are their prognoses in connection with "government interference." One of my patients constantly predicted, with malice toward everyone, including himself, that the "unhappy time will come when most of the profits will disappear, because products will be tested objectively by the government, and only those passing the test will be allowed to be popularized." The more solid concerns abstain, even today, from too unscrupulous advertising. Another patient spoke with bitter irony of a manufacturer who wanted his product to be advertised as a "life prolonger." He countered objections to this with actual sales figures, achieved through advertising, which ran high. Said the patient to me: "First you make a million dollar baby out of nothing, and afterward you have to use your own fake as objective proof. Do you understand why I call my profession a lot of hullabaloo?"

The feeling of being unjustly treated (See "mechanism of orality") was constantly stressed by these patients, and used as an alibi for their "fake" professions. This was very obvious in the four advertisers. The journalist mentioned before had a similar approach. The dramatic critic justified his malicious aggression toward younger creative people in this fashion, using self-created artistic "standards" as an excuse for tearing down their work "on principle." Characterologically, some of these six patients were borderline cases of "psycho-pathic personalities," not too trustworthy in general. The majority had correctly functioning Egos, but, as is usual with orally regressed persons, were at times capable of strange pseudo-aggressions of which they were justifiably ashamed in moments of self-reproach. Sexually, all six had potency or orgastic disturbances.

The pseudo-humbug suffers from a complicated neurosis, basic-ally in the sphere of scopophilia,[10] and is curable analytically. He does not lose his "creative" ability in analysis, as he fears; he can be restored to inner satisfaction and may sometimes even become a writer.

One of these patients, in his constant self-reproaches, quoted Thackeray's statement in "The Second Funeral of Napoleon":

> "Humbug they will have. Humbug themselves, they will respect Humbug. Their daily victuals of life must be seasoned with humbug."

But the patient was mistaken even here. He did not even respect humbug.

[10]Scopophilia has been, until now, a stepchild in psychoanalysis. I suggested that three neurotic entities in which scopophilia plays the decisive role, deper-sonalization, erythrophobia, and boredom, should be subsumed under "scopo-philiac diseases." See "On the Disease Entity Boredom (Alysosis) and its Psychopathology," Psychiat. Quart., Vol. 18, No. 2, 1944.

Chapter XII

POETIC JUSTICE AND THE UNCONSCIOUS BACKGROUND

I. Descriptive Signs.

One of the most consoling fantasies of humanity centers around the expectation that "poetic justice"[1] does exist and comes true eventually. Slight doubt remains, though, whether or not retribution for experienced wrongs shall arrive on schedule. This is visible even in the formulation ("*poetic* justice") which contains a suspicious connotation to the effect that that type of justice is more often encountered in poetry than in real life:

> "Poetic Justice, with her lifted scale,
>   Where in nice balance truth with gold she weighs,
>   And solid pudding against empty praise."
>   A. Pope, "The Dunciad," I. 52.

What are the descriptive signs of that fantasy of automatic retributive justice? That belief focuses its attention on the future of the malefactor, assuming that exactly the same evil will befall him which he meted out to the innocent victim. The proponents of poetic justice are not satisfied with punishment *per se* of the malefactor; the punishment must be exactly the same as the original offense. A complete reversal is asked for; technique and means remaining—absurd as it may sound—exclusively the malefactor's choice. By setting the evil example, the malefactor automatically determines the technique of his own undoing—in the fantasy of "perfect" poetic justice.

Poetic justice is further characterized by omitting the time element. Otherwise the victim would depreciate any pleasure in his retributive fantasy: even the ardent believer in poetic justice knows that years and decades may pass until the great moment of revenge comes. The omission of the time element guarantees that unconsumed hatred of the powerless variety can be endured.

A third sign of poetic justice is the assumption that the wrong-doer himself will be the manufacturer of his downfall. Somewhere

[1] First published in Medical Record 1946.

he will slip, make a mistake. Without knowing it, the victim places great emphasis on that point specifically.

To round up the fantasy of poetic justice, the victim depicts himself in his daydreams as executive organ of unavoidable vengeance. The malefactor has to slip and through his—of course, unintentional—mistake, come under complete dominance of the one-time victim. As years go by, more impersonal factors are introduced as executors in the fantasy: other victims, fate, death.

The "perfect" fantasy of poetic justice comprises therefore four elements:

(1) Punishment of the malefactor must contain a photographic copy of the original crime in reverse.
(2) Time element is stretched indefinitely.
(3) The malefactor himself must be unwillingly the manufacturer of his downfall.
(4) The original victim is the executive organ of punishment.

II. *Unconscious Background.*

Vengeance is one of the manifestations of aggressiveness and does not require any further explanation:

> "Now hatred is by far the longest pleasure;
> Men love in haste, but they detest at leisure."
>
> Byron.

The fantasy of poetic justice works with that clearly understandable psychic material which, when mobilized in self-defense, is not accompanied by inner guilt. In neurotic cases, the aggressive element in the fantasy of poetic justice is more complicated: the inner conscience of the victim accuses him of psychic masochism. To combat and counteract exactly that reproach, aggression is mobilized.

Not less obvious is the superficial motive for maintenance of the fantasy of poetic justice. It represents consolation of the helpless victim. The psychologic problem starts only where the four contributaries mentioned above are concerned.

ad 1) Why does the fantasy insist on a photographic copy of the original crime in reverse as punishment? The conception "an eye for an eye, a tooth for a tooth," is old. *"Poena talionis,"* punishment executed by the same means with which the original crime was performed, is an ancient precept, deeply anchored in the unconscious. It was only consistent that the Venetian Law of the Middle Ages prescribed that the murderer's right arm had to be cut off before capital punishment was performed. The idea behind it was that the murderer killed with the right arm, therefore he had to be punished at exactly the same organ. It is interesting that so many people felt deep satisfaction that Hitler's alleged suicide was executed through a shot through the mouth: his crimes had started with inflammatory-propagandistic words uttered by mouth, therefore the unconsciously self-provoked punishment was executed at the same organ. "Even if the story is not true and just Nazi propaganda," stated a patient of mine, "the fact that they thought exactly of the mouth, which is not a very heroic organ, is consoling."

It is likely that the problem embedded in *"poena talionis"* is not fully understandable without adducing Freud's conception of the "unconscious repetition compulsion." That mechanism stresses two sets of facts: the repetitions are beyond the pleasure principle and contain the tendency of *active* repetition of *passively* endured experiences. The purpose of the active reversal of what was passively experienced, is to restore the lesion of the victim's mortified narcissism. Freud gave the example of a little girl forced at the dentist's to open her mouth, who, after returning home, repeated the procedure in a game with a younger sister. At first glance it looks like a simple repetition; in reality there is more to it. At the dentist's, the girl was forced *passively* to open her mouth, in the game at playing the dentist she is *active*, assuming the dentist's part. This reversal nullifies the lesion in the child's self-esteem.

From this viewpoint it is understandable why the malefactor who seduced the victim's wife, is expected to become a cuckold himself. And the man who pushed a victim into bankruptcy must—to fulfill the victim's expectations—bankrupt himself. A deadly car accident would not satisfy the victim.

ad 2) The time element is amazingly elastic in the fantasy of poetic justice: no definite time-limit is set for the expected revenge. There are two reasons for that self-restraint; one is conscious, the other unconscious. The conscious part is obvious: without the proviso of indefinite time-limit the fantasy cannot be maintained in the first place, since the victim must witness the malefactor's triumph. The unconscious reason is less obvious. It has something to do with unconscious time-perception in general. In a longer essay[2] in collaboration with Dr. Roheim, I tried to prove that in every endeavor based on childlike megalomania, normal time perception is automatically disturbed. This applies to fantasy, games, intercourse, etc. Since the fantasy of poetic justice is primarily a—fantasy, fortunately one which sometimes, though seldom enough, becomes reality, the time-element can be indefinitely extended without losing its dynamic power.

ad 3)   The most puzzling element in the fantasy of poetic justice is the expectation that the malefactor himself will be the manufacturer of his own downfall. Analytically, the problem is not so mysterious. It expresses just the hope that the malefactor's guilty conscience will doom him. The malefactor gives, at first glance, the impression of a person without a conscience. This impression specifically is intolerable to the victim, because he himself is under pressure of his inner guilt. It is known that every defeat increases the power of conscience which accuses the victim. Defeat and unhappiness, said Freud ironically, heighten the moral sense. The victim's own feeling of guilt is *projected* upon the victor—thence the assumption that the latter will perish because of inner guilt. This process of projection explains also why people who in "quiet times" never take conscience into consideration, in situations of defeat are at once so "absolutely sure" that the victor will suffer from pangs of conscience.

Objectively, the subjective expectation of guilt in the victor—though starting as projection—is not so naive. Every human being has an inner conscience. The difference between normal and criminal conscience is this: the normal conscience prevents "impossible" actions from the start. The criminal conscience permits criminal actions on the unconscious condition that punishment will be meted out later. Every criminal bargains inwardly for the electric chair: without this inner stipulation no criminal action is possible.[3] It is an interesting problem for the future to determine whether the so amazing military and political mistakes of the Hitler-Mussolini-Hirohito gangs were thus explainable.

ad 4)   The last constituent of the fantasy is that the victim is the executive organ of punishment. Little is to be explained there, with the exception of a shift of the executive organ, as time passes

[2]"Psychology of Time-Perception." Psychoanalyt. Quart., XV, 2. 1946.
[3]See Chapter XV.

by, to fate or death. I knew a man of seventy-five whose wife, half a century before, had been "seduced" by the old man's partner. In a cruel and tactless way his acquaintances asked him regularly how his former partner was getting along. "I am only now in contact with him through the newspapers. Every morning I am looking up the death notices . . ." was the old man's answer.

The ubiquitious fantasy of poetic justice is so interesting because it can be used as an example of the fact that unconscious mechanisms are involved in every "simple" human reaction.

There is no such thing as a "simple human reaction." It just means that rationalizations in a specific case are so well furnished that the unconscious sub-structure is overlooked.

CHAPTER XIII

"SMALL CHANGE" OF GUILTY FEELING

The inner conscience, very aptly called by Milton "the hell within," manifests itself in the form of feeling of guilt, depression, and dissatisfaction. These manifestations are secondarily attached to rationalizations, with the result that the person feels guilty but for the wrong reason. The dynamic factor causing the trouble is typically repressed, as Freud proved time and again. A few banal examples:

A man with premature ejaculation felt "terribly guilty" because he could not satisfy his "poor wife"; his guilt pertained truly to the unconscious aggression displayed in his symptom, which in its effects led to refusing sexual satisfaction to her. Another patient complained that she felt guilty because she tortured her husband with a previous extramarital affair of his, though long forgiven and expiated. Her guilt pertained to her masochistic dwelling upon, and perpetuating of, an unhappy situation. A third patient stated that he felt guilty since he "mistreated" a girl of sixteen, the daughter of his wife by a former marriage. She could not satisfy him whatever she did: If the girl was doing her homework, she was told that she would remain an "old maid"; if she had a date, the stepfather reproached her with becoming a prostitute. The man understood the irrational factor in his behavior, but could not help himself, though his conscience bothered him. His real guilt pertained to his repressed sexual wishes toward the beautiful girl, shifted and warded off with anger.

The inner guilt is thus shifted and forces the unconscious Ego to create defense mechanisms. All of this is analytically well known. The purpose of this chapter is to describe a few specific clandestine mechanisms in which the inner guilt manifests itself in the form of repetitive "senseless" thoughts. Two subdivisions are proposed: (1) guilt disguised as repetitive thoughts and (2) defenses created because of guilt disguised in repetitive thoughts.

The remarkable feature of both types is that the whole contents of the reproach and defense, respectively, *do not reach consciousness,* with the exception of the mildly disturbing reiterant "senseless" thought or melody.

Type 1. Inner Guilt disguised in repetitive "senseless" thoughts.

It happens only too often that a thought, a name, a melody, a stanza, comes into mind which has no logical connection with conscious thoughts. This idea is at first not quite noticed, and only if it persists long enough does it become disagreeable, sometimes even painful, since the person involved cannot rid himself of it. Here is a representative example:

Example 1. A patient who came into analysis because of his masochistic personality difficulties based on unconscious feminine identification, resulting also in a potency disturbance, related the following incident in the stage of treatment in which he was already capable of having a successful relation with a girl: "I saw my girl yesterday, though I had had intercourse the two preceding days. As is easily understandable, I didn't have any wish to have intercourse. We petted, and without thinking, I aroused the girl. I didn't do anything and she was disappointed. At that moment Schubert's "Unfinished Symphony" came into my mind. That melody persecuted me during the whole evening. Even after having intercourse I couldn't get it out of my head. It was really bothersome. Could you explain the whole thing?"

The intercourse of the patient at that time was more an alibi than a real pleasure. The alibi was directed at a reproach stemming from his inner conscience to the effect that he was still passive, having feminine identification. The defense was his entirely too frequent coitus, which gave him no satisfaction. In very devious ways he tried to smuggle in his repressed wishes, which hinged on the "negative" oedipus.

The situation in which Schubert's melody came to his mind was this: He was dissatisfied even with the prospect of having intercourse instead of being sexually "mistreated" by a man (father). That conflict led to aggressions toward the innocent-guilty girl, whom he inwardly reproached with something senseless—not being a man. The defense against his passive wishes forced him to be aggressive by refusing intercourse. He aroused the girl but refused satisfaction by not "finishing" the job. There the reproach of his inner conscience set in: "Why don't you *finish* the episode which you started?" Instead of the reproach, the musical theme, "The *Unfinished* Symphony" appeared in consciousness embedding also the defense that the girl is "unfinished" (castration fantasies): hence not a man!

Type 2. Inner Guilt refuted in the form of repetitive "senseless" thoughts.

Example 2. A patient reported one day during his analysis that he had slept poorly during the preceding night, and had awakened very early. Asked of what he was thinking during that time (between 4 and 8 a.m.), he answered, "Something completely senseless—of all things—about the Boy Scouts!" This wealthy man contributed to many philanthropic organizations, including the Boy Scouts, since he believed that interracial tolerance could be promoted through this organization. In his thoughts he was mulling over a meeting in that connection the day before, which was for him personally unimportant. His thoughts were without emotion, just "stupid repetition," as he called it. The psychic conflict of that patient centered around his psychic masochism, mainly concentrated on his wife. She mistreated him greatly and he—enjoying it unconsciously—retaliated in his inner defense, with coldness toward her. But he stayed with her. The preceding day there had been once more a marital barrage of reproaches: "You are cold. You're not interested in anything but yourself," etc. A few hours later he had his "Boy Scout invasion," as he ironically called it. The analytic reconstruction led to the assumption that his wife's reproaches made a deeper impression than he consciously admitted—especially since his whole analysis was concerned with his defense, embodied in his pseudo-coldness, which represented his inner defense against his enjoyment of "being mistreated." The thoughts about the Boy Scouts represented an unconscious defense and alibi: "It is not true that I'm cold and feelingless—I give[1] even to people who are no concern of mine, as is visible in my large contribution to the Boy Scouts." At the same time he managed to shift the emphasis from the important to the unimportant point—his Super Ego accused him of psychic masochism, not at all of aggression.

Example 3. The same patient who had repressed the interpretation just mentioned found himself a second time thinking for hours during the night about the following insignificant event: The preceding day a casual acquaintance had called him up, asking for information about a competitor who wanted to rent a part of his summer estate. The man mentioned that another person whom both knew

---

[1] In a deeper layer a "magic gesture" was involved. See my paper "The Problem of Magic Gestures," The Psychiat. Quart. Vol. 19, No. 2, 1945.

had applied for the place but had not been accepted because of his foreign accent: "What I want is congenial company." The patient was slightly amused at the man's inconsistency, since he worked with him on different "tolerance" committees. He was also surprised at the man's stupidity in divulging his anti-Semitic tendencies to a gentile who fought anti-Semitism (the man who asked for information and the other applicant were Jewish). The patient then supplied the information required. That was the content of the conversation which came into his head during hours of sleeplessness. I suspected that a mechanism similar to that involved in the previous example was at work here. I asked him: "Did you have any reason to reproach yourself for being unwarrantedly aggressive toward somebody in your family?" "Not that I know of," was the precise answer. At that moment it occurred to me that the patient had mentioned a long time ago that he employed in one of his plants some of his poorer relatives. The possibility dawned on me that he could have fired one of these and was therefore feeling guilty. As a trial, I asked him laughingly: "Why didn't you tell me that you had to dismiss one of your family from your plant?" The patient looked surprised, suppressed quickly a "How did you know?" and explained that because of "lack of loyalty" he really had not prevented the dismissal of, among a few other employees, a brother-in-law, the husband of his wife's sister. "I had nothing to do with the dismissals directly. I'm sure that the whole incident did not cause any feeling of guilt, since I felt justified," argued the patient. "That is what you think. Your Super Ego accused you of deliberate aggression toward your wife, and so you defend yourself. Your inner defense runs somehow like this: 'If my acquaintance can have unjustified prejudices (foreign accent, anti-Semitism), I can certainly use justified self-defense, even if the malefactor is a distant member of the family.'" The patient was not convinced and reiterated that his action in dismissing the relative was a rational act and that even his wife was "neutral" in the matter. I explained that his conscience did not bother him because of his rational behavior but because of the displaced aggression toward his wife, warding off his masochistic attachment toward her; and suspected that he did not go out of his way to avoid the conflict with his relative. The patient still objected, though not too convincingly, and I told him the old joke of a man who eats in a restaurant and is interrupted by a bore who asks about his wife and son. "They are dead." "But that is impossible—I saw both of them only yesterday." "They are dead now; everyone is dead while I'm eating . . . ." The patient laughed, and understood that in situations of conflict we are all drawing the circle of enmity widely—that his anger toward his wife could include even her relatives.

Example 4. A Jewish patient, a physician, complained that he could not help whistling all day long the Nazi song "Horst Wessel." He was rather indignant, but could not get rid of that melody. "It all started after I had a disagreeable experience a few days ago. Two months ago a woman consulted me, suspecting pregnancy. The examination of the uterus was negative, as was the Aschheim-Zondek test. I told her that she was not pregnant. Two months later she presented herself—she was pregnant." He consoled himself with the fact that the A.Z. test was ninety-seven per cent correct, and everyone could be mistaken. Then "Horst Wessel" started to "persecute" him. The explanation was that his Super Ego reproached him because of his ignorance, and he inwardly used the alibi of the current atrocity reports in concentration camps: "If the Nazis killed millions of people, I'm not so terribly guilty in bringing, through my mistake, one more child into this world. . . ."[2]

Other examples of "small change" of guilty feelings are parapraxes—slips of the tongue eliciting confessions, "mistakes" in writing, "forgetting" of all types and so on. All of these were described by Freud nearly fifty years ago in "Psychopathology of Every Day Life."

[2]It is even possible that the defense went one step further. The patient had the vague feeling that the woman originally wanted an abortion, though she did not dare mention it. Then the Nazi song would mean also: "I'm not a killer like the Nazis," and at the same time represent irony against his "ironclad" objection to abortion, reminding him of certain incidents in his life in which only fear of conflict with the law prevented him from performing abortions.

CHAPTER XIV

TORTURING DREAMS AND INSOMNIA BECAUSE OF INNER GUILT

"A good conscience is the best pillow to sleep on" claims an old adage. Clinical facts confirm this. Insomnia is, of course, a complicated phenomenon, having many reasons. *Psychologically*[1] two stand out: unfulfilled wishes and guilty feelings.

The problem of insomnia is not comprehensible without a short summary of analytic theories concerning sleep and dreams.

One of Freud's greatest achievements was the unraveling of the mystery of dreams. Freud proved in his famous book, "Interpretation of Dreams" (1899) that dreams represent nightly hallucinatory wish fulfillments of *repressed* infantile desires expressed in a symbolic language. Only after decoding the manifest contents of a dream does the decisive, latent purpose become apparent. This part of his investigations is so well known that elaboration seems superfluous.

The difficulty in fitting in newer analytic theories—especially Freud's own Eros-Thanatos theory—was responsible for the strange fact that the importance of inner guilt in dreams was, even in psychoanalysis, underestimated for a long time. Dr. Jekels and I tried to remedy that lack of coordinating newer analytic experiences in a paper entitled "Instinct Dualism in Dreams," read at the XIII International Psychoanalytic Convention in Lucerne, August 1934.[2]

In accordance with Freud's "Eros-Thanatos" theory, our whole life is a constant intrapsychic struggle between these two giants. We do not see, of course, life and death instinct in pure states. Only the constant mixture of derivatives of both tendencies is clinically observable.

Applying these thoughts to the phenomenon of sleep, one comes to the conclusion that sleep and death are unconsciously identified. It is interesting to note that many popular expressions point intuitively in that direction: "to sleep like the dead," "like a stone," "sleep is a little death." The ancient Greeks depicted sleep and death as twin brothers. Cicero stated: *"Habes somnum imaginem*

---

[1] There are also more organic reasons for sleeplessness, although the phenomenon sleep is always a combination of organic and psychic factors.

[2] Later published in Imago, 1934, and (translated) in Psychoanalyt. Quart., Vol. 9, No. 4, 1940.

mortis." To quote more modern statements, Schopenhauer believed that each night we anticipate death. And so on.

The fact that we dream, then, has also another connotation, than the originally assumed one by Freud—that of fulfillment of repressed wishes. It is *also* the mobilization of the "last reserves" of the life instinct. That interaction explains the neutralization of thanatic elements—we wake up refreshed, the biologic "recharging" of energy is fulfilled. Without that counteraction, to go to sleep would really be a dangerous undertaking, calling for the undertaker.

The frantic attempt of the death-instinct to use its advantage, however, leaves other imprints, too. It was never explained why sleep and dream are practically identical. If dream represents the counteraction of the life instinct against the sinister designs of the death instinct, then dreams are a necessary measure of defense.

The second advantage of these assumptions is the possibility of explaining why everybody dreams of remnants of infantile sexuality. Are people so insatiable? Are the quantities to be discharged so overdimensional? More likely is the assumption that the last reserves are mobilized in the death-like emergency. The greatest clinical importance of these assumptions lies in the fact that every human being has such an abundance of punitive dreams. One could say: "Daimonion" is on the loose. It is the counteraction of erotic tendencies which counteract that, too.

In "Transference and Love,"[3] we attempted to separate more sharply the component parts of the Super Ego, frequently insufficiently differentiated, by applying the theory of the life and death instincts. We arrived at the conclusion that the two parts of the Super Ego, the Ego Ideal (Thou shalt) and the Daimonion (Thou shalt not), differ psychologically, instinctually and genetically.[4]

In the dream, too, the Ego Ideal is constantly maintained as a model. Nor is this holding up of the Ego Ideal as a silent model by the Daimonion innocuous. Every deviation from the self-established Ego Ideal appears in the Ego in the form of feelings of guilt. The strange thing about this process is that the torments which the Daimonion inflicts on the Ego always detour via the Ego Ideal. A discrepancy between Ego and Ego Ideal must always exist before feelings of guilt and need for punishment can arise in the Ego. By

[3]Jekels in collaboration with myself. Imago, XX, 1934, pp. 5-31.
[4]See Chapter II.

thus putting the desexualized Eros in service against Eros, the destructive instinct conquers Eros with its own weapons.

If we try to apply this point of view which we derive from the Eros-Thanatos theory to the Freudian theory of the wish fulfilling tendency of the dream, we reach the conclusion that this early concept still stands firm. In the light of the newer material bearing on the struggle between the two original instincts in sleep, it becomes apparent that in the Freudian formula, "The dream is a wish fulfillment," only the erotic component of the instinct fusion appears to be considered. Unshakable as is the concept of wish fulfillment in the dream, if one seriously wishes to apply the Eros-Thanatos theory to the dream, which as far as we know no one has yet attempted, a supplement is required. It is this: besides the Id wishes in every dream, there is to be found a second, equally important group of tendencies which center around the Super Ego. One arrives at the amazing conclusion that this second, most frequent and regular constituent of every dream is a more or less successful *defense against a reproach of the Super Ego.*

In order to reduce misunderstanding one should state immediately that reference is not made to the punishment dreams which have been described by Freud and Alexander and whose existence is today analytically recognized. We are speaking here of the typical wish fulfillment dream, and postulate that it has a double mechanism. That is, we deduce from our experience that the driving force of every dream derives from a repressed wish of the Id and an unconscious reproach of the Super Ego, from which the Ego then creates the psychic structure which is known to us as a dream. Which of the two instincts becomes master of the situation following their collision depends on whether the unconscious Id wish or the unconscious Super Ego reproach succeeds in taking possession of the Ego Ideal and its undifferentiated narcissistic energy. Thus every dream must fulfill two functions: (1) to refute the unconscious reproach of the Daimonion, and (2) to satisfy a repressed infantile Id wish.

In proof of our thesis we select Freud's famous dream of July 23-24, 1895, "The Dream of Irma's Injection,"[5] which has initiated whole generations of analysts into the understanding of dreams, and which may serve as a paradigm for wish dreams.

---

[5]Freud: The Interpretation of Dreams in "The Basic Writings of Sigmund Freud." New York: The Modern Library, 1938, pp. 196-207.

As we recall, the incident preceding the dream which is later used as the day's residue, is that an individual designated as "friend Otto" replies to a question of Professor Freud, somewhat hesitantly and ironically, that Freud's patient, Irma, is better but not entirely well. "I realized," says Freud, "that these words of my friend Otto's, or the tone of voice in which they were spoken, annoyed me. I thought I heard reproach in the words, perhaps to the effect that I had promised the patient too much. . . . This *disagreeable impression,* however, did not become clear to me, nor did I speak of it. That same evening I wrote the clinical history of Irma's case, in order to give it, as though to justify myself, to Dr. M., a mutual friend, who was at that time the leading personality in our circle."[6]

The dream consists of a complicated refutation of reproaches by the Ego Ideal, which had cast an aspersion of inadequate professional conscientiousness. The wish fulfilling refutation is known: not the dreamer, but Otto who had administered an injection with a dirty syringe, is to blame for Irma's illness. The young widow is incurable because of the damming up of sexuality through living in abstinence; her illness as a matter of fact is not psychogenic but organic; she rejects the analytic interpretation, etc. Thus we find a series of refutations of the accusation of inadequate professional conscientiousness linked with aggression against Otto and Dr. M., the representative of the Ego Ideal, and buttressed by the opposed authority of another, sympathetic friend. In short, the dreamer is exonerated.

The question remains: exonerated by whom? The answer is unequivocal: by his own conscience. Freud is justified in calling the argumentation in this dream "a defense in court." The plea is made before the inner tribunal of his conscience. What is a token of his amazing genius is that Freud, although he did not give it direct expression, sensed this as long as forty years ago. At a certain point in the interpretation of this dream he says: "Curiously enough, there are also some painful memories in this material, which confirm the blame attached to Otto rather than my own exculpation. The material is apparently impartial. . . ." And in another place, in reference to the use in the dream material of three cases in which his medical treatment had been followed by dire results, Freud says: "It seems

'Freud: Ibid., page 196. Italics in this and further quotations are mine.

as though I were looking for excuses for accusing myself of inadequate professional conscientiousness."

From that new viewpoint one can understand these contradictions. The Ego Ideal makes use, or rather misuse, of the day's experiences to accuse the Ego of the dreamer of inadequate professional conscientiousness. By means of a regular legal defense, turning the plaintiff's arguments against himself, making use of refutations, alibis, qualifications, derision of the Ego Ideal, citation of exonerating witnesses, the acquittal is achieved. The reproaches which seem so strange to Freud in a wish dream, belong to the bill of particulars of the district attorney, the Daimonion, and this must be answered.

Yet the dream of Irma's injection admirably fulfills its second function, hallucinatory gratification of repressed infantile wishes. There are certain easily discernible erotic and aggressive wishes whose interpretation is merely hinted at and into which we need not go more fully.

We postulate for *every* dream this double mechanism—defense against the unconscious reproach of the Ego Ideal, dictated by the Daimonion, plus fulfillment of repressed Id wishes. In this dualism we see Thanatos and Eros at work, each attempting to gain possession of the Ego Ideal. In the typical wish fulfillment dreams it is Eros which succeeds. But in the "resignation dreams," which are to be discussed later, Thanatos is successful.

We now see the question of "the day's residue" in the dream in a new light. The "residue" up to now has had the significance of an acceptable package wrapping in which contraband articles are smuggled across a border. "We . . . learn," says Freud, "that an unconscious idea, as such, is quite incapable of entering into the preconscious, and that it can exert an influence there only by establishing touch with a harmless idea already belonging to the preconscious, to which it transfers its intensity, and by which it allows itself to be screened."[7] Freud gives the example of a dentist practicing in a foreign land who protects himself against the law by associating himself with a native dentist who then serves him as a signboard and legal "cover." "We thus see that the day-residue, among which we may now include the indifferent impressions, not only borrow something from the unconscious when they secure a share in dream-formation—namely, the motive-power at the dis-

[7]Ibid., page 507.

posal of the repressed wish—but they also offer to the unconscious something that is indispensable to it, namely, the points of attachment necessary for transference."[8] On the other hand, the cathexis of the unpleasant residue is offset by the wish fulfillment of the dream, and so the dream is preserved as the protector of sleep. "We may succeed in provisionally disposing of the energetic cathexis of our waking thoughts by deciding to go to sleep. . . . But we do not always succeed in doing it, or in doing it completely. Unsolved problems, harassing cares, overwhelming impressions, continue the activity of our thought even during sleep, maintaining psychic processes in the system which we have termed the preconscious. The thought-impulses continued into sleep may be divided into the following groups:

1. Those which have not been completed during the day owing to some accidental cause.

2. Those which have been left uncompleted because our mental powers have failed us, i.e. unsolved problems.

3. Those which have been turned back and suppressed during the day. This is reinforced by a powerful fourth group:

4. Those which have been excited in our unconscious during the day by the workings of the preconscious; and finally we may add a fifth, consisting of:

5. The indifferent impressions of the day which have therefore been left unsettled. . . . But what is the relation of the preconscious day-residues to the dream? There is no doubt that they penetrate abundantly into the dream; that they utilize the dream-content to obtrude themselves upon consciousness even during the night; indeed, they sometimes even dominate the dream-content, and impel it to continue the work of the day; it is also certain that the day-residues may just as well have any other character as that of wishes."[9]

All these assertions of Freud about the day's residue are incontestable. We suggest, however, that the residues have a still wider meaning. *The residue is, among other things, the reproach in direct or symbolic form, to the Ego by the Ego Ideal*, a reproach misused by the Daimonion for its antilibidinal purposes by holding up the "silent model" of the Ego Ideal. At bottom we are dealing with ramifications of a chronic tendency to feel reproached, due to the domination of the Daimonion.

[8]Ibid., page 508.
[9]Ibid., pp. 500, 501.

The diametric opposite of the wish dream, in which Eros succeeds in appropriating the undifferentiated energy of the Ego Ideal, is found in the so-called dream of failure or resignation. Here the adversary of Eros, Thanatos, succeeds in annexing the desexualized psychic energy of the Ego Ideal, with the result that the hopelessness of all its erotic endeavors is demonstrated to the Ego which then resignedly abandons them and even life itself. These dreams can be reduced to a common denominator, "give up all hope." An example of such a dream is:

> "Because of the frost, the water supply and also the drain were shut off. I suffer from terrible thirst. . . . At last I am given a glass of lemonade, which turns out to be unhygienic, since it is made with old, stagnant water from my sister's canteen. Nor is there any water in the thermos flask, and I almost drank Sidol by mistake. I awaken in a deep depression, which lasts all day."

This is a dream[10] of a patient who had regressed orally and who had an orally determined ejaculatory disturbance. The starting point of the dream is the stimulus of thirst. But how differently the patient elaborates this wish from the normal person who would perhaps comfort himself with the dream that he was drinking from a spring. The word "thirst" is the cue which releases in our patient a whole witch's brew of Super Ego reproaches which are heaped on the intimidated Ego: oral wishes directed toward his sister and mother (who was in the habit of sending the sister to the office every day with a thermos bottle of coffee for the patient). The last phase of the dream is to be equated with a suicide: Sidol is a poisonous, white metal polish. It is as though the Daimonion wished to embitter the Ego against every oral wish, as though it had said to the resigned Ego, "What can life mean to you? Give it up and die; you will never fulfill your true wishes."

In this dream, too, the day's residue is a reproach of the Ego Ideal. The sister's canteen, out of which the patient had repeatedly drunk during a mountain climbing trip on the preceding day, and the mother's thermos bottle are both symbolic representations of the breast or female penis which are held up to the patient as reminders,

[10]Cf. my papers: "Some Special Varieties of Ejaculatory Disturbances Not Hitherto Described." Internat. J. Psycho-Analysis, XVI, 1935, pp. 84-95; and Chapter C of the monograph: "Psychic Impotence in the Male." Berne: Verlag Hans Huber, 1937.

and which represent to a certain extent the derisive answer of the Daimonion to the patient's apparently harmless wish to drink.[11]

Between these extremes, the wish dream and the resignation dream, lie great possibilities of variation. Someone with an inclination for classifying and systematizing could pick out the two sharply characterized dream types from the wealth of compromise possibilities on the erotic and thanatotic parts of the scale; on the erotic side: aggression against the Ego Ideal and the dream of "undisguised acknowledgment"; on the thanatotic side, the anxiety dream and the punishment dream.

Let us begin with the dream of aggression against the Ego Ideal. One of the possibilities of defense of Eros against the advances of the Daimonion is aggression against the bothersome Ego Ideal. Examples of such aggression against the Ego Ideal are: mania, wit, comedy, hypocrisy, humor. Each of these techniques is employed according to its nature by Eros, to wrest from the Daimonion its instrument of torture, the Ego Ideal.

The showing up of the fragility and hypocrisy of the Ego Ideal also takes place in the dream, and is indispensable for the psychic economy of many people. This is shown by the following example:

A patient came into analysis after he lost his position because of antagonizing his superiors too successfully. His wife reproached him bitterly because his "impossible behavior" once more endangered her and her children's existence. The husband was indignant, deciding however to "try analysis." During the first days of treatment, he dreamt:

"I enter in gay company a restaurant, situated somewhere in a cellar. A large group of Chinese dines at a table. The moment I enter the room they greet me with the Hitler-salute. I am amused."

The patient had no associations to that dream, and was greatly amused at the "inconsistency" that Chinese should use the Hitler-salute. Asked, what his relations to Chinese were, he replied that he had none, with exception of knowing his laundryman superficially. I showed him the possible symbolic connotation between "washing one's dirty linen" and his analysis. "That's far fetched. Assuming, that there is a slight connection, I still don't see the implication."— "Well, perhaps you wanted to express that there are people who for

<hr/>

[11]The attainment of the repressed Id wish fails, unless we take the white color of the suicide potion, Sidol, a milk substitute, to be a triumph of Eros, paid for, indeed, with death.

a square meal are capable of anything, even accepting humiliating conditions?"—"Why do you want to drag my problem into that dream?"—"Every dream must contain the dreamer's problem. A dream is like a business concern in which only the most important matters are brought to the president's attention."—"In this case, the Chinese would represent Jews whom I accuse of bowing to Hitler. I am not antisemitic. Some of my best friends are Jews."—"That does not change anything. You are under severe reproach of your inner conscience, projected upon me. I explained to you that you damaged yourself with your masochistic technique. Your repartee is that you are a proud and independent person who would not sacrifice his principles. That's exactly what you told me. In your despair in the dream, you discard my interpretation, taken up by your conscience, by ridiculing me."

The anxiety dream, too, lies on the border between the erotic and thanatotic sections of the scale. We know from experience that it appears when the Ego is pressed too hard by the Daimonion. It is an erotic attempt at rescue and prevention. In agreement with a number of authors, we are of the opinion that anxiety is the reaction of the Ego to the destructive instinct which has been turned back against the individual. Certainly anxiety can be secondarily misused by Thanatos for purposes of torment.

Punishment dreams are not identical with the previously discussed resignation dreams. Both are thanatotic, but they differ from each other in their effect. Fundamentally the punishment dream still serves the pleasure principle since its solution is, "Expiation to achieve release," and it generally extracts some masochistic pleasure from its misery. In the true resignation dream this is not the case to any appreciable degree.

In the last stages of successful analyses, the unconscious sense of guilt is tremendously increased, for, in advanced stages of the treatment, the guilty feelings which were lodged in the symptoms, depressions, self-provoked punishments, Ego-limitations, etc., are activated, thus transforming the *bound*, unconscious sense of guilt into a *free-floating* one. When the analysis is far advanced, this sense of guilt, released from its former positions, temporarily increases the patient's sense of depression, his subjective uneasiness, and his aggressive impulses toward the analyst, although the symptoms have subsided. In its free-floating form it now fastens with all of its force on the reproach leveled by the patient's conscience. "Why are you not well yet?" It is difficult to determine what part is played here by psychic-economic factors—the provision of a better outlet for the sense of guilt or indeed of any outlet at all. Of course, that part of the unconscious sense of guilt which represents the patient's reaction to his sexual and aggressive pre-oedipal and oedipal wishes is resolved by the analysis; besides, analysis destroys these wishes.

This reproach of conscience, "Why are you not well yet," finds expression in typical dreams, in which the Ego seeks to reject the Super Ego's accusations. I proposed that we should call dreams of this type "dreams embodying a sense of guilt in connection with recovery."[12]

I shall give one example: A young girl suffering from agoraphobia and hypochondria, dreamed in a late stage of analysis in which her street fear diminished to a negligible degree for a longer time:

> A person resembling the patient's sister declares during a quarrel that, if the patient does not get well, she will not feel bound any more to secrecy and divulge the reason why the patient came to the city from her distant home-town. The patient curses the sister's child.

Situation on the day preceding the dream: The patient did not feel happy at all at her improvement. She shifted the emphasis from the disappearing street fear to the shape of her breasts. Even if analysis could completely eliminate her street fear,—so she argued—this alone would not help her, since the shape of her breasts was irreparable. The problem was thoroughly discussed in analysis and it was proven to the patient that her pre-occupation with the breast was based on masculinity wishes. Her main objection to her breasts was their "softness" and smallness—she just compared them inwardly with an erected penis. Neither the diagnostician nor the gynecologist could detect anything abnormal or even cosmetically objectionable in her normally shaped breasts. During the last analytic appointment preceding the dream, she was shown how she sabotaged recovery, since she did not want health at all and clung to her masochistically tinged complaints, covering materialization of infantile wishes. In the dream the sister takes over the role of the analyst and of her own

[12]First stated in the authors contribution to the Symposium on Theory of Therapy, held at the XIV Internat. Psychoanal. Convention, Marienbad 1936. Published in Internat. J. of Psycho-Analysis 1937.

Super Ego, respectively, because the patient had consulted her sister about her breasts before entering treatment; her sister had declared that she was imagining things. She knew about the patient's "great secret," her analysis. The patient did not want to give any information to her sister and the latter used the technique of taking a great oath of secrecy. Since both sisters were superstitious the oath had the formulation: "I swear that my child shall die, should I divulge my sister's secret."

The dream could thus be interpreted:

Id-Wish: I want masochistic exhibitionism continued, want a penis and hate everybody who has a penis-substitute (child).

Super Ego Reproach: You don't want to change at all. First you centered your complaints around street fear, now you are stressing the breasts. You don't want the cure at all, but indulgence in exhibitionism, masculinity and hatred, masochistically misused.

Ego-Compromise: It is not true that I don't want recovery, it is not true that I am jealous of my sister's child and what it represents. Quite the contrary! I am not exhibitionistic, my sister is: she wants to misuse my secret for exhibiting at my expense. I therefore have the right to curse her child since I am acting in self-defense. My complaints about my breast are real enough! I am neither masochistic nor aggressive, I defend myself in self-defense.

The patient's dream satisfies both purposes: fulfillment of unconscious wishes and rebuff of Super Ego reproaches.

The correct handling of the transference and resistance via "working through" activates the unconscious feeling of guilt and makes it a *vis a tergo* which pushes the patient out of his or her neurosis.

In summarizing, we ascribe to the *second* component of *every* dream (the above-described refutation of the reproach of the Daimonion, held up to the Ego in the form of the day's residues through the interrelation of the Ego Ideal) *the same psychic valence as the repressed infantile Id wish which is hallucinatorily fulfilled*. It is this dualism, the combination of both tendencies, which finally creates the dream which thus emerges as a typical example of instinct fusion. Accordingly as the two basic instincts succeed in gaining control of the undifferentiated psychic energy of the Ego Ideal, there arises one of the many possible variations between the wish and resignation dreams.

The connection between the "day-residue" of dreams was found to be even more intimately connected with inner guilt by a further investigation of mine.[13]

In discovering the meaning of the "day residue" in dreams, Freud has provided us with one of the most significant guiding posts in the interpretation of dreams. In the first edition of his "Traumdeutung," published in 1899, the founder of psychoanalysis was already able to prove that there was no simple repetition of the day's events in sleep, but that a selection took place. From the multitudinous mass of thoughts, things read, things experienced, only those were chosen which seemed particularly suited to represent unconscious material. Hence the significance of the "day residue" could be described as an "acceptable package wrapping in which contraband articles are smuggled across the border."

To this first function of the "day residue," Jekels and I added a second function, which was described above. It was shown that the day residue also represents, either in direct or symbolic form, *a reproach* of the *Super Ego*. We came to the conclusion that every dream not only gratifies the repressed wish, but *also refutes the repressed reproaches of the conscience*, hence fulfills *two* functions.

Twelve years have passed since this report was made on this second function of the day residue in dreams. Since that time I have had occasion to analyse several thousand dreams, and in them I found the above-mentioned findings confirmed. With the exception of two colleagues who have also fully confirmed these findings, I am unaware to what extent others have been able to verify or disprove our assumptions. Nevertheless, I am now venturing to propose a third function which seems to be contained in the "day residue" of the dream. This third function serves the purpose of *contradicting the reproach of the conscience which is contained in every dream*. This formulation may seem confusing, since it has been pointed out that the day residue represents a reproach of the Super Ego as well. How can the day residue represent such a reproach and at the same time contradict it? The answer is that a high degree of condensation takes place involving contradictory tendencies having their origin in different regions of the unconscious part of the personality.

Accordingly we can say that the day residue present in dreams contains three elements condensed into one, varying only in a quantitative sense. In other words, three functions are served by the day residue:

1. "Package-wrapping for contraband articles," that is, Id wishes (Freud).

2. "Symbolic representation of Super Ego reproach" (Jekels-Bergler).

3. An attempt to refute the reproaches of conscience (Bergler).

In what follows, I will analyse six dreams which serve to illustrate this third function.

First Dream

"I was in Prague, and bought a pillow made of rubber, and a pair of spectacles."

This patient suffered from ejaculatio praecox. Through his analysis and just previous to the time he had this dream, he had slowly been gaining insight into his aggressive feelings toward his wife covering deep masochistic attachment. These became especially clear to him after he was forced to admit that he had no special reason for being constantly unfaithful to her. He had first explained it by saying that she failed to satisfy him, but then he admitted that he also suffered from premature ejaculation with his present mistress. This mechanism of playing one woman against the other for aggressive reasons, and the realization that it had its roots in a childhood situation, invoked in him intensive feelings of guilt. These increased when he began to understand that the symptom itself contained this chronic act of denying pleasure out of oral revenge [14]: what he gave was only a caricature of the act of giving, since it came at a time when his wife could have no pleasure from it.

His associations to the dream were as follows: The element "spectacles" he related to a residue of the day before, namely a letter he had received from his eleven-year-old son, who was away on a ski trip. The son wrote that he had lost his sun glasses, and asked his father to send him another pair via special delivery. This angered the father but he complied with the request. Furthermore, the patient had strong scopophilic tendencies, especially of the voyeur

---

[14] "Ejaculatio Praecox." Psychiat. neurol. bl., Amsterdam, 1936; and "Psychic Impotence in the Male." Berne: Hans Huber Verlag, 1937.

type, but also at times exhibitionistic. The day before, although in the company of his wife, he had turned around rather pointedly to look at some woman. His wife upbraided him for this.

To "rubber pillow" he associated a joke that he had in common with his mistress. During a *coitus a tergo*, he had compared her buttocks to rubber pillows. This woman's name, by the way, contained the word "brown." It had already become evident that the anal-urethral wish to soil (Abraham) was an important issue with the patient.

The element "Prague" was significant because the patient had been brought up there as a child.

Interpretation:

The Id wishes: Voyeurism, and aggressive soiling of the woman.

The Super Ego reproach: You are only interested in satisfying your vulgar desires, and do not pay attention to your family (son).

The Ego compromise: I am neither a voyeur nor aggressive toward women. I am a good family man, the proof being that I sent the glasses to my son. Anyhow, why shouldn't one "lie soft"? (rubber pillow). It is true that my relations with Mrs. Brown speak against me, but why should I be held responsible for my childhood neurosis (Prague)? Furthermore I am doing everything I can to cure myself, since I am being analysed, which helps me to see (glasses). And for the rest, my relationship to Mrs. Brown is of no importance since I only regard her as an object for sexual gratification (rubber pillow, for sleeping). It is not true that I *deny*; I give (I bought the glasses). And finally, if I were such an evil person, I would have married for money and not for love.

Accordingly, the dream attempts to function as a fulfillment of the Id wishes, and a refutation of the reproaches of the Super Ego. For our purpose, the dream element "glasses" is of the greatest significance. It contains all three of the elements characteristic of the "day residue," as described above.

1. "Package wrapping for contraband articles" (the Id wishes). voyeurism.

2. The reproach of the Super Ego: You are only interested in your lowly voyeur wishes (as indicated in the street scene with his wife); you are aggressive, and a bad father.

3. Refutation of the Super Ego reproaches: I bought the spectacles, therefore I am a good father; furthermore I am being

analysed (opening up my eyes), hence I am struggling against my neurosis.

Second Dream:

"I was in a museum, where they were exhibiting early American living quarters and furniture. A provincial-looking couple spoke to me. I explained, with a great display of authority and self-assurance, that one could draw conclusions regarding the characteristics of the occupants of the house from their furniture. For instance, one could judge their height from the height of the chairs and height of the ceilings. The woman looked at me admiringly, and declared that I had given her more information in a few minutes than her husband had done during many years. The husband had described himself as a steel magnate of high standing; in reality however, he merely had a subordinate position as salesman. He gave the impression of being a boastful person."

This dream occurred in the third week of analysis. This patient's situation at that time was as follows: He had lost, by reason of his provocative behavior, a position which he had held for some time. Consequently his wife had urged him to undergo an analysis, to which he consented. She had previously been treated by me, and she feared quite rightly that her husband would be continually ruining his chances through his masochistic provocative behavior. This was the third time he had lost a position in this manner. He was a talented man and had repeatedly obtained important and remunerative positions which he retained for some little time, only to lose them in a logically incomprehensible manner as a result of his quarrelsomeness. In his last position he was discharged with the explanation, "Your personality does not fit into our organization."

He entered analysis shortly after this occurrence, although he was of the opinion that there was nothing wrong with him, but rather that he was the victim of adverse circumstances. What he did admit was that he had a "perverted sense of humor" which led him into difficulties. He also asserted that he was a very independent person, never lowering himself for others, and, perhaps, "nice with the wrong people." He always got along well with his subordinates; it was only with his superiors that the difficulties began. Towards analysis he adapted an attitude of ironic incredulity. He considered nonsensical the idea of a connection between "real" conflicts and childhood fantasies and experiences. He was of the opinion that analysts complicated things unnecessarily. After he had been to see the musical comedy, "Lady in the Dark," he declared ironically to his wife that even he could be an analyst. He did not believe at all in the therapeutic value of analysis, and as far as the theory was concerned, "one could argue about that."

The patient demanded that I tell him how I knew he had a neurosis, since he denied that there was any sure evidence of it (namely, the fact of chronically losing his position because of his provocative behavior). I told him that his neurosis must be complementary to his wife's neurosis. I showed him how he and his wife played into each other's hand, so to speak, with regard to their conflicts; then I explained that this could not be merely the result of chance. The man was exceedingly astonished, had no answer to this, but said instead that I could never understand him because I was not an expert in the steel industry (this was his occupation). Without any special knowledge of his field I would not be able to help him, he felt. In this he remained obdurate, treating me with contempt because of my ignorance of his branch of business. I pointed out to him that his argument was a rather futile one, since it was impossible for an analyst to become acquainted with all occupations and fields of endeavor. I suggested, however, that he explain to me the particularly complicated facts in his field, and that we would both learn something then, for he in turn would be learning something about analysis.

To return now to the dream, the patient had no associations, was blocked completely, except for the statement: "The only thing I can say is that I live in the neighborhood of a museum."

Interpretation:

The dream was intended to make fun of analysis (reconstruction), and to offer the patient narcissistic gratification by making him the object of admiration and respect. At the same time, his conscience did not allow him to draw a very complimentary picture of himself.

Reproach of the Super Ego: You are a boastful windbag, who pretends to be a steel expert, although you are hardly anything more than an agent. (The patient is obviously represented both by himself and by the provincial gentleman in the dream.) You have grandiose ideas that you can do everything better than another person. (Remark about the "Lady in the Dark," and his covert sarcasm about the "reconstructions.") Furthermore, in reality, you do not know anything about yourself. This stranger (analyst) knows more about you than you do yourself.

The Id-wishes: These are only evident indirectly, most likely the retention of the masochistic wishes.

The Ego defenses and the compromise: It is not true that there is such an art to analysis, that it requires special knowledge. Any lay person can produce those ridiculous "reconstructions" (the irony about the reconstructions in the museum). One can impress a provincial woman (referring to, and belittling his wife) with such nonsense, but not me. In addition, this foreigner (the analyst) knows nothing about an American's childhood ("*early* American living rooms"). Accordingly it is all a fraud, and I need not fear any narcissistic mortification.

The three functions of the "day residue" (here the "reconstruction" or the "museum") can be described as follows:

1. "Package wrapping for the Id wishes": concealed behind the mask of narcissistic superiority lie masochistic tendencies.

2. The reproach of the Super Ego: You are a fraud, who pretends to know everything better than everyone else; it is valuable and informative to reconstruct the history of your childhood during analysis; the analyst can tell you more in an hour than you can tell in years of your idle talk.

3. Refutation of the Super Ego: I do not believe that such reconstructions are of any significance, but even if this should be true, any one could do it; it leads to a nonsensical result, which can only make one laugh. And even if it did make sense, such a reconstruction could certainly not be made by this ignorant foreigner, who puts on airs (the husband in the dream evidently combines the figures of the patient *and* the analyst). And finally, even if these reconstructions of my childhood were correct, their only value is that of a historical (museum) document. ("Analysis has no therapeutic value.")

Third Dream:

He is in an automobile somewhere in London during an air attack. A policeman stops him, accusing him of having parked in a "No Parking" area. He is ordered to appear in court on Saturday.

The same patient had the above dream. Associations to the dream element "London": The patient, unemployed for the reasons given before, informed his wife on the day preceding the dream that a friend of his had offered him a job in London for the postwar days. His wife, who is quite worried about her husband's future, suggested moving to London immediately, that is, still in time of war. The patient reiterated that the job is intended only for the postwar days. To the dream element "Saturday," the patient had no associations. I reminded him, however, that his wife, who had been visiting her family for some time and had returned only the day before, had requested her husband to make an appointment for her with me. He had suggested Saturday. He was rather opposed to this visit because he assumed that his wife intended to complain about him. He suggested Saturday because he thought I did not have my regular appointment schedule on that day, since he himself came five days a week, Monday through Friday.

Interpretation:

The dream is an attempt to refute the reproach of the Super Ego that he had masochistically provoked his discharge from employment. His aggression, that of denying (money, position, social contacts), is "justified" if he can "prove" that his wife is unjust, and that he consequently must be aggressive in self-defense.[15] In his attempts at justification, he is saying: "My wife is so cruel that she is even willing to send me to London, although she realizes my life would be in danger, just in order to have security and money." At the same time, the dream is supposed to indicate to what extent he is sacrificing himself for his family. The policeman (analyst) is going to call him to account on Saturday. In reality, however, his wife is the one who is going to pay me a visit on Saturday. The (feminine) identification with his wife means here, among other things, "We are both ill, and nobody can be held responsible for a neurosis."

The function of the "day residue" (London, Saturday):

1. "Package wrapping" for Id wishes: Saturday is the day of

[15] See Chapter VI.

the analytic Criminal Court. The element London represents the masochistic situation.

2. Reproach of the Super Ego: You wish to be masochistic after you have again proved that your wife is "cruel." You are distorting the facts, since she does not intend to send you to London alone, but to accompany you.

3. Refutation of the Super Ego reproaches: My wife is cruel; she just wishes to take advantage of me. She never seriously intended to go to London with me. (In the dream, his wife is not with him.) I do not aggressively deny my family; on the contrary, I am sacrificing myself for them (London). And for the rest, if my actions are neurotic (parking in the wrong place), then I am neurotic, and, as a result, absolved from blame. For that matter, we are both neurotic.

Fourth Dream:

"I have dirty feet."

This patient entered analysis because of a complicated potency disturbance of oral aspermia.[16] Besides some anal-urethral components, his difficulties were centered in a revenge pattern (denying) because of supposedly not having received enough love (milk, etc.) in the pre-oedipal phase of his development. Those revenge patterns covered deeper repressed masochistic attachment.

His occupation kept him on his feet all day long. He suffered from excessive perspiration of his feet, because of which he took a foot bath daily. His wife was very sensitive to the odor of perspiration.

Interpretation:

The reproach of the Super Ego: you are acting aggressively towards your wife in denying her everything (sexual pleasure, potency, sperm). The only thing you do not deny her is the odor which she abhors.

Id wish: ridiculing aggression toward his wife (denying).

Ego compromise and defense: It is not true that I am aggressive and denying toward my wife; on the contrary, I work myself

---

[16]"Some Special Varieties of Ejaculatory Disturbance Not Hitherto Described." Internat. J. Psycho-Analysis., XVI, 1935; also "Further Observations on the Clinical Picture of 'Psychogenic Oral Aspermia.'" Internat. J. Psycho-Analysis, XVIII, 1937.

to the bone for this parasite. It is only my hard-earned money that interests her, whereas my sore feet and their perspiration revolt her. Naturally her reaction to money is different: *non olet* (an allusion to the familiar words of Vespasian in regard to the taxes imposed on public comfort stations in Rome.) Furthermore, it is not true that I deny my wife sexual gratification (foot-penis); I'm merely tired in the evening. It is not my intention to make her endure the obnoxious odor, but how can I help it if I suffer from excessive perspiration?

The function of the "day residue" (here, foot=urethral-anal conception of the penis):

1. "Package-wrapping" for the Id wish: aggressive use of the pregenital penis.

2. Super Ego reproach: You wish to be aggressive in that you offer your wife your penis merely in the form of an obnoxious odor (an anal-urethral use of the penis).

3. Refutation of the Super Ego reproach: *"Non olet,"* I am ill, and really suffer from excessive perspiration of the feet; I sacrifice myself for my wife; she is unjust. I do not wish to play with my penis through anal-urethral fantasies, but rather I want to "wash myself clean" (analysis).

Fifth Dream:

"Something about an undershirt. I was supposed to go to the tailor."

This patient's analysis was centered around his exhibitionistic difficulties. He was an opera singer, that is, he studied singing, but had such strong inhibitions with regard to performing in public that his singing teacher suggested that he undergo an analysis. When I began to interpret his repressed exhibitionistic tendencies, he was both astonished and furious, especially with reference to their connection with castration fantasies on the one hand, and, simultaneously, with the denial of castration. Through the act of opening his mouth on the stage (identification of mouth and vagina), he indicates his castration and at the same time denies it by showing his tongue and producing song.

Associations: For weeks he had been intending to go to the tailor but had continually postponed it, presumedly because he had no time. He admitted that he hated to go for fittings, and especially to undress "in the presence of others."

To the dream element "something about an undershirt," it suddenly occurred to him that as a child he had been teased for years in regard to a certain incident. He had once walked into the parlor wearing only an undershirt while his parents were entertaining, and had been greeted with uproarious laughter. His next association was not an association at all, but a long argument in an attempt to depreciate the fact of exhibitionism, and an expounding of the theme: "You will naturally try to exploit this harmless memory for your own purposes, whereas it really means nothing at all."

Interpretation:

Due to the pressure of the analytic situation, feelings of guilt regarding exhibitionistic impulses had been mobilized. The dream described above represents at the same time a confession, and the attempt to refute or at least to dilute the confession.

The reproach of the Super Ego: Why do you deny the existence of these exhibitionistic tendencies and castration wishes? Don't you remember the incident of your childhood in which you exhibited yourself? And what about your "queer feelings" when you have to go to the tailor? Also, you are exhibiting yourself in analysis, in that your mind is thrown open to the analyst.

Id wishes: Exhibition, and castration wishes (tailor).[17]

Ego compromise and defense: It is not true that I wish to exhibit myself; on the contrary, I am ashamed to undress myself in front of my tailor, and to appear in my undershirt before a man (!). However, the reason I do not go to the tailor is because I have no time. I am a serious-minded person who has no time to indulge his vanity (exhibitionism). And for the rest, I do not exhibit myself in analysis, but am here for the purpose of being cured.

Function of the "day residue" (tailor):

1. "Package-wrapping" for the Id wish: exhibition and passive castration wishes.

2. Reproach to the Super Ego: The warning of the scene in his childhood where he had exhibited himself; furthermore, symbolic representation of castration.

---

[17]In German, the word "schneiden" means "to cut," and "Schneider" means "tailor." This play on words, here referring to castration, cannot be reproduced in English.

3. Refutation of the Super Ego reproach: It is not true that I wish to be castrated and to exhibit myself. The only reason I do not go to the tailor is that I have no time. And for the rest I am allowing myself to be treated.

Sixth Dream:

> "I attempt to take a bus to Boston, but an employee informs me sullenly that trips are cancelled because the company is on strike. I upbraid him."

This female patient is a frigid hysteric. In her analysis she is struggling desperately for male status. It angers her, although able to understand it, that male identification and the possibility of having an orgasm could not be achieved simultaneously; at the time she had the above dream, she was going through a period of extreme antagonism toward men, and collected details to demonstrate how despicable they were and how they never "entirely accepted" the woman. On the one hand she would like to have the respect due her as a woman, but on the other, she resents any intimation that would suggest to her that there is still some distinction between a man and a woman. For instance, she was infuriated by the following article in the New York Times which reported a lecture given by Sinclair Lewis, entitled "Has Modern Woman Made Good?"[18] Mr. Lewis felt that a man should be able to talk to a woman as he would to a man on any subject without the woman interrupting with the reminder, "I am a lady." In answer to a question from the floor later he gave his definition of a "lady" as "a woman so incompetent as to have to take refuge in a secluded clan like kings and idiots who have to be treated with special kindness because they can't take it."

Associations: The patient is a native of Boston, and comes from an "aristocratic" family. She had had no contact with them for many years, and is proud of being a "self-made *man*." Although she hated them she had incorporated most of their prejudices, which were hidden only by a very thin layer of "revolutionary" ideas. On the day preceding her dream, she had read the following newspaper article:

[18]The New York Times, November 20, 1941.

"Ohio Charwomen's Pay Fight Halts Line's
Buses Here and in Boston

"All Service Out of Cities on Two Branches of Greyhound System
Is Stopped in Sympathy with 7 in
Cleveland

"A dispute over the wages of seven cleaning women in a Cleveland garage halted all service out of New York and Boston yesterday on buses of the Central and New England Greyhound Lines. The sympathy walkout affected 125 drivers and 70 mechanics in this city and 100 drivers in Boston. All strikers are members of the Amalgamated Association of Street, Electric Railway and Motor Coach Operators, A. F. of L.

"Although the stoppage forced cancellation of all runs out of this city after 2:15 P.M., Jay L. Sheppard, vice-president of the two bus companies, said there had been little real inconvenience to passengers. The terminal at 245 West Fiftieth Street remained open and ticketholders got transportation on other bus lines or railroads to Buffalo, Syracuse, Rochester and other points where they could pick up Greyhound buses.

"There was no interference with operations of buses of the Pennsylvania Greyhound Lines.

"In Cleveland, where the controversy over the cleaning women arose, Dan F. Hurley, a Federal conciliator, began conferences with union leaders and representatives of Central Greyhound Lines. The union contends that the seven women, hired at the company's Cleveland garage two weeks ago, were receiving only 40 cents an hour, against a 60-cent minimum fixed in the union's contract with the company. The management maintains that the women were not covered by the contract.

"Mr. Sheppard said the union posted a picket line outside the Central Greyhound garage at 12-12 Forty-third Avenue, Long Island City, Queens, early yesterday afternoon and that *all but twenty of the ninety mechanics employed there walked out in sympathy with the Cleveland charwomen.*"[19]

Immediately upon reading this article the patient was extremely put out, first because she had the impression that the newspaper was making fun of women, second because only seventy of the ninety employees went on the sympathy strike for the seven charwomen. She herself remarked with a certain irony, however, that here she was complaining about the fact that too few men went on strike, whereas usually she was criticizing labor severely for creating too many strikes. This reminded her of a remark that I had made to the effect

[19]The New York Times, December 6, 1941.

that her anger was primary and the search for some object upon which to abreact this anger was secondary. Her anger and the object of her anger had little in common, since the anger itself originated from some other source.

In connection with this lack of stability in her behavior a recent incident in her analysis occurred to her. In order to demonstrate to her that her opinion that all married women were slaves was a fantasy and no more, I repeated to her what another patient had said to me. This man, who had been treated ignobly by his wife, and who had been analyzing his passive-masochistic tendencies, remarked, "You seem to have very Continental ideas about marriage relationships. In this country, the man does not wear a wedding ring on his finger but through his nose!" My patient was amused at the other's rationalization of his condition of "slavery," but added at once indignantly that women only received that respect which they "deserved."

To "employee whom I upbraided," she had the following associations: "He was a cross between my husband and a cousin of mine." This cousin had been present at one of the typical scenes between her husband and herself, to which he had remarked that her husband had an astonishing amount of patience with her. Her husband had responded by "nodding his head sullenly." This remark infuriated her, because it agreed in essence with a similar remark made by the analyst. The "employee" is evidently the analyst as well, since she repeatedly asked me if I was not going to lose patience with her.

Interpretation:

Id-wish: I wish to return to my family (Boston), even if it would not be as a successful woman but in a more humble role. (She was contemptuous of persons who traveled by bus, considering them "paupers.") To this we must add the symbolic sexual meaning of bus and pauper. The first element represents coitus which, however, she assumed as only done by "paupers." Part of her hostility toward working men is unconscious envy regarding their sexuality, which was denied to "aristocrats" in her childhood fantasies.

Reproach of the Super Ego: Your hatred of the family is not justified; your neurotic fantasies about men's tyranny is nonsense and only conceals your penis envy; here for instance, men strike to aid women. You envy those who are active sexually (bus). You will continue to play with fire until your husband becomes "sullen" and repulses you. You are not very logical in your desire to identify yourself with the male, since you wish to be treated both as man *and* woman at the same time.

The compromise created by the unconscious Ego: It is not true that I wish to return to my family in Boston. I would never travel in a bus (which means to accept "vulgar" sexuality). I was merely interested in the bus because I wanted to gather some information. I wished to see to what extent the men on strike were standing solidly in back of the women on strike. If I find out that they are only half-heartedly in sympathy with the women on strike (70 to 20), I will have a valid reason for hating them, and not a neurotic one.

Function of the "day residue" ("bus" and the "injustices connected with being a woman") :

1. "Package-wrapping" for Id wishes: bus as a means of returning to her family and infantile sexuality.

2. The reproach of the Super Ego: the bus strike is proof of the fact that men are not such despicable and tyrannical creatures as you have assumed them to be. All your hostility is merely neurotic penis envy.

3. Refutation of the reproach of the Super Ego: Men are unjust, since not all of them (70 out of 90) are willing to offer assistance to women. And if they do do it, they are "sullen" about it. Therefore I am justified in despising and upbraiding them.

It is only to be expected that this threefold function of the "day residue" can be demonstrated fully on "perfect" dreams, that is, dreams which are complete and successful wish fulfillments *and* refutations of Super Ego reproaches. Some dreams end with a defeat for the Ego, and in the same way the Ego is not always successful in building up its defenses in the dream. This might almost lead one to the assumption that the more completely the "day residue" fulfills the third function, that of refuting the reproaches of the Super Ego, the more successful a dream it is. Consequently, the *choice* of the "day residue" could also be used as an indicator as to which of the three functions had been victorious in any given dream.

In situations in which guilty conscience is quantitatively strong, sleep, with its accompanying dreams and specific solutions, is prevented. Even the layman knows that "worries" prevent sleep.

Here are a few examples of insomnia because of neurotic guilt.

A forty-year-old patient (Mr. A.) suffering from insomnia consulted me in a highly excited state. His one and only complaint was that he was sleeping exactly six hours every night and as a result of "missing" three hours (previously having slept nine hours), was constantly tired, could not concentrate, and was concerned for his health. He had consulted various diagnosticians without benefit, and had become especially agitated after one such consultant had told him that six hours' sleep was "not so tragic" and wondered why he had not accustomed himself to his "new routine," which had persisted already for eight months. The patient had started to brood about his health and to use sleeping pills of various sorts, to no avail. He had tried to change his hours of rest, but whether he went to bed at 9 P.M. or at 1 A.M., after his six fateful hours he was fully awake although tired and full of "sleep deficit," to quote him. In his despair he had consulted a neurologist, who had recommended psychoanalysis to him.

The patient could not give any precise information about the origin of his sleeplessness. He just knew that about a year before entering analysis he had begun to sleep poorly. Since this "insomnia" had repeated itself regularly, he had started to observe his hours of sleep and had come to the conclusion that there was something wrong with him.

The man was a successful businessman, without obvious neurotic symptoms and signs. He described his marriage as satisfactory, and showed impatience at the analyst's attempt to "find out something" about him. "You can probe as much as you want, but you won't find more than sleeplessness." He described his father as a "harmless, boisterous hypocrite" who preached a good deal to other people on how they should behave without sticking to his rules himself. He gave as an example that his father, a physician, would recommend moderate eating to his patients while he himself ate great quantities. He described his mother as submissive toward his father, admiring him and "never seeing through his hollowness." The patient spoke about his parents, both of whom were dead, rather ironically; his father especially was the object of his satiric scorn. Said the patient: "He lived after Oscar Wilde's aphorism to the effect that duty is exactly what *other* people should do." The man parried every attempt to unearth his childhood with an impatient nonchalance, and exclaimed one day: "As a child I had the measles, too; my whole childhood seems to me one such child's disease, without any actual importance." He knew theoretically even before starting analysis that analysts consider childhood experiences and fantasies important, but had no respect for this emphasis. The same guardedness was visible with respect to dreams: He never remembered having any. During the first few weeks of analysis he could not remember a single dream. One day, after four weeks, he told me ironically: "You should admit two things: first, that you overcharge, and, second, that you are at a loss in my case." The next day he suggested: "How about reducing my fee since I don't dream, I don't produce free associations, and you don't know what's the matter with me?"

His allusion to not producing free associations referred to the fact that he regarded that "form of approach" as "silly." He actually spent his appointment hour either complaining or describing daily happenings. The fact was that for a few weeks he provided no opening either for an interpretation or for a preliminary understanding of his personality—which remained a colorless and nondescript mass.

I had the vague feeling that his irony might provide me with an opening, that it was perhaps a covering cloak for inner fears, and suggested analysing it. "There is nothing to it; all people tease each other."

"But you seem to overdo it," I objected. "Do you ever express a thought directly?"

"Seldom," he admitted. "You have to be ironical because people would be offended if you told them bluntly what fools they were."

"Why tell them at all?" I asked. "Don't you think that the necessity of proving to people what fools they are is in itself suspicious? Why not simply smile condescendingly and keep quiet?"

The patient was surprised at such a possibility; he always felt tempted to tell people to their faces their respective "foolishness," and since he did not want, or more precisely, did not dare to offend them openly, used irony. He even had an exaggerated opinion about the truth allegedly automatically inherent in irony. When I quoted Voltaire's "A witty saying proves nothing," he was genuinely surprised. He was no less surprised over Disraeli's statement: "It is much easier to be critical than to be correct." For him criticism and truth were more or less synonymous.

It became possible to suggest that his constant irony was an inner defense. Against what? was the next question. I drew his attention to the fact that the first person to whom his irony in analysis was openly directed was his father, and that he repeated this with the analyst. I showed him how I had become suspicious that his constant irony signified more than the usual teasing: on the one hand he treated his childhood as he did his long-forgotten measles; on the other hand, he wasted great irony on his father. Were his statements correct that his past was "deader than dead," then his high-pitched irony was superfluous. That this was an unaccountable expenditure of psychic energy the patient could understand. "I am against senseless office expenses," he remarked ironically.

"What do you suspect?" was the patient's first question the next day.

I replied: "If I wanted to reduce to absurdity your constant irony toward me, I would show surprise that you give me credit for suspecting anything. Did you not ask for a reduction of the fee just a few days ago since I didn't have the slightest idea of what was the matter with you?"

The patient was not exactly a good sport, and was rather sensitive when treated with a dose of his own medicine. He sullenly replied: "Oh, you're making fun of me."

"Not at all," was the answer, "I just want to show you that your constant irony is but a window dressing."

"Let's call it at least defense in depth," recoiled the patient. Still, his moment of sullenness had confirmed my suspicion of the defensive element in his pseudo-irony.

During the next days the irony disappeared—"just disappeared," the patient would have said in his previous mood, to make way for an accusing tone referring to recollections concerning his father. These accusations all boiled down to the fact that he had wanted his father's attention very much but had never been able to get it. In his case the "negative" ("inverted") oedipus played a leading role. He had wanted his father's love and had not gotten it despite his identification with his mother. As is usual in such cases, a normal oedipus preceding the inverted one could be proven, later shattered by castration fear. Instead of identifying—as end result of the oedipal conflict—with his father and building up thus a strong inner conscience, he had identified with his mother in order to be seduced by his father. He remembered specifically one situation which had hurt him deeply and which was at the same time *the first recollection he had of directing irony at his father*. He was six or seven years old and spending his vacation in the country with his parents. An aviator (it was 1910!) was giving a performance in the nearby city. The patient wanted very much to see it, and it was therefore arranged that the whole family would go to town. But at the last moment the patient's sister became sick, and the mother had to stay home with her. There was some talk of giving up the whole expedition, but finally it was decided that the boy would accompany his father, since the man had to go to the city on business anyway. The first day of the excursion was a good one, the boy taking his mother's place even to the extent of sleeping in his mother's bed next to his father. Everything went well, the spectacle of the aviator, the dinner, the night. In the morning, his father awoke late, saying: "I must buy your mother a present." This offended the boy deeply; he felt "nullified." He remembered looking at his father at that moment rather critically and thinking: "What a swindler he is. *He always preaches that you don't need to sleep long, in any case not more than six hours, yet he slept nine hours.*" And thus in his mind the foundation was laid for his accusation of hypocrisy, later so pro-nounced in his description of his father. Of course, it could be proven later that his accusations of hypocrisy pertained chiefly to sexual matters. These were forbidden the child, while the father could indulge in them. The recollection just described was a typical "cover memory."

I was curious as to whether the patient, a very intelligent per-son, would be capable of connecting this recollection with the present. Here was the explanation of his nine hours' sleep—identification with his father, and of his six hours' sleep—irony directed against his father and attempt to reduce him to absurdity. The patient had only to connect the loose ends to see that he was acting out in his insomnia his irony against his father, based on the unconscious thought: "*How tired you would be if you really slept only the six hours that you preach, you hypocrite!*" The strange thing was that he was *dramatizing on his own body an irony directed against his father* and at the same time was identifying with his father's "official" preachings.

The patient did not connect the loose ends. He experienced,

however, a really dramatic highpoint when he understood what I meant. Such dramatic highpoints occur seldom in analysis; when they do, they have the cumulative effect of lightning.

I shall interrupt the description of the case at this point, since further details are not necessary. I should mention, however, the fact that understanding of the situation just described gave the clue to the patient's personality, or, to be more cautious, to his "insomnia." It became clear, for instance, that the boy had wanted to see the acrobatics of the flier so desperately because they were to him a symbolic argument that erections were permitted and even exhibited and also as negation of castration. His analysis progressed satisfactorily from that time on; especially after he had worked through his queer identification of irony directed against his father. His "insomnia" disappeared, not to reappear, according to a letter received from him seven years later.

Miss B. was a bed-wetter in her childhood. The symptoms occurred in sleep only. Later she remained a poor sleeper. Said she: "I practically don't sleep at all." In reality she got four or five hours of "restless" sleep. The unconscious reason for her sleeplessness was that it furnished the alibi of "being a good girl" to present to her inner conscience. Since bedwetting was stigmatized by her conscience as neurotic pleasure, she unconsciously avoided sleep, the prerequisite of that "pleasure."

Mr. C., suffering from premature ejaculation, informed me that he had slept poorly all of his life. Of his complicated analysis I will mention only one pertinent fact: when he was about four, one of the games which he would indulge in with his brother consisted of "playing dead." The patient would say, "Now you are dead," and the brother would stretch out, hold his breath, and simulate a corpse. After a few seconds the next command, "Now you're alive again," would make him stir again. In our unconscious, death wish and death are synonymous. Since the patient hated his brother, the game became a materialization of his desire to kill his brother. Because of inner guilt, he identified with the victim, and in remaining awake, he defended himself symbolically, the unconscious argument being: "I didn't kill my brother; he is fully awake." Sleep and death were —once more—synonymous in the patient's unconscious vocabulary.

Another man (Mr. D.) woke up every half-hour with a terrifying dream: his wife was raped by a man. In this dream the sleeper fought against an unconscious feminine identification.

A patient of forty-two (Mr. E.) woke up every night at 2:45 a.m. His sleeplessness started after a not-too-severe heart failure was discovered by an insurance doctor. Analysis could prove that this man—who "retired" from his family for fifteen years because of complicated quarrels—received eight years before the onset of his insomnia a letter from his mother informing him of the death of his father. The letter was not answered by the man; the fact of the death of his father did not make any perceptible impression—for years. The moment he himself felt ill, he started unconsciously to be bothered by his old guilt: "So you were not interested in your father's death, now you will die yourself." Only in analysis did the patient remember that his mother's letter contained the precise time of his father's death—2:45!

If we compare the last two examples we see in the former the fulfillment of a libidinous wish against which the Super Ego protested. In the latter case, however, sleep was avoided because unconsciously sleep was identified with death; insomnia was therefore a protective mechanism of the unconscious Ego against a punishment meted out by the stern Super Ego.[20] These two types don't comprise all possible cases. There are many additional factors, as seen in the case of the girl with the bedwetting.

All cases of psychogenic insomnia have one feature in common: unconscious guilt feelings are directly or indirectly responsible.

---

[20] Dr. S. Rothenberg came—independently—to similar conclusions concerning the connection of unconscious guilt because of death wishes and insomnia. "Psychoanalytic Insight into Insomnia Disturbances" Lecture, delivered Feb. 28, 1946, at the Society of Psychotherapy and Psychopathology, N. Y. C.

CHAPTER XV

THE NEUROTIC WHO BARGAINS UNCONSCIOUSLY FOR THE ELECTRIC CHAIR: THE CRIMINAL[1]

It is not exactly a flattering psychiatric truism that we are ignorant of the psychologic reasons leading to criminality. It is agreed, however, that social *and* psychologic reasons often work together in the constitution of the phenomenon, crime. No reasonable person denies sociologic facts. That acknowledgment does not imply, however, that one should exaggerate their importance in *every* case, especially in those in which psychologic factors play the prime role. In some cases the social factor in criminal actions is either an excuse, or, more often, a rationalization for hidden unconscious motives, or the hitching point for the repetition of injustices experienced in reality or in fantasy in the child-mother-father relationship, afterward projected and perpetuated masochistically upon society or the social order in general. The more superficial rationalizations are often generally accepted *because* they seem "obvious." To avoid the old controversy in criminology — here, medical psychology, there, sociology—let us concentrate exclusively on cases in which the social facts play a practically unimportant role, the psychologic factors the decisive one, and let us ask whether we know something about the *genetic* factors.

Where does our ignorance in genetic criminology arise? Are there any reasons to assume that our transitory ignorance will remain in the future as a static factor as well? Our present ignorance is based first on lack of experience.[2] This seems strange, since tens of

---

[1] First published under the title, "Suppositions about the mechanism of criminosis" in J. Crim. Psychopath. V, 2, 1943.
[2] One could mention an additional factor, a curious reserve against psychiatric research of criminality among many scientists. An amusing example is the introduction which J. B. S. Haldane, Fullerian Professor of Physiology, Royal Institution, London, wrote to J. Lange's "Crime and Destiny" (Charles Boni. N. Y., 1930): "Why do people commit crimes? This question has been asked, and answered, ever since we have any record of human thoughts. In the Bible we find answers of various kinds. Evil acts are sometimes put down to supernatural intervention, as when the serpent tempted Eve, and the Lord hardened Pharaoh's heart. Sometimes they are ascribed to the influence of another man, as when Jeroboam, the son of Nebat, made Israel sin. In other passages the source of evil is placed quite emphatically within us. According to Jeremiah, 'The heart is deceitful above all things, and desperately wicked: 'Who can know it?' And Jesus said, 'Out of the heart proceed evil thoughts, murders,

thousands are inmates in different penal and corrective institutions in every country every single year. The material to be studied seems abundant: the means and the personnel are lacking. The only way of changing our deplorable ignorance would be a donation enabling, let us say, fifty psychoanalytically-trained psychiatrists to analyze in prisons for two years, five hundred criminals of all types. A cross section of the material obtained in that mass experiment might reasonably give the hope of coming to some compromise in conclusions. Strangely enough, no millionaire or group of millionaires has thought of that type of contribution. Until now there have been only two attempts of that kind, which enabled one, later two analysts to work with a few cases for some time.[3] The results of these attempts were neither encouraging nor discouraging, since first, the cases selected by Alexander and Healy were one-sided (in general, stealing), second, the length of time was inadequate, and third, a few cases are not a sufficient basis for conclusions. On the other hand, material was gathered which showed the specific difficulties of exploratory analysis in prisons and also confirmed indirectly an old suspicion concerning therapy of "criminosis" — the exaggerated amount of self-damaging tendencies. Especially significant seems to me a case described by one of the physicians: of a young man, who hearing of the possibility of being analysed in prison, gave himself up in order to undergo psychoanalysis, received two years' prison term for previous offenses (there were warrants out for him), but discontinued analysis after a short time, with threadbare excuses. In general, Dr. Foxe's cases are more revealing.[4]

Since it is not possible to induce millionaires to devote money to criminologic research, we can, in the meantime, use only the tan-

---

adulteries, fornications, thefts, things which defile a man.' Now in the Bible spiritual things are described in parables, that is to say, symbolically. We know today that the heart has very little to do with moral behavior. Heart disease does not lead to evil conduct . . . ." Haldane takes the word "heart" literally, despite the fact that it was always used allegorically as the seat of feelings. When, for instance, the famous French writer, Stendhal, made his statement: "Je suis observateur du coeur humain," he did not mean that his profession was that of a cardiologist. The word "heart" meant in olden times with regard to feelings something similar, though naively expressed, to what we would call in more modern terminology the "unconscious."

[3]Alexander and Healy, "Roots of Crime," Alfred Knopf, 1935. Even more important is the pioneer work of Dr. A. N. Foxe who was the first analyst to analyze convicts in prison. See his valuable book, "Crime and Sexual Development," 1936.

[4]See Foxe's paper, "Psychoanalysis of a Sodomist," Am. J. of Orthopsychiat. 11, 1, 1941.

gential material which comes to our attention in private practice, or we can draw hypothetical "conclusions." The criticism that neurosis and criminosis[5] was identified—a fact first stressed by B. Karpman in his book "The Individual Criminal"—is justified. In a previous paper[6] I emphasized the banal fact that neurosis and criminosis are by no means identical, a fact known and *theoretically* acknowledged but *practically* often overlooked. I explained that misunderstanding, which can be found between the lines of many a publication, by pointing out the fallacy of analogies. Since Freud's psychoanalysis has proved that in neurosis unconscious mechanisms are used, it is attempted to use the same approach in explaining criminosis. Unfortunately, the psychologic *contents* of an action do not explain the actual *motor act* executing the action itself. The motor act, however, is the real conundrum of crime. An additional factor or factors explaining the motor act must be found to explain a criminal action. Since the direct means, observation through the analytic microscope, is unavailable—the "microscope" is ready, the trained eyes of hundreds of observers are accessible, but the money necessary to put them into action is lacking—we still have the possibility of imagining. Scientifically speaking, we can build theories and hypotheses.

I do not know if my teacher in English was correct when he answered my question, "How do you express in English something which is *even less founded than an hypothesis?*" with the laconic, precise, and firm statement, "Supposition." If he informed me correctly, I want to speak about "suppositions," I cannot be accused of having any illusions about the groundwork of sand on which I build my "suppositions."

First, let us clarify the issue. *In every criminal action two factors are involved*—a varying one and a constant one. The *variable factor* is the *psychologic content*, which is multitudinous in form and may be different and must be specifically determined in every specific case. The variety of motives is as great as the variety of unconscious motives in general. The *constant factor* in crime is the unknown X which explains the *motor act* executing the criminal move itself.

In every criminal action, therefore, two things must be determined: the psychic contents (variable factor) and the constant and

[5]The term "criminosis" was coined by Dr. Foxe and is today a part of psychiatric nomenclature.
[6]Hypocrisy: "Its Implications in Neurosis and Criminal Psychopathology," J. Crim. Psychopath., IV, 4, 1943.

pathognomonic factor accounting for the motor act. This constant and pathognomonic factor I propose to call the "mechanism of criminosis." Our investigation pertains solely to that constant and additional factor or factors.

Since in every crime we deal with *two* factors (the variable one and the constant one), in approaching the problem we have to differentiate between the two in the following way: The *variable* factor explains the unconscious *contents* of a criminal action. To explain these contents we must use all of the knowledge of unconscious mechanisms with which Freud has provided us, so successfully applied to the explanation of human conduct in general: unconscious wishes, defense mechanisms, projection, identification, atonement of unconscious guilt feeling, etc. The *constant* factor, which I call the "mechanism of criminosis," is concerned, not with the varying psychologic contents of a specific crime, but with the *motor act* itself executing the results of the variable factor. The real riddle in crime is the motor act. It borrows from the inexhaustible source of aggression, using it as the most primitive of human trends without revealing whether that aggression is primary or secondary (defense-aggression).

The problem resolves itself to finding the additional specific factor or factors explaining the motor act. The result up to date is not exactly promising. A few examples: Sheldon and Eleanor Glueck[7] speak about "numerous factors, various circumstances, and uncontrollable forces either of psychologic or social origin," as well as biologic factors, responsible for the fact of crime. Michael and Adler[8] state: "There is no scientific knowledge in the field of criminology. We have no knowledge of the causes of criminal behavior. . . ." Alexander and Healy[9] describe the oral regression in their criminologic material and believe that the "universal basis of criminal inclinations is the instability in the psychologic balance between social restrictions and gratifications" (p. 279), but in addition to using the "unknown selective principle in the social sphere" (p. 275), recur to *biologic factors:* "Thus, one cannot discard an earlier assumption of Alexander that certain unacquired bases of the instinctive life (constitution), apart from environmental influences, must be partly responsible for the fact that similar emotional conflicts

[7]"500 Criminal Careers," Knopf, New York.
[8]"Crime, Law, and Social Science," Harcourt, Brace, New York, 1933.
[9]"Roots of Crime," I.c.

may, depending on the make-up of the individual, result either in criminality or in neurosis" (p. 289). The authors lay great stress on an "inner prestige motive"; "Criminality, especially stealing or robbery, is, then, an attempt to regain the lost self-esteem by a kind of pseudo-masculinity, but at the same time the criminality offers means of self-support and avoidance of the systematic effort involved in working" (p. 285). They answer the question as to why the same emotional conflict which in certain cases finds expression in psycho-neurotic symptoms in other cases leads to criminal behavior as follows: "The chief difference between neurosis and criminal behavior is that in neurosis the emotional conflict results in symbolic gratification of unsatisfied urges, whereas in criminal behavior it leads to overt misdeeds. The emotional conflicts and deprivations of childhood, the resentment against parents and siblings, find a powerful ally in resentment against the social situation, and this combined emotional tension seeks a *realistic expression* in criminal acts and *cannot be relieved by mere fantasy* products that are exhibited in neurotic symptoms" (p. 288).

Despite all of these multitudinous explanations, one has the impression that no satisfactory answer is given, and that impression is best summed up in the words in which the authors themselves describe the results of their investigation of one case: "The question why the oral fixation in this case led to stealing and did not find its expression in neurotic symptoms remains unsolved" (p.251). Bernard Glueck in a criticism[10] of that book points out that the enthusiasm which such a first attempt provokes does not pertain to the results of that attempt. The original drives, as shown in the cases of Alexander and Healy, especially the oral ones, cannot be, as Glueck believes, the reasons for the criminal actions. Glueck reiterates the connection between environment and subjective factors in crime. He is very optimistic about the future possibilities of psychoanalytic investigations in criminology, but shows clearly his disappointment with the results so far.

Schilder and Keiser published in 1936 "A Study in Criminal Aggressiveness."[11] They studied the cases of male criminals committed to the Bellevue Psychiatric Hospital for observation, either before or after conviction for crime. The material, which was not

[10]Imago, 1936. Pp. 476-477.
[11]Genetic Psychology Monographs, XVIII, Nos. 5, 6.

analysed because of limitation in time, covers nine cases. Further-more, a questionnaire was submitted to fifty criminals and twenty-five non-criminals. The authors come to the following conclusions:

> "We conclude that in many instances *aggressive action is a re-active state resulting from a sense of passivity*. This passivity is frequently felt as identical with homosexual trends and fears of anal abuse, and is often felt by the individual to be synonym-ous with femininity. He therefore attempts to overcome his sense of femininity by acting out those attributes which are commonly considered the earmarks of masculinity, that is, aggressive behavior.

> "This original sense of passivity is at times reactive to over-whelming severity of the educative forces in childhood, so that none of the native aggressiveness can be expressed, but only held in storage. This energy when released shatters all of the hitherto restraining forces and frequently becomes an exquisite expression of masculinity and aggressiveness.

> "In others, a native physical weakness, or some abnormality, is so stressed that the individual feels forced psychically into a submissive role. But his aggressive forces also will not accept a denial of all outlets.

> "That non-criminals can so easily express verbally their aggres-sive desires is indicative of the smoother flow of tension from aggressivity to passivity. There are no wide swings of the pend-ulum, but a moderate arc is described in the swing of their ag-gressive and passive impulses. The criminal expresses and fre-quently lives a markedly passive existence, save for, or until, his criminally aggressive acts. This is frequently observed in the adolescent hold-up boy. A fundamental causative factor seems to be our socially conditioned concepts regarding masculinity and femininity. A male needs to fight off any sense of femin-inity by physical activity—a masculine trait. Perhaps we can teach that both are present in all and that the one is no more ex-pressive of femininity than the other is of masculinity.

> "The organization of the Ego plays an important part in the problem. The Ego function can be impaired either by libi-dinous conflicts in childhood or by structural impairment. But the ideology plays an important part, as when the individual values physical fitness or prowess greatly, or when the environ-ment approves of illegal violent behavior."

The paper of Schilder and Keiser is of greatest clinical value. The idea that aggressive criminality is "not a release but a counter-reaction" introduces for the first time the element of the defense mech-anism into the explanation of criminal behavior of actual *mur-*

derers.[12] The conclusion is of such indisputable merit that it over-weighs all objections to that paper. The most important objections to the paper are the two following: First, the reason for the use of criminal channels by that defense mechanism and the factor which distinguishes it from a neurotic mechanism are not given in the general formulation, "One would conclude that aggressiveness comes to criminal acts when we deal either with specific defects in the Ego structure or with an overpowering of the Ego system by particular libidinous conflicts of especial strength or primitiveness." Second, in my opinion the mechanisms described by the authors are correct but represent only the *superficial layer*. Beneath it orality of a specific type is buried. However, if we thus enlarge their approach, we can perhaps reach one of the most important cores of criminality. Despite the objections to the paper, it represents pioneering and high originality, showing clearly the touch of Schilder's genius.

Zilboorg, in his shortly to be published book. "Mind, Medicine and Man," devotes a whole chapter to the problem of "crime and judgment." These fifty pages represent a highly impressive analysis of the psychologic contradictions of the criminal law, showing also its historic development, its emphasis on the revenge-idea, and presenting a plea for acceptance of newer psychiatric findings. Pointedly Zilboorg states; "The law punishing the criminal has as much to do with the prevention of crime as the prohibition of the sale of firearms with the prevention of homicides" (p. 283). Strangely enough, Zilboorg's explanation of the phenomenon of crime itself is disappointing: "The criminal commits the criminal act when his instinctual drives temporarily overcome the resistance of the Super Ego and thus overwhelm the Ego, which is forced to do the bidding of the Id" (p. 253). In other words, Zilboorg goes back far beyond Schilder-Keiser and Alexander-Healy, the former having assumed that the criminal action is an inner defense against passivity and femininity, the latter stressing the oral regression. As explained previously, Schilder and Keiser, in my opinion, merely scratch the surface; they do correctly observe the surface reverberations of a subterranean conflict, mistaking these reflections for the conflict itself. In Zilboorg's formulation crime is simply a volcanic eruption of Id-wishes in specific circumstances. The whole problem of inner

[12]That the pseudo-masculinity plays a role was previously hinted at by Alexander and Healy in their report on the cases of stealing.

defense in crime is not mentioned. In my opinion, however, the direct eruption of Id-wishes is never clinically visible; what appears on the psychic surface is always the defense mechanism. In another paper[13] Zilboorg comes to an optimistic conclusion with regard to future psychiatric therapeutic possibilities in criminality: "The brief experience in Sing-Sing seems to suggest in a rather convincing manner that psychiatry could be therapeutically most effective in criminal cases if it were organized for this purpose independently of any agencies of criminal law."

The present situation can be summarized by saying that the following attempts have been made to explain the unexplained specific factor in criminal actions: shifting from the psychologic to the social side of the problem, involuntary or non-admitted identification of neurosis and criminosis (previously, of psychosis and criminosis), emphasis on unknown biologic factors, stressing of quantitative increase of effective elements showing up in neuroses.[14] All of these attempts, with the exception of the significant and important papers quoted above and many others not mentioned here— it is, of course, not my intention to give a review of the literature— are either fallacious, or avoid the issue, or shift the responsibility for finding the reasons for criminosis to other sciences. We cannot escape the obligation that only medical psychopathology must solve the medical psychiatric issue involved in the specific qualitative factor in criminosis.

We have reason to suspect that a criminal action represents an attempt to solve an *inner* conflict with *qualitatively* specific means

[13]"Investigative Psychotherapy in Certain Types of Criminals," New York State J. Med., May 1943.

[14]Another more tragic example of that fallacy is the "cause celebre" of Halsmann. The reactionary medical faculty of Innsbruck, Austria, was asked to express its opinion of the reason that a young Latvian Jew, Halsmann, killed his father, a crime which the defendant denied and which could be "proven" only by doubtful circumstantial evidence. The partly Nazi faculty decided that Halsmann had an oedipus complex which was operative ("wirksam"). Freud objected to that biased nonsense, pointing out the universality of that complex. Said Freud: "Even if the conflict between father and son could be proven, one must say that there is a long distance between that conflict and the causative factors of such a crime." Freud illustrated his point by a joke. A man was sentenced for robbery on the ground of circumstantial evidence, having been arrested near the robbed apartment with a skeleton key in his pocket. Asked if he had anything to add when his sentence had been passed, he replied that he wanted to be sentenced also because of adultery, having that "key," too, in his pocket. "Das Fakultaetsgutachten im Prozess Halsmann," (Ges. Schr. XII, p.412). The long distance mentioned by Freud is exactly the distance between our present ignorance and the finding of the "specific factor" in crime.

which are different from every known type of neurotic, perverse, and psychotic "solution."

My personal experience has taught me, to my surprise, that all cases[15] which I have observed in private practice who either came chronically in conflict with the law or were only by chance or favorable external circumstances not detected or prosecuted by the law were persons regressed *orally*. This finding seems to confirm Alexander and Healy's statement that the receptive-oral tendency is of greatest importance for criminal actions. However, our definition of "orality" differs. According to those two authors, orality seems to be simply the expression of the getting desire, stemming from the oral phase, in combination with the aggressive wish of taking away. In my conception of orality the getting wish is entirely substituted by the *masochistically* centered revenge desire. I regard it as a clinical necessity to acknowledge the clinical fact that oral patients in their neurotic behavior no longer pursue the fulfilment of their infantile wish—the getting desire—but are rather set entirely upon *revenge* for the oral denial. (1) Unconsciously, they are constantly constructing and concocting situations in which they are disappointed. (2) Then, so to speak in self-defense, they throw themselves upon their self-constructed or imaginary enemies with the sharpest aggression, repressing everything but the feeling of "righteous indignation," especially repressing the unconscious provocation. (3) As the final act, they revel in self-pity; expressed analytically, they unconsciously psychically enjoy "masochistic pleasure." I have described this triad several times. I have called it the mechanism of orality and I assume it to be pathognomonic for all oral neuroses.

That mechanism was found by me in *neurotic* cases. It is *not* directly applicable to *criminal* cases, since it does not explain the motor act. The mechanism of orality exhausts itself in the constant unconscious constellation of situations in which someone is unjust, giving the person who provoked the injustice the alibi of defense-aggression and producing the unconscious pleasure of self-pity. The mechanism of criminosis differs in the following points:

1. Despite the fact that the starting point—feeling of being unjustly treated by the pre-oedipal mother—is identical in both the

---

[15] I exclude the psychotic cases as well as cases in which justified doubt is permissible as to what degree social factors enter the picture, obscuring the psychologic aspects.

oral and criminosis mechanisms, it leads to different reactions. The *oral neurotic* sufferer creates the triad comprising the mechanism of orality. His feeling of helplessness is overcome by two devices. First, he repeats *actively* what he experienced originally *passively*, using the "unconscious repetition compulsion" (Freud), which restores the mortified narcissism. Second, he seems to overcome his feeling of helplessness toward the pre-oedipal mother by feeling consciously that he is aggressive in self-defense, despite the fact that he enjoys unconsciously psychic masochistic pleasure. The *criminotic sufferer* acts similarly to begin with, but his feeling of helplessness is seemingly not overcome. The motor action in criminosis is based on the inner feeling of *being incapable of making the mother even feel that he seeks revenge on her.* The situation is that of a dwarf trying to annoy a giant who refuses to see these attempts. *There is a direct relation between the herostratic tendency in criminosis and the feeling of helplessness in making evident that revenge.* Because of his feeling of being a dwarf, the criminal uses, so to speak, dynamite. Of that the giant must take cognizance. This feeling of helplessness has nothing to do with "feeling of inferiority," feeling of being unmanly and feminine, with aggression in defense against it. It is a sensation which the child has *before* these other terms have any meaning for him. It is this deep feeling of dwarfism which the child in the criminal cannot "take." Secondarily, masculine and feminine identification and defense against passivity take place, as Schilder and Keiser have shown; however, they represent a *later* reflection of an early development.

Every criminal action has something herostratic about it. Herostratos was the individual who, in 356 B.C., burned the famous temple of Artemis in Ephesos in order to become "renowned." Our herostratic criminals perform similar acts with another purpose; to force the mother of their first childhood to acknowledge that they are at least *capable of taking revenge upon her.* The deepest core of the criminal's conflict is the pre-oedipal helplessness and the feeling that the mother and her successive representatives do not believe that the child can help himself, even in revenge. That is the basis of the criminal's not being able to "take it." Characteristically enough, sometimes that problem appears on the surface with rationalizations. For instance, Schilder and Keiser report (l.c.p. 368): D.N., a boy of sixteen was admitted to the Bellevue Psychiatric Hospital for observation, charged with assault and robbery. In company with another boy, he held up and shot a *female* subway agent. *His reason for shooting her was to convince her that he was not fooling* . . . . In the foreground is a fear of passivity . . . ."

2. The disproportion between the official reason for a criminal action and the exaggerated crime itself is explainable when we take into account that the underlying unconscious motive is the herostratic compensation for that deep feeling of helplessness to take revenge masochistically.

3. The unconscious acceptance of punishment is an inner prerequisite of every criminal action. One must not be fooled by the fact that this need of punishment does not appear on the surface. There are reasons to believe that the amount of self-damaging tendencies in criminosis is far greater than in every known neurosis.

4. The role of inner exhibitionism in criminal actions seems to have a disproportionate importance. The criminal's sense of self-preservation directs him to hide his crime, since *consciously* he does not want to be punished. His unconscious exhibitionistic-masochism, on the other hand, wants to show up his deed, to prove to the mother that he was able to take revenge. The typical self-betraying "mistakes" of criminals are determined, not only by their unconscious need for punishment, but also by their unconscious need to exhibit the negation of their helplessness.

A more detailed differential diagnosis of the mechanism of orality and criminosis is found in the tabulation on page 272.

The idea that the criminal has not developed an inner conscience seems absurd to me. If his conscience does not prevent criminal deeds—as does a normal person's—the question arises as to what specific means he uses to appease his conscience. The problem is complicated, since the whole development of the Super Ego is still controversial, even in psychoanalytic literature. The very few facts known and more or less accepted are these: The core of the Super Ego consists of the introjected educational authority (mother-father and their successive representatives), as shown by Freud. What is introjected, however, is by no means the real mother and father, but the mother and father as the child sees them, through the spectacles of his own projections, as has been stressed by English analysts. When, therefore, the child projects a great deal of his own aggression upon his parents, he later introjects them as cruel and

Mechanism of orality in neurosis	*Mechanism of criminosis*
1. Starting point: the feeling that the mother of the pre-oedipal period (or her representatives) is unjust and denying.	Starting point: identical.
2. The feeling of deep injustice leads to the *triad*: (a) Construction or misuse of situations to force someone identified with the phallic mother into the role of being unjust and denying. (b) Repression of the provocation, with conscious feeling only of righteous indignation and resultant counter-aggression, seemingly in self-defense. (c) Punishment from the outer world, unconsciously enjoyed masochistically, for that counter-aggression. The triad helps the neurotic to overcome his deep feeling of passivity by the facade of pseudo-aggression.	The feeling of deep injustice leads to the triad of the "mechanism of orality," with the following modification: The real or fancied frustration in early childhood results in absolute helplessness with regard to forcing the mother to acknowledge the child's ability of taking revenge. That inner helplessness is counteracted by a *herostratic act* (crime in its different phases) to force the mother (or her successive representatives) to acknowledge the child's ability to take revenge.
3. Symptomatic and characterologic difficulties exhaust the need for punishment.	Social ostracism, prison or capital punishment, unconsciously desired.
4. Exhibitionism plays a relatively unimportant role.	Exhibitionism is indispensable; it is used to demonstrate to the phallic mother — representative that the child is powerful enough to force her to *see* that he is not helpless. (See next point.)
5. Super Ego is appeased by unhappiness resulting from self-constructed defeats which do not endanger the life.	Super Ego is appeased by expectation of punishment; therefore allows the "proof" of the mother's evilness. Self-betraying "mistakes" are necessary to appease unconscious need for punishment and also unconscious need to exhibit denial of helplessness to take revenge.

Mechanism of orality in neurosis	Mechanism of criminosis
6. Quantitative amount of inner passivity: insufficient to disrupt the Ego.	Inner passivity present in greater amount; defense against it stronger, in form of herostratic criminal deed. Paradoxically, the most passive of persons is the criminal with an over-inflated defense.
7. Sense of depression prevails.	Sense of depression is absorbed by herostratic act and expectation of punishment.
8. Childlike megalomania is satisfied in concoction of masochistic situation.	Childlike megalomania prevents the criminal action from being a "perfect crime," since the assumption, "Nothing can happen to me," based on the unconscious wish to be punished, and lack of complete thinking through of all possibilities, based on the same self-damaging f a c t o r, work against that goal.

malicious, even though in reality they are mild and benevolent. To complicate matters further, the whole structure of the inner conscience is not fully understandable unless one takes into account Freud's Eros-Thanatos theory.

The Super Ego makes itself clinically visible in its effects: feeling of guilt, need for punishment, sense of depression. In criminal action that need for punishment is clearly visible. All of the little mistakes which criminals make leading to their detection have also their effective basis in the need for punishment. Th. Reik has devoted two excellent books to that problem,[16] which represent a brilliant and informative approach to the subject of the need of punishment.

The next problem is to what degree the feeling of guilt is the simple consequence of a criminal deed. How complicated this problem is becomes visible in comparing the following statements:

[16]"Compulsion to Confess and Need of Punishment," Internat. Psychoanal. Verlag, Vienna, 1925. "The Unknown Murderer," Ibid., 1932.

Schilder and Keiser: "We have no definite reason to believe that the wish for punishment, although present, is one of the outstanding factors . . . ." (l.c., p. 368). "As with most criminals, he wants to be punished, but not too severely. It is the attitude of the child, who regains the love of his parent after punishment." (P. 367.)

Zilboorg: ". .. . As soon as the impulse is discharged and the special Id drives are thus temporarily gratified and silenced, the Super Ego re-establishes itself and asserts its demands. Even the hard, defiant criminal then feels unconsciously repentant. His challenging, snarling, boisterous defiance of the law, or his sullen, apparently indifferent, emotionless attitude is in most cases but an automatic covering, boastful or humbled, of the sense of guilt. The writer has never failed to find it deeply buried in the unconscious of apparently confirmed criminals of whom he had the opportunity to make a psychological study within the wall of a prison. Many criminals, as a result of this inner penance, kill themselves soon after the crime . . . ." (l.c., pp. 253-4).

I personally disagree with all three authors with regard to the deposition of the feeling of guilt. I disagree with Schilder and Keiser since I believe that the *unconscious feeling of guilt has the place of pivotal importance in criminal deeds and is automatically included in the deeds.* If the criminal did not know unconsciously that he would be punished, if he did not project his expected punishment upon the juridical and penal authorities, making them the executive organ of his own Super Ego, his feeling of guilt would prevent his deed in the first place. Only *because* he projects that expectation of punishment does he appear often detached and sometimes without penitence.[17] I disagree with Zilboorg because of his conception of crime. For him, the criminal action represents a volcanic eruption of repressed Id-wishes followed by feeling of guilt. In my opinion, crime is not the outburst of an Id-wish but a defense against it executed by highly complicated means. The feeling of guilt does not appear *post facto* but is embedded in the deed itself. *Only that unconscious expectation of punishment makes the criminal action possible.*

It is confusing to try to realize that the criminal is not the

[17]However, should the Schilder-Keiser assumption prove correct, to my surprise, it would give the possibility for a successful therapy of criminosis.

embodiment of aggression but of passivity, with an over-inflated pseudo-aggressive defense. We are often confronted with the question: "Why is the criminal so aggressive?" That impression is the result of his cruel *action* and not of his genetic *structure*. Basically, we have to resign ourselves to the fact that aggression is one of the inborn drives. Every cultural development tends to restrict murderous aggression and to sublimate it. In this respect Freud was very explicit, as is proven in his work, "Civilization and Its Discontent." Child-analysis has contributed further proof of this natural aggressive drive. Melanie Klein and her followers have good work on the subject, despite the fact that many of their interpretations are controversial. From the psychiatric field a highly important work on that subject should be stressed, "Aggressiveness in Children," by L. Bender and P. Schilder.[18]

The technique with which the criminal's unconscious Ego appeases the Super Ego has already been described. I would like to stress one of the techniques of disarming the Super Ego as described in my study on "Hypocrisy."[19]

Schilder and Keiser believe that aggressive criminal deeds are a reaction to an "enormous passivity." They point to the ideologically-based idea in our culture that masculinity and virility, passivity and femininity are identical. As a defense against that femininity criminal aggression is used. They may be right, but they are stressing only the superficial layer, Buried deep beneath that oedipal defense is the pre-oedipal passivity. The best proof is in the fact which the authors mention repeatedly—that the criminal is afraid of homosexual relations. They do not take into account, however, the oral, pre-oedipal basis of homosexuality.[20]

The appearance in rationalizations of the desire to show the mother-representative one's ability to take revenge on her is illustrated in one of the best psychologic descriptions of a murder in belles lettres, Dostoevski's "Crime and Punishment." In this Raskolnikof doubts consistently his ability to go through with his plan of killing the old *female* pound-broker, and convinces himself only by means of actually committing the murder. The same holds true in

[18]Gen. Psychoanal. Monograph, 1936. Nos. 5, 6.
[19]J. Crim. Psychopath., 1943. IV.
[20]See my paper in collaboration with Eidelberg, "The Breast Complex in the Male," Internal. Ztschr. f. Psychoanal., 1933.

the logically-senseless murder in Aldanow's "The Fifth Seal," to mention a "modern" description.

One of the results of Freud's work is the clinical proof that the psychologic gap between the normal and criminal personality is not so wide as previously assumed. The unconscious of even the most normal person harbors enough forbidden wishes. Great psychologists have always known this fact, best expressed in Goethe's statement that there is no crime he could not have *imagined* having committed. Another example is the allusion of Balzac in "Père Goriot" to a passage of J. J. Rousseau, in which that author asks the reader how he would behave if, without leaving Paris and without being detected, he could kill with his thoughts only an old mandarin in Pekin whose death would be of great advantage for him. Balzac lets us suspect that he is not of the opinion that the mandarin's life is very secure. "Tuer son mandarin" has remained, as Freud once remarked, the prototype for that inner preparedness for aggression in the cultured human being. W. Stekel was so impressed by these "criminal" tendencies that he wanted to enlarge Freud's statement that the child is endowed with a "polymorph perversion," by saying that he is also equipped with "universal criminality." His pupils, for instance Gutheil, elaborated on that assumption. There are strong objections to that assumption. The most precise objection was formulated by Schilder, Bender, and Keiser: "It has been said that children are criminals, but such a formulation is of course senseless. Human actions and attitudes are what they are merely in *specific social setting,* and the *social setting of the child and the criminal are fundamentally different.* It is true that fundamental trends of human psychology are particularly expressed in children, and the understanding of these trends may help in the analysis of the aggressive criminal."[21]

The following are short excerpts from case histories in which problems of criminology were discussed in a tangential manner. In other words, the patients did not come into treatment because of their criminal deeds; quite the contrary. The material was accidentally or involuntarily produced and often accompanied by secrecy and conscious non-collaboration on the part of the patient. Still, in it can be found certain clues to our problem.

Case 1. A man of fifty-three entered psychoanalysis without his volition. He had developed a writer's cramp and was sent by his

[21]"Studies in Aggressiveness," p. 554.

health insurance company for analysis. (Health insurance was obligatory in pre-Hitler Austria.) The patient received benefit payments and would have forfeited them if he had not submitted to any prescribed treatment. He openly admitted that that was the only reason for his permitting "such nonsense as psychiatry." He refused to give any information about himself, was deeply suspicious, and proposed that if the physician would testify every time to his coming, he would save the physician's time by leaving at once. Since that simplification was rejected, he spent six weeks in sullen silence, obstructing all treatment consciously. The few "facts" which he revealed were that he did not remember his parents, was happily married, had no conflicts, was a well-paid employee of a large concern. He claimed that his duties were purely representative, paying visits to important old customers, having a friendly chat with them, and getting orders which the concern would get anyhow. One day, he said, he wanted to write the order of a customer and discovered that he could no longer write. He was alarmed about his cramp, consulted his physician, who recommended rest and after that electric treatment and injections. After a few weeks the suspicion arose that the symptom was psychosomatic in origin, and the patient was sent to me. No further information could be elicited from him. Neither free associations, nor dreams, nor any other information were forthcoming. It was obvious that the man was consciously withholding information, but nothing could persuade him to be less reserved. Every attempt to break down his conscious sabotage was hopeless. I told him that in these circumstances further attempts at treatment were senseless and that I should have to discontinue the treatment. As a reaction the patient volunteered two dreams, the only two dreams which he did reveal, having denied previously that he ever dreamed. In the first he received an anonymous letter stating that his wife was a prostitute. In the second he was on trial before a court martial, for a crime which was not clear to him but which had something to do with money. No associations could be obtained from him; he sank once more into his sullen and suspicious silence. I attempted to gain some insight from them, having the following trend of thought. He harbored some unconscious aggression toward his wife, with resultant feeling of guilt which he tried to appease by finding her a "bad" woman. From the second dream one could surmise that his aggression toward his wife had some connection with a deep conflict about money (of course *not* in the trivial sense, that she wanted a new dress, which he refused). Since his symptom—writer's cramp—suggested inhibition of repressed aggression, I concluded that his conflict was perhaps a repetition of childhood aggression projected upon his wife, the supposed conflict about money playing the role of a provocative agent, bringing to the surface old oral refusal fantasies. I told the patient that it was, of course, impossible to interpret the dreams without his cooperation, but ventured to guess: "I suspect that you hate your wife because of some unexpected and grave conflict about money." The patient's reaction was one of complete surprise. "How did you know?" Under the influence of "magic" as he called it, he then gave me a little information which was even more fantastic. The first part of his story was true. He loved his wife, who had waited for him for years when he was a prisoner of war in Siberia. Everything went well until her father, who had always been badly off financially, died suddenly and left a large sum of cash in a hidden place. No one knew where that money had come from. The suspicion arose that he had accumulated it during the War, perhaps by smuggling on the Swiss border. At any rate, the money was there, and the patient's wife and her sister began to quarrel over it. The latter's husband pretended to have always known about the hidden treasure; indeed, he even claimed that the old man had promised him half of it. He suggested that he receive fifty percent and the sisters divide the remainder; in other words, he and his wife proposed to receive seventy-five percent, conceding twenty-five percent to my patient and his wife. After many conflicts the Treasury Department confiscated the money because of unpaid taxes, permitting the sisters only a part of it provided that both sign the checks. A complete stalemate resulted. A further quarrel arose between my patient and his wife over her share of the money. He wanted her to buy him a café, hoping to quit his job immediately. His wife consented to buy it on the condition that he continue his job for two years, when he would become eligible for a pension. During one scene between them, the man became so furious that he "nearly killed her," as he expressed it. He threw at her a burning lamp filled with petrol (they lived at that time in the country and had no electric light). Her clothes caught fire, but it was extinguished. The man declared that he had thrown the lamp at a rat. With that obvious lie he patched up the quarrel, but he could not alleviate her suspicion, which she expressed precisely: "You wanted to kill me." After that manslaughter-assault he became "dizzy" and fell into "some kind of coma or sleep" lasting for twenty hours. Two days later he resumed his duties, but shortly thereafter produced his writer's cramp.

In the superficial layer his cramp had the purpose of forcing his wife to let him give up his position and buy the café. His choice of the right hand had a deeper significance, though. If his problem had been only about his work, he would more conveniently have produced a speech difficulty, since his main business was talking. Undoubtedly the cramp of the right hand, the hand of aggressive deeds, such as throwing the lamp, meant an unconscious inhibition of that murderous aggresion. Deeper determining factors could not be found, since the patient discontinued treatment after asking me to convince his wife to buy his café. I did this, and perhaps they even lived happily afterward. The patient was not interested in having his symptom cured. The secondary gain was too great, since to be cured meant at the moment to be an agent once more; to remain sick meant to become the proprietor of a café.

The case is interesting because in it is seen the transition between a murderous deed and a neurotic symptom. The report is incomplete since analysis could not be performed. Only the suspicion could be expressed that repressed oral material was operative. His deep feeling of injustice at not being given the café and his choice of a café in itself pointed in that direction. Nothing could be elicited about his childhood history. He did admit, though, that at the height of the conflict he had consciously thought of killing his wife.

Case 2. A homosexual woman killed her three-year-old child many years before entering analysis in the following manner: On a vacation trip by car she refused to consult a physician when the child became sick, despite being warned by inn-keepers that the infant was seriously ill. She wanted to reach a certain place and did reach it, but the child, who had diphtheria, died soon afterward. That "incident with the child," as the patient called it, was not her reason for seeking treatment. She sought treatment only because of her homosexuality and her personality difficulties. Her family history was one frequently encountered in oral cases: aggressive mother, weak father. Her mother beat the children mercilessly and was in general a sadistic educator. Analysis of the patient showed the typical oral substructure of female homosexuality (Jones and other English authors, H. Deutsch, myself). She was attached to that mother with a deep oral masochistic attitude (mechanism of orality). Partly to deny her masochistic attachment and partly to diminish her exorbitant feeling of guilt because of the defense-aggression, she produced in her homosexuality the alibi: "I don't hate her; I love her and her successive representatives." She repeated in her relation toward her own child a "negative magic gesture"; her behavior represented an unconscious caricaturistic demonstration directed toward her mother: "I shall show you how badly you treated me; you would even let me die." In that identification the child was unconsciously identified with herself; on the other hand, she, as a real person, played unconsciously the role of the sadistic mother.

As mentioned before, the killing of the child in a round-about way was not the reason for her entering analysis. She admitted, however, that she had feelings of guilt after its death, but could never be brought to explain whether the killing was intentional or not. The weakness of her protests aroused suspicion. She went only so far as to admit that she had "sometimes played with the idea of being rid of her burden."

Case 3. A patient sought analysis because of kleptomania. He treated his difficulties rather as a joke, and only through his uncle's persuasion did he see an analyst. In addition to being a kleptomaniac, he was a pathologic gambler and suffered from koprophemia.

He was the only child of a marriage of only a few months' duration. His father drowned before his birth. His mother, an energetic, high-strung, and obstinate woman, earned her living after her husband's death by managing a canteen near an army camp. She was promiscuous, and changed her lovers every few weeks. Of greatest importance in the patient's childhood was a scene which he witnessed in which a huge soldier, trying to force his mother to submit to intercourse, took out her right breast and squeezed it until the woman, half-conscious with pain, gave in. That recollection was repressed and came to the fore in the course of analysing the patient's strange tendency in his late 'teens to try to seduce women by pressing their buttocks with force. The young man was at that time of the opinion that that technique represented the seduction par excellence, which no woman could resist. It became clear that he had shifted the emphasis from the breast to the buttocks, very likely because the original technique of seduction—as used by the soldier—had to be eliminated from consciousness since it activated old oral-sadistic wishes directed toward his mother.

His kleptomaniac activities started during puberty. They pertained first to electric bulbs only, which he destroyed in the lavatory, defecating upon them. Later, all manner of round objects were substituted; and finally, he stole without discrimination. One could prove in analysis that in every kleptomanic action his oral hatred of the breast was repeated.

His Super Ego was "not unified." In childhood he was highly submissive to his "uncles" as his mother called her lovers. They constantly gave him different and contradictory commands. The case seems to substantiate Reich's opinion.[22] He spoiled every possibility for himself by his habitual provocations. His whole life was based on the mechanism of orality. No *conscious* feeling of guilt was visible; constant expectation of punishment absorbed all unconscious feeling of guilt. Though he came repeatedly into conflict with the law, his good humor was not disturbed by it.

I have analysed five cases of kleptomania, including the one just mentioned. In every case the oral substructure was visible. Other authors have come independently to this same conclusion of the oral genesis of kleptomania (M. Klein and her followers, Staub, Alexander, and others).

Case 4. A male homosexual entered analysis because his friend was being treated analytically. Despite his pretences, he had no real desire at all to get rid of his homosexuality, his inner reason for coming being simply to be "nearer the enemy." He believed inwardly that he would thus be better prepared to counteract the change wrought analytically in his friend, especially by having the same analyst. The analysis revealed the typical oral substructure of male homosexuality. The patient informed me after the first four weeks that he would have difficulty in paying next time, since his sick benefit payment had expired and he would have to pay the next fee for the first time out of his own pocket. To explain his financial embarassment, he said that his employer would be present in the city at this time. At first I did not understand, and asked if he meant to say that he would not receive his salary because his chief would be absent. "No," he replied, "I mean present." The situation sounded sus-

[22]"Der Triebhafte Character."

picious and I pressed him for an explanation. Hesitating and yet laughing cynically, he informed me that in recent months he had been stealing money regularly from his office, and that this was possible only in his boss's absence. He had spent the stolen money on his homosexual friend, but now, as he graciously added, he wanted to make use of it for his analysis. I explained that I would not make myself his accomplice by permitting myself to be paid with stolen money. Hitherto the treatment had been paid by the sick-benefit money from his health insurance. If this source of payment was no longer available and he himself could not pay from his regular salary, the treatment would have to be postponed. In any case, I would break off treatment immediately. The patient was furious and told me that it was none of my business where the money for my fee was obtained; indeed, he accused me of hampering his cure. That he had provoked the entire affair himself he refused to see. His behavior was a typical example of the described mechanism of orality.

Case 5. A patient had the habit of attacking policemen when drunk, thereby causing himself to be repeatedly arrested. The case cannot be explained without discussing the psychology of dipsomania, which is orally based. In my studies on dipsomania[23] I enumerated a series of reasons for the illness based on the breast complex, one of these being a specific form of oral revenge: Via unconscious identification with the pre-oedipal, denying mother, the drunkard fills her with poison, an interpretation partly in accord with statements of English colleagues. In other respects, also, my patient showed an abundance of parasitic-revengeful tendencies. He lived on his wife's money. Sexually, he was completely uninterested in her; in other situations, too, genital sexuality seemed to play a subordinate role. Only occasionally did he treat himself, *using his wife's money*, to the "luxury" of hunting up a prostitute, with whom he would get drunk and have intercourse. The decisive factor in his case was not sex, however, but revenge on his mother (wife); he used her money for the prostitute and the alcohol. The idea that alchol enhances sex is erroneous; what it really effects is the revival of oral aggression as a defense against which genitality is used, to save the individual from oral murderous fantasies on the one

*Published f.i. in Quart. J. Stud. on Alcohol V. 3. 1944.

hand and self-destructive masochism on the other. The aggression displayed, covers but a deeper repressed masochistic attachment.

The patient's choice of police officers in particular as the object of his aggression when drunk represented only in the superficial layer an oedipal conflict; in the deeper layer it was a defense against his real problem—desire to attack the woman (mother) and also satisfied his masochism—it was the shortest way to jail.

Case 6. A woman patient of thirty repeatedly, without any justification, accused men of rape, and three times went to the police over such "incidents." The last of these occasions could be observed in the first weeks of her treatment. She had a room to rent, and a young Rumanian student came to look at it. He immediately started to make love to her. At first she denied to me, but later admitted, that she was perhaps "a little coquettish" toward him. Knowing the patient, who entered anlysis because of nymphomania and frigidity, one could assume that she tried to seduce the man, not he to seduce her. She warded him off, saying that she expected her son home from school at any moment (a true statement, by the way), so the young man promised to return the next day at 1 p.m. At first she intended to be away from home when he came, struggled hard with him but finally submitted to intercourse. Then she immediately went to the police and denounced him. She was asked if she realized the consequences for the man. "Yes," was her reply, "I know all about that." Something in her behavior must have made the official suspicious. He began to ask her about the details and inquired whether she was not afraid of pregnancy as a result of the rape. "No," answered the woman, "he used a rubber, as I requested." Homeric laughter was the effect. A rape in which the man had the possibility to use a rubber, especially at the woman's request, could not be considered a rape, since it presupposed the woman's consent, was the official's opinion. The whole affair could be settled. The official wanted first to press charges against her for being a prostitute, but could be convinced that he was dealing with a sick person.

What was the reason for the patient's queer behavior? Her nymphomania was, in the superficial layer, a posthumous revenge on the oedipal father, based on the idea, "If you don't want me, I shall take revenge by being a prostitute." In a deeper layer a pre-oedipal hatred of the mother was discernible. This was evident very soon in her fantasies in analysis; for instance, in the patient's pathologic attitude toward sperm. On the one hand, she was offended if the man did not ejaculate vaginally, as she interpreted the ejaculation unconsciously as castration of the man. On the other hand, she had an unconquerable fear of impregnation, and regarded sperm as if it were a sort of concentrated poison. From her transference it became clear that she projected the idea of being deprived and even poisoned by her mother. She expressed, for instance, her idea that the physician wanted to spoil her orgasm and to deprive her of every pleasure, despite the fact that consciously she knew that analysis was attempting to restore her sex life, and especially that it could not deprive her of an orgasm which, being frigid, she did not have. The sperm-poison idea was orally determined (penis-breast; sperm-milk); from the "bad" mother she could expect only spoiled milk.

Her masochistic hatred of her mother was counteracted by an immense feeling of guilt. That feeling of guilt gave her away when she confessed to the police official the man's use of a rubber during the "rape." The same feeling of guilt was responsible for her sense of depression after every promiscuous act. She lived for years the life of a prostitute, despite having an income and throwing away the money men gave her or using it to play "magic gestures," buying toys for children in the street. Her feeling of guilt was visible also in her avoidance of her first name. Asked what it was, she became enraged and swore that nothing on earth could force her to tell it. It happened to be Mary and was a constant reproach to her, a Roman Catholic, because of her promiscuous behavior.

In her life she acted out typically the mechanism of orality. Her hatred of her mother was so intense, her feeling of being unjustly treated so magnified, that she did not produce any visible feeling of remorse toward her victims; for instance, the unjustly-accused student.

Case 7. In the Psychoanalytic Clinic in Vienna we had, many years ago, the possibility to observe a "mass experiment" on a small scale, supplied strangely enough, by a regular court. There was at that time a judge who harbored the naive idea that psychoanalysis could cure any perversion, even *without* the patient's cooperation. For a time, therefore, he did not sentence perverse exhibitionists who repeatedly offended, to the rather long prison term usually imposed. Instead, he passed a suspended sentence and remitted their punishment if they could prove after six months that they were under psychoanalytic treatment. Five cases were sent to the Clinic, where they were to be treated free of charge. Of these five persons, who faced the alternatives of imprisonment or psychoanalysis, one began analysis with one of our colleagues and promptly gave it up a few days after receiving the written confirmation that he had begun treatment. Two others did not appear after the first interview with the head of the Clinic. With the two remaining I spoke once or twice. After being told that they could start treatment, they withdrew with the most threadbare excuses. All four allowed themselves to be imprisoned. How can this grotesque situation be explained? Even fear of the alleged unpleasantness of the treatment cannot be used as the reason for the behavior of these four individuals, since they had no idea of what the treatment consisted. They could not have had any antipathy for the particular physician who would treat them, since each spoke with three physicians on the staff at the Clinic. Nor was there a conspiracy, for there was no proof that they even knew each other. From the discussions I had with two of them, I received the impression that imprisonment from time to time was an inseparable part of their psychic equilibrium. It gave them the opportunity to atone for their inward feeling of guilt. The prison term gave them, so to speak, the ticket permitting their next perverse action. Also striking was the awkwardness of their behavior when they were caught. They actually provoked arrest. One of them, for instance, was threatened by an old woman who saw his exhibitionistic act with a child from the window of a third floor. The man ran away, but returned in a few minutes, his rationalization being that he wanted to see if the old woman was still there. She was exactly where he suspected she would be, but had with her a police officer, who arrested the man.

Not only was imprisonment preferred by these two sick individuals, but it had become a part of the routine of their lives. One of them had a small business delivering packages by car; when the occasion arose for a prison term, he told his family that he had to make a business trip into the country. The "business trip" was undertaken in jail. Another worked in his brother-in-law's print shop, and he was able to convince him that he occasionally had to take a trip to the mountains in order to keep fit. In this instance, the vacation was spent in jail. One could not but feel that treatment would obviously have disturbed the vicious circle of unconsciously self-provoked punishment, with the license it gave unconsciously to continue the perversion.

The five cases show why one must have some doubts in respect to a future therapy of criminal actions. Judicial punishment is in some cases not punishment at all but unconscious temporary solution of a guilt-conflict.[24] The punishment is unconsciously not dreaded but expected by these sick persons.

Another case of perversion exhibitionism which I treated proved to be orally based. Independently similar findings have been reported by Alexander and Christoffel.

Case 8. A schizoid man of thirty-eight, a citizen of a highly puritanic country, entered analysis because of his neurotic attachment to a woman who constantly tortured him with ironic or aggressive reproaches, treating him "like dirt." Unconsciously he liked to be treated that way, consciously he pretended to continue the relationship only because of pity. He convinced himself that the girl would commit suicide should he leave her. When I first saw him, he had stopped sexual relations with her; he acted oral refusal with a pseudo-aggressive facade, pitying himself extensively. He had some knowledge of analysis and could be convinced that his relation with the girl was neurotic. First his deep passivity stemming from the negative oedipus complex was worked through. The result was that within a few months he changed his external behavior, becoming a very aggressive businessman. He claimed to be cured, but I proposed to analyse his paranoiac ideas and his more deeply rooted oral regression. One day the following incident of his previous years was discussed. He had exchanged a few words with a man at the bar of a restaurant. The stranger, in a jovial mood, invited him to his table, where three women were sitting. After some time the man was unexpectedly called away, leaving the patient with the women. Someone suggested another bar, and the patient paid the bill for the dinner of all five. At the next bar he became better acquainted with one of the women, who was a divorcee with a child. She was coquettish, and the patient had the impression that she "wanted" him. He asked her if he could see her the next day. She consented and appeared

---

[24]Interestingly enough, Freud suspected as long as thirty years ago that some criminal actions were performed because the criminal had an unconscious feeling of guilt stemming from other sources. He spoke of "Verbrecher aus Schuldgefuehl." In these cases the feeling of guilt was not the result of the criminal deed but the criminal deed the result of feeling of guilt.

at the rendezvous on the following day with two other women, whom he had not met before. The patient became suspicious and was of the opinion that she was using him for a "sucker." All four went to an expensive restaurant, and once again the patient, who was a person of some means, paid the bill. He tried afterward to get rid of the other women, without success. Finally he cornered the woman and told her furiously that she had taken advantage of him, that she was a cold woman who had promised to sleep with him without intending to do so. The woman protested that she had promised him nothing. "You did," replied the man angrily, "through your behavior. You are a bad woman only interested in exhibiting your power before your girl friends." His fury mounted, and he presented her with the ultimatum that she either sleep with him or return every cent he had spent on both evenings. At first the woman believed that he was joking, and started to plead with him. "And if I don't do what you want?" she asked. "I shall besiege you and you shall go to bed with me or pay back every cent." The besiegement began that very night. For hours he called her by telephone, waking both her and her son. The next morning she saw him and pleaded with him once more. "You don't really want me in bed," she objected. "True, after I've slept with you I don't want to see you again. This will be your punishment." Finally in her despair the obviously neurotic woman returned all of his expenses.

The patient did not understand that his behavior at that time was criminal. "Serves that whore right!" was his only reaction. Asked whether he was aware that his behavior could bring him to jail should the woman press charges, he replied that it was necessary to take chances in life. "Don't you see that she took me for a sucker?" "That was undeniable," I replied, "but if you allow yourself to be pushed into that position, you must pay for such a misinterpretation on the part of your partner." "You're wrong there; one has to take revenge" was his stubborn answer. And in that viewpoint he persisted, even later calling his action only a proof to himself that he was "not weak" and had acted boldly. It was also interesting that his fury toward the woman was still present, despite the fact that the incident took place many years before analysis.

The next girl whom he found was, as he proudly announced, a "baby." The baby turned out to be a calculating elderly woman who wanted to marry him because of his money and her neurosis.

In his case it was characteristic, as in the cases described previously, that no feeling of guilt with regard to the criminal action was visible on the *surface*. The sense of being unjustly treated seemingly consumed every feeling of guilt, and, as far as such feeling was present, it was projected upon the expectation of punishment.

Case 9. A man of twenty-one entered analysis because of potency disturbance. He reported that his potency had been normal until he had had a "strange experience" with a girl whom he had met in an amusement park in the capital of his country. That experience took place two years before he entered treatment, and was as follows. He tried to persuade the girl, a chambermaid, to have intercourse with him on the evening they met. She refused, and he forced her to masturbate him in some dark street corner, threatening to choke her to death if she refused. The girl was really frightened, and after a few minutes ran away. He caught her and started to strangle her. The girl freed herself and began to scream. A policeman arrested both. The man pretended that she had attacked him, trying to rob him; the girl told the true story with some exaggerations. The whole affair looked unfavorable for the young man, and only the girl's police record saved him. It seemed that a few weeks earlier she had been accused of stealing a ring from her employer but had been freed on lack of definite proof of her guilt. The man was of a higher social circle, well-dressed, and amiable in his manner; his family lawyer was able to convince the officials that such a well-bred person was incapable of committing a crime. No charges were pressed, and the girl was sent back to her own community.

After that incident the boy's family sent him abroad to continue his studies. He decided to use this time for analysis.

Since that incident with the girl he had become impotent and in the end avoided women. Every time he approached one sexually he failed, thinking of the scene in which he had really wanted to strangle the girl. He crystallized in his mind even the fear that he could kill a girl in intercourse. In analysis he pretended at first that the story he had told the police was true. He broke down the moment he understood that his lies would not solve his problem in analysis. He did not produce any conscious feeling of guilt for having harmed the girl. He hated her consciously and always referred to her as "that tart."

His family situation was the following. He hated his mother for being "cold and unmotherly." After his disappointment in her, he shifted his libidinous wishes toward his father, and developed a strong negative-oedipus attachment (feminine identification). His feeling of being unjustly treated was very predominant throughout his childhood. He remembered a journey of his parents to Paris and his feeling of being abandoned and lonely. In the period of maturation he had the feeling that all woman were denying and refusing. He regarded them with hatred. His attempts at genital sexuality failed at first. Later he found a girl who allowed intercourse, but was made to feel humiliated by a contemptuous remark of the girl, who said, "Deeper, stupid boy," when he looked for the vagina somewhere near the navel. Another girl told him that his manner of persuading her to have intercourse was enough to defeat his purpose, that instead of being tender, he was "complaining and demanding." In his other activities he showed the typical "mechanism of orality." He was a collector of self-provoked injustices, not satisfied until he had his daily dosage of that psychic poison. Then came the "strange experience." It was amazing to what a degree that man was convinced that he was one hundred percent justified in his actions toward her. "She was a bad, aggressive girl, and that I hate most in women." His behavior upon being arrested seemed perfectly correct to him. "She was stupid to yell." When I asked him if he believed he would have strangled her, he answered in the affirmative. "I was so furious that I would have killed her, and it would have served her right."

It was clear that he saw in the girl he attached the embodiment of all the motherly injustice done to him. He dwelt upon the different methods with which he had tried to attract his mother's attention as a child. "She was cold—cold—cold!" he cried with furious hatred. "And I was so helpless—nothing could move her."

Why he had wanted to strangle the girl, using that method, remained unclarified for a long time. In some of his repetitive dreams this situation would often occur: An enormous ball (sometimes a stone) would be pressed into his mouth. He would be suspended in mid-air, face downward, his feet bound together on the ceiling, like a reversed fixture. These dreams could not be interpreted, as no associations were given. Having met similar dreams before, I suspected orality as the basis, but did not mention this to the patient.

However, one day he mentioned an incident which seemed to bear out the accuracy of this suspicion. He had entered by chance the room in which his landlady's daughter was nursing her baby; he retired immediately with apologies and thought, "It looks as if she would choke the baby with her enormous breast." One could only guess that for some infants the discrepancy in size between their mouth and the mother's breast could cause such a misconstruction of the harmless act of suckling. A good example of the child's ability to change its mother's gesture of benevolence and kindness into one of malice! It is possible that the choking of the girl was an active repetition of this passive experience.

The patient's symptom changed quickly; his erective potency was established. He did not ejaculate, however, having for some time a "psychogenic oral aspermia," which was his way of denying. Eventually he was cured of this too. Characterologically, however, he was difficult to attack, since he lacked insight of his situation. His hatred of his mother subsided; he became more friendly in his outlook toward life; but he was by no means a benevolent person. His feeling of guilt toward the girl he had damaged never came to the fore. Simply to appease me, he inquired about her and learned that she had died of tuberculosis. He "closed that chapter" without visible feeling of guilt, which was seemingly completely appeased by his feeling of being unjustly treated in life and by the expectation of punishment.

We have so far not the slightest inkling as to whether or not criminals are therapeutically accessible. Despite a few optimistic expressions of hope on the part of scientific authors, I personally have my doubts as to the possibility of changing them. These doubts are based on the difficulty of changing even those neurotic patients who have a great amount of self-damaging tendencies, and the most neurotic individual uses a different, *less* self-damaging technique than the criminal. The amount of psychic masochism in criminals makes one suspicious of their curability. On the other hand, we are still not even at the beginning of clinical-criminal investigations. *At the moment clinical knowledge is the thing we lack.* Every prognosis about the future therapy of criminals is simply guesswork. The therapeutic solution will perhaps be child-analysis; early treatment of "difficult" children will prevent more criminal actions.

One fact is clear: no punishment prevents crime. Responsible for that fact is the unconscious calculation on punishment in the criminal's deed. It is an integral part of the crime. The dread of punishment can therefore not prevent crime. Paradoxically, to quote an ironically-inclined patient of mine, a criminal lawyer, dread of punishment is more necessary for non-criminals than for criminals. The non-criminal needs unconscious recompense for being a life-long good boy. Therefore public opinion asks for severe punishment of criminals. The majority of habitual criminals is unchangeable. This is only a reminder to be less optimistic about the penal results—especially in the case of second and third offenders—and to have less illusions about persons having "learned their lesson." People in general and criminals in particular do not learn so easily.

Every society must protect itself against individuals who do not accept the rule of the community. Criminal deeds are outside of the social game; they represent specific solutions of a specific inner conflict and endanger the community as a whole. The habitual criminal himself has nothing to hope for from the solution of the enigma of crime. He will very likely be treated *morally* differently; he will be acknowledged to be a sick person. *De facto* he will pay for the omission of the moral odium with disadvantages, for instance, lifelong detention. The moment the illusion of betterment and re-habilitation of habitual criminals through punishment is abandoned because it does not work, society will regretfully impose lifelong detention on the habitual criminal, not because he is "bad" but because he is a danger to the community.

The problem of "betterment" of criminals is in general approached either from the practical or the humanitarian angle. What is going on theoretically is still *terra incognita*. The fact that "habitual criminals" ("criminel d'habitude," "Gewohnheitsver-brecher") are not changeable is sometimes acknowledged. What happens, however, in the mind of first offenders, who seemingly change after a prison term, and those who are helped and restored by the parole system? Since we know so little about the inner working of the criminal's psyche, that question is for the time being unanswerable. It is possible that the childish part of the personality, confronted with the reality of prison, exhausts its feeling of guilt in the actual punishment. That theory would agree with Schilder and Keiser's previously-discussed assumption that the criminal wants punishment, "but not too much." On the other hand, these first and single-time offenders are perhaps criminal "borderline cases" from the beginning. In contrast to these cases is the legion of others —undoubtedly the majority—who, despite punishment, continue their criminal careers.

The future generations of criminologists will learn more and more about the psychology of criminality. One can guess, however, even today that crime is not an atavism of jungle aggression but a maladjusted unconscious defense mechanism. Scientific progress in criminology is possible only if the theoretic issues are clarified on the basis of clinical experience, and the confusion between the two indispensable factors of every criminal action—the *variable* contents of a single crime characteristic of that crime alone and the *constant*, specific and pathognomonic factor explaining the motor act —is cleared away. It is perhaps too much to hope that this clarification will take place in the near future. Every confusion, not excluding the scientific one, has a self-perpetuating and self-propelling life of its own.

Chapter XVI

"LET YOUR CONSCIENCE BE YOUR GUIDE"—
ESPECIALLY IN THE ATOMIC AGE

What are we to expect from the development of conscience? Is there any reasonable chance that human beings will ever act according to the prescription of civilized mores? Where does the development of conscience lead? How are we to explain that the amount of criminality increases? That whole nations are driven by criminals which they call their "Führer," "Duce," and "Emperor" into brutalities beyond description, culminating in slaughters, concentration and extermination camps?

Human conscience provides the "unpredictable factor" in human conduct. Its working does not always benefit the victim, but its existence is undeniable. To give a clinical example: Many years ago a young girl with hysteric neurosis and serious ideas of suicide consulted me. Her chief acute conflict centered around an uncle, her mother's brother, who was pressing her to start a sexual relation with him. This uncle was very wealthy and tyrannized the whole family. I suggested that she confess to the uncle that she had consulted me and ask for help to finance her analysis, since she was penniless. Whereupon her uncle visited me and declared: "Analysis is nonsense! My niece suffers from epilepsy and can be cured only by a sexual relation with me."

My reply was: "Analysis is correct. Your niece never suffered from epilepsy, and if you press her into your bed, you will be responsible for incest and the girl's probable suicide."

Agreement was impossible with this conceited psychopath, who emphatically declared that he would never pay for psychoanalytic treatment. Fortunately for the patient, the money necessary for the treatment could be secured from friends. The moment the uncle heard of this, he did two things. First, he broke off his "friendly" relations with the girl. Second, the stingy man, who had never given the smallest present to his sister, the girl's mother, and even extracted rent from her, presented her with a monthly endowment. *He gave his sister, during the whole duration of the analysis, the same amount of money he had been asked to pay for it*—and had refused. The patient's mother, unaware of the circumstances, suspected that her brother had "gone crazy."

In discussing the problem one must take into account over and over again that the majority of people are overtly or latently neurotic. And neurotics have a conscience which can be bribed. If a criminal establishes himself as a Super Ego by usurping power, wrapping himself into pseudo-officiality, and allowing slaughter, his masochistic dupes follow him. Of course, without deep-seated inner aggression *and* inner masochism in the make-up of these dupes, no Hitler, Mussolini, or Hirohito could have mobilized his followers. Nothing is more characteristic than the battle-cry of early Hitlerism: "Heil Hitler, Juda verrecke" (Heil Hitler, death to Jews). The slogan, expressed psychologically, signifies: "Bow in masochistic submission to Hitler and you acquire the right to live out your aggression toward the Jew, who can't defend himself anyhow." The right to murder was promised on the condition of allegiance to a gangster. Even in the Hitlerian battle-cry was included the appeal to self-destruction: All of his followers knew unconsciously that in the end they would be punished. In other words, the psychology of Hitler and his gang was not different from that of the typical candidate for the electric chair, to be studied in penitentiaries, as described in the previous chapter.

This parallelism of increase of psychic masochism executed via pseudo-aggression and, at the same time, acceptance of the voice of the inner conscience in unconscious expectation of punishment, is typical for the present times. Decency in human conduct is no fantasy. This does not exclude the fact that there will always be a group of psychopaths whose unconscious aim is self-destruction via pseudo-aggression. These desperadoes must be isolated or legally exterminated. A well-known psychiatrist, Kretschmer, in pre-Hitler times presented a psychotic Nazi to his students and remarked: "In quieter times we pass psychiatric judgment on such people; in less quiet times, these people rule us."

One of the amazing facts in the manifestations of inner conscience is that even criminals use rationalizations. Theoretically speaking, they could commit their crimes without rationalizations. They don't; a rationalization is always adduced. It doesn't help the victim, but it is, *per se*, a remarkable feat of "bribing" their inner conscience.

Self-destruction in criminal disguise is no argument against the existence of conscience. It is a proof that the conscience of the neurotic, of the criminotic and that of the psychotic work differently. True, what decent people want to achieve is the prevention of criminal actions from the start by means of conscience. Conscience does achieve this, in not-too-neurotic people. The tragedy of the man killed by a gangster is not mitigated by the knowledge that the gangster was capable of killing him only because of the unconscious precept that he himself would be killed too, via legal authorities. Whether psychic masochism will find other outlets is a matter of hope and conjecture. I do not see any reason for pessimism because of recent experiences with the Axis gang. The fact that decency was victorious in this war in itself warrants an optimistic outlook.

The scientific approach automatically abhors "big words." That attitude, however, cannot detract from the fact that in the *atomic age* the future of the population of this planet *depends exactly on the working of the inner conscience in a normal or criminotic way.* Atomic power will determine either greater progress and ease of living for millions or destruction of exactly these millions depending on how that new power is used. Should the neurotic-criminotic appeasement of conscience prevail in decisive moments—there is no hope. Should, however, as optimists assume, the normal functioning of conscience work, the future is more than "rosy." Only a naive person would dare predict the "shape of things to come." Psychologically, one can state only that thus far there have been no clinical proofs to the effect that the human race will destroy itself. There is little reason to assume that people really learn something decisive from mere experience. Common sense will not preserve the world from an atomic deluge. Normal workings of the inner conscience might.

The increase in religious feeling observable all over the world points in the direction of activation of inner conscience. Whether or not a specific observer of culture as reflected in newspapers and magazines is religious himself is irrelevant for the understanding that inner guilt is one of the promoters of religious feeling. This being so, increase of religious feeling points to increase of the working of the conscience.

To sum up: The basic elements of conscience are indestructible. True, we do not yet know all the details which make the conscience "tick and click"; we do not know enough of the prevention of criminal deviation of conscience. But we do know enough to state that conscience is a dynamic force which—under specific conditions— may lead humanity to a better and safer world in which to live. Optimists assure us that the battle of the conscience will be won. We have psychiatrically no reason to contradict them—until further notice.

CPSIA information can be obtained at www.ICGtesting.com
Printed in the USA
LVOW062353190313

325028LV00028B/1356/P